The LAW
of PROPERTY
IN NORTHERN
IRELAND

CATHERINE TURNER, LAUREN QUINN
& THOMAS MURPHY
with Richard Shields

Published 2014 by Colourpoint Educational
an imprint of Colourpoint Creative Ltd
Colourpoint House, Jubilee Business Park
21 Jubilee Road, Newtownards, BT23 4YH
Tel: 028 9182 6339
Fax: 028 9182 1900
E-mail: info@colourpoint.co.uk
Web: www.colourpoint.co.uk

First Edition
First Impression

Copyright © Colourpoint Creative Ltd, 2014
Text © University of Ulster, Catherine Turner and Lauren Quinn, 2014
Chapters 14 and 15 © Richard Shields, 2014

All rights reserved. No part of this publication may be reproduced,
stored in a retrieval system or transmitted in any form or by any means, electronic,
mechanical, photocopying, scanning, recording or otherwise, without the prior
written permission of the copyright owners and publisher of this book.

The authors have asserted their right under the Copyright,
Designs and Patents Act, 1988, to be identified as authors of this work.

A catalogue record for this book is available from the British Library.

Designed by April Sky Design, Newtownards
Tel: 028 9182 7195 Web: www.aprilsky.co.uk

Printed by GPS Colour Graphics Ltd, Belfast

ISBN 978-1-78073-058-5

Law is correct as of June 2013. While this publication has been written and checked carefully, neither
the authors nor the publishers are able to guarantee that the material is entirely error-free. For this
reason, and because legislation and case law can change at any time, all readers are advised to obtain the
services of a suitably qualified solicitor prior to making any decisions based on this material. Readers
are advised to check all appropriate references for themselves, and satisfy themselves that they fully
understand the current legal position, prior to making any decisions. The publisher and the authors
accept no responsibility or liability for any losses incurred in connection with any decision made or action
or inaction on the part of any party in reliance upon this publication. In particular, the publisher and
authors do not accept any responsibility or liability for any economic loss or any indirect or consequential
loss or damage including, without limitation, loss of business and loss of profits, as a direct or indirect
consequence of, or in connection with, the information contained in this publication by any person.

Contents

The Authors

Catherine Turner is a lecturer in property law at Durham Law School. Prior to joining Durham she was a lecturer in law at the University of Ulster, where she taught Introduction to Property Law for a number of years. She holds a degree in law from Trinity College Dublin (2002) and an LLM from the London School of Economics (2004).

Lauren Quinn studied law at Queen's University Belfast (2007) and has been a practising Barrister at the Bar of Northern Ireland since 2008. She has recently been called to the Bar of Ireland and the Bar of England and Wales (Gray's Inn). She is an accredited mediator and is currently undertaking a PhD in the Department of Land Economy at Queens' College, Cambridge. Lauren has lectured widely in the property law field and in many institutions including University College Dublin, Griffith College Dublin and the University of Ulster. She specialises in the areas of chancery, insolvency and probate law.

Richard Shields studied law at Trinity College, Dublin (2000) and obtained a Masters degree in American literature from Kings College, London (2002). He has been in practice at the Bar of Northern Ireland since 2002, specialising in chancery and commercial law.

Acknowledgements

Catherine Turner

When first asked to teach property law as a newly appointed lecturer a shiver ran down my spine. Few students remember land and property as the easiest or most engaging of the subjects studied in the course of their degree. However as the years passed I developed a deep respect for the subject, with its own internal logic and rules. This respect gradually turned to love, and I now find it difficult to understand why students find this a difficult or tedious subject. I hope some of this enthusiasm for the subject has been communicated in the book.

Inevitably my journey in property law has been influenced along the way by a number of colleagues. The book is aimed first and foremost at undergraduate students. The syllabus on which it is based was developed with Thomas Murphy and Kathy Sinclair at the University of Ulster. Together we faced the challenges of teaching property, and their knowledge and good humour made the journey enjoyable. More recently Robin Hickey, now of Queen's University, provided valuable advice and encouragement on the need for this book. This, along with his infectious enthusiasm for property law, helped keep me going through the writing process. Thanks are due to Adam Reilly of Durham Law School who provided meticulous research assistance. Michelle Cully and John Greer both read and commented from a practitioner perspective on individual chapters for which I am very grateful. Heather Conway helpfully provided materials that informed the chapter on co-ownership in particular. Last but not least, Richard Ross proofread multiple drafts of this manuscript, for which I am eternally grateful.

For many years those teaching property law in Northern Ireland have struggled to teach the subject in the absence of any dedicated text. Particular thanks must therefore be extended to Colourpoint for their willingness to take a chance on this venture and to publish an accessible and affordable text for the Northern Ireland student market. Thanks also to Rachel Irwin for her editorial attention to detail and her hard work on this project.

My final thanks are reserved for Mr Justice Deeny. His generous comments on the draft text and his support and encouragement in our endeavour have strengthened the book significantly.

Lauren Quinn

Firstly, I would like to extend my gratitude to Catherine Turner for inviting me to co-author this text with her, while we were both teaching at the University of Ulster. I am very grateful to the staff there, in particular Kathy Sinclair, for the enthusiastic discussions we had about the need for a book such as this one. I hope that, through my involvement, this book is of benefit to both students and fellow practitioners.

My love for property law began in my undergraduate years sitting in land law lectures delivered by Dr Alan Dowling and Dr Heather Conway in Queen's University Belfast. This fascination with the subject has stayed with me and I am truly thankful for the inspiration they both gave me. I am also grateful for the insightful wisdom of the many students I have taught over the last five years and to former colleagues who have helped and supported me. In particular, I would like to thank Professor Fiona de Londras, now of Durham Law School, whose work is a fount of knowledge in all things Irish land law.

Throughout my career, I have been most fortunate to have benefited from the co-operation and assistance kindly provided by a number of people. Those individuals continued to motivate me throughout this project. In particular, I would like to thank Mr James Johnston BL, my master at the bar, who still teaches me something new every day; Mr Richard Shields BL, who took up my offer of coming on board as our co-author; Mrs Sheena Grattan BL; Mr John Coyle BL and Councillor Stephen Martin. Furthermore, I will always be indebted to Mr Justice Deeny for his continued support, for agreeing to write the foreword and for his kind comments on the first draft of the text.

Special thanks must also go to Dr Fiona Marshall and to Ryan Quinn for reading and considering draft chapters and providing useful feedback. Finally, on a personal note, a word of thanks to my parents and to Andrew Fullerton for their patience and continuous encouragement throughout this journey.

Foreword

By

The Honourable Mr Justice Deeny, Presiding Judge of the Chancery Division of the High Court of Justice in Northern Ireland

The law of property in Northern Ireland has always been of importance to a significant section of the public both rural and urban. The numbers interested in it will have widened significantly during the property boom and bust which this jurisdiction has experienced over the last decade. Although there has been a trickle of valuable texts and reports on certain aspects of our land law these authors can justifiably say that this is the first exercise in providing a concise text of the applicable land law in Northern Ireland. It is all the more welcome in that Professor JCW Wylie has acknowledged that recent editions of his Irish Conveyancing Law and Irish Land Law were not dealing with the law of Northern Ireland, save in brief notes for comparison purposes.

The learned authors have not sought to replicate Wylie's works but have provided an accessible and interesting text of value to those practicing or wishing to practice land law in Northern Ireland. This is of particular importance given the unique features of our land law, retaining features no longer to be found in the other jurisdictions in these islands. Indeed the Law of Property in Northern Ireland also seeks to provide a comparative analysis of some of the differences between our law and that of England and Wales, and to a degree the Republic of Ireland. It will be of interest to any student of the law and good lawyers remain students of their profession up to and often beyond retirement. All will benefit from a careful reference to the relevant statute law with up-to-date coverage of the leading Northern Ireland cases. This is particularly so as the book helpfully addresses a number of topics, such as wills and inheritance, not necessarily included in a land law textbook but clearly of value to likely readers. This lucid text is sure to take its place alongside the valuable productions of SLS in the recent past and be of great assistance to those addressing property law in this jurisdiction or in universities elsewhere.

Table of Cases

Table of Legislation

Glossary

Adverse possession A process by which title to land can be acquired through acts of possessing land of another until such time as the real owner is statute barred from recovering the land or the adverse possessor is registered as owner.

Assignment A transfer of a proprietary interest (used, for example, in relation to a transfer of a lease or reversionary interest or in relation to the transfer of a benefit of a restrictive covenant).

Beneficiary A person who holds an equitable interest in property held by way of a trust.

Chattel An item of personal property usually not fixed to the land and not regarded as forming part of the land (as opposed to a fixture).

Conveyance The deed used to transfer a legal estate where title is unregistered.

Covenant A promise made by deed (either requiring someone to do something ie positive, or not to do something ie negative).

Covenantee The person in whose favour a covenant is made and thus who has the benefit of a covenant and may enforce it if breached.

Covenantor The person from whom a covenant is extracted and who has the burden of the obligation.

Deed A document normally required to create a legal estate or interest in land.

Disposition A dealing with land (for example sale of a freehold estate).

Dominant tenement A piece of land that is benefited by a proprietary right in respect of the land of a third party (usually an easement).

Easement A proprietary right that falls short of ownership, exercised over one piece of land (the servient tenement) for the benefit of another piece of land (the dominant tenement); can be positive or negative in nature.

Equity of redemption A mortgagor's interest in mortgaged property.

Estate The duration of proprietary right in land entitling the holder to possess, use, and enjoy land for a period of time, be it unlimited (freehold) or fixed (leasehold) to the exclusion of others.

Estate contract A contract to grant an estate in land (includes options to purchase and rights of pre-emption).

Fee simple absolute in possession The greatest of the freehold estates; lasts indefinitely until such times as the owner dies without heirs; the only legal freehold estate that can be created in England and Wales.

Fixture An item that has been fixed to land so that it becomes part of the land (as opposed to chattel).

Freehold estate The largest estate in land; there is no other person with a better claim to the land between the owner of the estate and the crown.

Incorporeal hereditaments Proprietary rights that are intangible and which benefit land; interests in land that fall short of ownership.

In gross Where a right exists in gross, it is not for the benefit of a dominant piece of land but merely for the benefit of an individual (for example profits à prendre can exist in gross, easements cannot).

Injunction An equitable remedy that forbids someone from doing something (for example erecting a fence that would obstruct a right of way).

Interest A type of proprietary right entitling the holder to use and enjoy land of another.

Inter vivos A disposition which takes place during the lifetime of the grantor (rather than by operation of his/her will upon his/her death).

Joint tenancy A way of holding co-owned property, where co-owners are seen as a single legal entity holding the whole of the property as a single owner (contrast tenant in common). The right of survivorship operates between joint tenants.

Lease The legal agreement or contract that creates a leasehold estate (often referred to as creating a 'tenancy').

Leasehold estate The second largest of the estates in land that have legal capacity; a limited form of estate carved from a greater estate; subject to a reversionary interest.

Licence Permission given by a land owner (the licensor) to another (the licensee) to use his/her land; does not normally create a proprietary interest.

Mortgage The grant of an interest in property as security for a loan.

Mortgagee The person to whom a mortgage is granted and who acquires an interest in the property of the mortgagor as security for money lent.

Mortgagor The person who creates the mortgage and grants an interest in his/her property to the mortgagee as security for a loan.

Negative equity Where the value of a mortgaged property is worth less than the debt secured on the property.

Notice An equitable concept which refers to (i) knowledge of an existing interest in property: actual (real knowledge); constructive (knowledge of things you could have found out about if you had made reasonable enquiries); imputed (knowledge acquired by an agent is deemed in the knowledge of his/her agent); (ii) a type of entry that appears in the charges section of the register of title protecting certain interests in registered land.

Overreaching A procedure by which a purchaser of a legal estate can take that estate free from certain equitable interests, notably beneficial interests under a trust, provided purchase monies are paid to at least two trustees or a trust corporation.

Overriding interest An interest in registered land that binds third parties coming to the land without any need to be protected by being entered onto the register; a feature of Land Registration in England and Wales but not in Northern Ireland; In Northern Ireland such interests are known as interests that bind without registration.

Partition The process by which property is divided to allow the enforcement of a judgment against the property of the co-owner who has undertaken the debt but not that of the other co-owner.

Personal right A right not exercised against the land itself (as opposed to a proprietary right) and (generally) can only be enforced against the person who gave it to you.

Prescription A method by which easements and profits can be acquired by evidence of long use.

Privity of contract The existence of a contractual relationship between the parties; the basis on which obligations can be enforced between the parties.

Privity of estate A direct relationship of landlord and tenant between the parties.

Profit à prendre A proprietary right that allows a person to go onto the land of another and take something from that land, be it natural produce of the land or animals.

Proprietary right A right governing a person's ability to use and enjoy land that is potentially enforceable against third parties (as opposed to a personal right).

Puisne mortgage A legal mortgage of unregistered land that is not secured by the deposit of title deeds. Usually a second or subsequent mortgage.

Purchaser When used in its technical sense, a person who acquires an estate or interest in land through the action of another, rather than automatically by operation of law.

Quasi easement A right exercised over, and for the benefit of, your own land which has the potential to develop into a proper easement should that land be divided into two plots that are separately owned and/or occupied.

Registered land Land where title has been registered at the Land Registry.

Registered proprietor The person registered as owner of a legal estate in registered land.

Remainder An interest in land granted under a settlement which takes effect after some previous interest has expired.

Rentcharge Similar to rent paid in respect of a lease but rather it relates to a freehold estate.

Restriction A type of entry that appears in the proprietorship section of the register of title limiting the way in which the registered proprietor can deal with the land.

Reversion The right remaining in a grantor after he/she has granted some interest to another that is shorter in duration to his/her own (for example landlord retains a reversionary interest upon granting a lease).

Right of survivorship A process which occurs automatically upon the death of a joint tenant of co-owned property whereby his/her entitlement to the property extinguishes and the co-owned estate passes to the remaining joint tenants.

Servient tenement The piece of land that is burdened by a proprietary interest such as an easement.

Settlement A disposition of land which creates successive interests in that land.

Severance A procedure whereby a joint tenant becomes a tenant in common.

Specific performance An equitable remedy that requires someone to do something (for example perform a contract for the transfer of a freehold estate).

Sub-let Creation of a sub-lease, a lease granted by a landlord who is him/herself a tenant of another lease (the headlease).

Tenancy in common A way of holding co-owned property where each co-owner holds a distinct, individual but as yet undivided share of the property (contrast joint tenancy); the right of survivorship does not operate between tenants in common.

Tenure services Provided by a tenant in return for holding land from his feudal lord.

Term of years absolute The technical title for a leasehold estate.

Title A person's proof of ownership of property.

Transfer The deed used to transfer the legal estate where title is registered.

Trust A way of holding property whereby legal title vests in the trustee(s) and the beneficial interest vests in the beneficiaries.

Trustee A person who holds legal title to property on behalf of another person.

Unregistered land Land where title has not been registered at the Land Registry.

Introduction

Land law in Northern Ireland is somewhat akin to a jigsaw puzzle, made up of a number of different pieces that must be fitted together to form the complete picture. This is due in large part to the history of the jurisdiction and the varied historical and legal conditions that have combined to shape the law. The origins of land law in Northern Ireland are varied. Historically Ireland, both North and South, was subjected to the feudal system of government introduced by the Normans. Feudalism introduced a centralised system of land ownership with all title to land deriving ultimately from the Crown. This resulted in the integral linking of land law in Ireland with that in England and Wales, and indeed many features of this common system remain to this day. For example, the doctrine of tenure introduced by the feudal system continues to provide the foundation for the system of land law in place in Northern Ireland. Over the centuries the corpus of land law in Ireland evolved to include a mixture of statutes passed by Parliament in England whose operation was extended to Ireland; statutes passed expressly for Ireland which spoke to the specific political and social conditions in Ireland at the time, and more recently, of legislation passed specifically for the separate jurisdictions of the Republic of Ireland and Northern Ireland.[1] All of these sources of law have been subject to interpretation and application in context, shaping the law to suit the political, economic and social conditions of the time. The history of land law is inescapably linked to political and social struggle and that history is reflected in the law as we have inherited it. The turbulent history of Ireland is also reflected in the incoherence that remains within land law. The absence until now of any concerted process of consolidation or reform of the law in force in Northern Ireland has resulted in the situation whereby land law in Northern Ireland must effectively be pieced together from a range of sources taken from land law as it applies in England and Wales, and in the Republic of Ireland, whilst also searching for the missing piece – a piece of legislation or a judicial decision – which represents the unique Northern Ireland position. This is not an easy task.

The difficulty of this task is also compounded by the fact that the law in Northern Ireland has by in large failed to keep pace with developments in the laws applicable in England and Wales and in the Republic of Ireland. While it is not desirable that reform be introduced for reform's sake, particularly where the context of land use differs, land

---

1   See JCW Wylie *Irish Land Law* (4th Edn) (Dublin, Bloomsbury Professional, 2010) [1.06]

law in Northern Ireland is replete with rules and doctrines which have long since been abolished in other jurisdictions. At the time of writing a process of reform addressing some of the anachronisms and inconsistencies that exist within the law has been proposed.[2] It is hoped that the proposed reforms would modernise the law applicable in Northern Ireland, making it more easily understood and accessible. Nevertheless, these suggestions remain as proposals. Time will tell how successful they are in modernising and simplifying the law.

The applicable law is also now complicated by the increasing application of the provisions of article 1 Protocol 1 to the European Convention on Human Rights to questions of property. The applicability of human rights law to matters of private law is seen in diverse areas of property law, from the protection of social tenancies to the ability of lenders to enforce mortgage security. Indeed the influence of human rights now pervades so many different areas of property law that rather than include a chapter on 'Human Rights and Property', human rights concerns have been identified throughout the book as they arise. This adds a further layer of complexity to establishing the scope of property law in this jurisdiction.

In addition to having to engage in this process of piecing together the law, the student of land law in Northern Ireland is in the unenviable position of having to learn not only the law applicable in Northern Ireland, but also of having to be able to compare that law with the law that applies in England and Wales. While the historical origins and basic doctrines of land law are the same, reform of the law in England and Wales, coupled with reform processes undertaken in pre-partition Ireland, means that there are significant differences between certain aspects of land law in Northern Ireland and England and Wales.

The aim of this textbook is therefore twofold. The first aim is to provide a concise text that outlines the principles of law applicable to the ownership of property in Northern Ireland. It does not aim to be an exhaustive work that delves into the finer intricacies of the law. Professor Wylie has already undertaken that task. Nor does it seek to be a practitioner guide to specific legislation. Rather it seeks to provide a clear and concise overview of land law in Northern Ireland, drawing as far as possible on decisions of the Northern Ireland courts, that makes it accessible to the law student. This is not a project that has been undertaken before, with the result that the student in Northern Ireland is reliant on texts from either England or the Republic of Ireland, neither of which adequately address their key issue of concern – the law as it applies in Northern Ireland.

---

2   Northern Ireland Law Commission, *Land Law* (NI Law Com No 8, 2010)

The second aim of the text is to provide an introduction to comparative analysis of the law that applies in Northern Ireland with that applicable in England and Wales. This comparative element is a core component of all law degrees in Northern Ireland and is one which adds a further layer of complexity to the study of land law. The book aims to highlight to students the key differences that exist between the two jurisdictions and to guide the student's own comparative study of the subject.

Of course in some areas the law in the two jurisdictions is strikingly similar. As Lord Justice Girvan has noted:

> "The practice of the courts in this jurisdiction is normally to follow and apply the most recent decision of the English Court of Appeal."[3]

This means that in most areas of law the fundamental principles remain the same between the two jurisdictions. For example, there is little divergence between the basic doctrine of adverse possession between the two jurisdictions, or of the law of licences or easements. This means that the jurisprudence of the Northern Ireland courts has tended to confirm the applicability of rules developed in the English courts to Northern Ireland and to apply those rules to the specific circumstances of the case. In some areas of law there is a very distinctive application of common rules. For example, the doctrine of proprietary estoppel is relied on heavily in the Northern Ireland courts as an informal means of regulating title to land in a way that is not so common in England and Wales. There is therefore a rich vein of case law that addresses the operation of the doctrine in the unique context of Northern Ireland. Similarly the approach of the courts and also of the Northern Ireland Law Commission to adverse possession demonstrates a localised appreciation of the importance of possession of land as the root of title. While recent reforms in England and Wales have emasculated the doctrine to a significant extent, the role it plays in the regulation of title to farmland in particular is recognised in this jurisdiction.

There are similarly areas of law where the law diverges in Northern Ireland simply because historic features of land law that have been abolished in England and Wales continue to exist in Northern Ireland. The inclusion of an entire chapter on the doctrine of estates testifies to the lingering presence of legal concepts that were abolished nearly a century ago in England. Similarly the law on co-ownership retains distinct qualities, such as the existence of the legal tenancy in common, that mark the law out as different from that which pertains in England and Wales.

However this divergence is not always simply a matter of inaction. Returning to Lord Justice Girvan, as a matter of strict legal theory, with the exception of the Supreme

---

3   *National Provincial Building Society v Lynd and Another* [1996] NI 47 (Girvan J)

Court, the decisions of the English courts are not binding on the courts in Northern Ireland. While they provide persuasive authority they do not prevent the development of the law in Northern Ireland in ways that better reflect the nature of land ownership in the jurisdiction.[4]

For all these reasons it is important to be aware not only of the common heritage of land law in the two jurisdictions, but also to be aware that Northern Ireland is a distinct jurisdiction legally and culturally, and this is reflected in the land law. It is important to consider the significance of key concepts of land law in context and to appreciate why the law exists as it does. The recent Northern Ireland Law Commission consultation on land law confirmed that while there are some aspects of the law that are outdated and could be reformed in line with the law in other jurisdictions, there are elements that continue to serve the jurisdiction well, and that we should not therefore embark on a programme of reform simply for the sake of reform.

Although texts on land law would not traditionally include provision on the law relating to wills and intestacy, we have included them here to provide an introduction to the means by which property is transferred on death. This is a subject that has been of great interest to local students over the years and we hope this continues to be the case.

This book seeks to provide a clear picture of land law in Northern Ireland, highlighting the law as it has developed in this jurisdiction. While in many cases it is necessary to explain basic concepts with reference to their evolution in the English courts, where possible case law from the Northern Ireland courts has been used to illustrate key legal points and principles. The book is authored by a combination of teachers and practitioners, ensuring that an up-to-date knowledge of the proceedings of the Chancery Division is combined with the skills of explaining difficult legal concepts to students. The book therefore provides a user-friendly introduction to a rather opaque system of law.

The text is the result of a number of years experience of teaching property law and land law in universities in Ireland North and South, witnessing the difficulties confronted by students in attempting to piece together the law and catch a glimpse of the bigger picture. The piecemeal nature of the law makes this a steep hill for the student to climb. It is hoped that this text will aid the journey.

---

4   Ibid 63

CHAPTER 1

Estates and Interests in Land

1.1 Introduction

Land law in Northern Ireland is rooted in the feudal system brought to England by the Normans in 1066 and imported into Ireland in the late 12th century. Many of the basic concepts that underpinned feudal systems of land holding continue to underpin modern land law. The central feature of the feudal system is the doctrine of tenure. Under this doctrine all land is owned by the Crown, and there is no other concept of ownership of land other than from the Crown. There are two lingering effects of this doctrine on modern land law in Northern Ireland. The first is that to this day there is no system of outright or 'allodial' ownership of land. All land in Northern Ireland, as in England and Wales, is still deemed, ultimately, to belong to the Crown. Second, the historical origins of modern land law in the feudal system remain visible in many key aspects of land law. This means that although these concepts may seem "complex, outdated and opaque",[1] familiarity with the doctrines of tenure and estates is nevertheless essential to an understanding of modern land law.

1.2 Tenure

Under the feudal system, the King would grant land to his loyal subjects. These grants would be subject to services and incidences that were known as feudal dues. The terms

---

1   Northern Ireland Law Commission, *Land Law* (NI Law Com No 8, 2010) para 1.1

and conditions of the grant would be determined by the King, and could include duties such as providing military service[2] or agricultural service.[3] This system of making grants of land was known as subinfeudation, and was a way both of rewarding loyalty, but also of raising revenue for the Crown. These feudal incidences were therefore an early form of taxation which provided an income for the grantor. The lords to whom grants were made could in turn make smaller grants to other individuals by the process of subinfeudation. In this way the land came to be sub-divided into smaller plots. The sub-division of the land did not have the effect of transferring the grant, but rather of creating a new layer each time. Landholding was therefore characterised by a hierarchical structure of ownership referred to as a feudal 'pyramid'. The King would remain at the top of the pyramid, followed by the tenant in chief and so on. As land continued to be sub-divided the number of people with an interest in the land increased. Each grant and sub-grant would add to the pyramid structure until eventually all land in the Kingdom was covered.[4]

However, while the influence of the feudal system remains in modern land law, the system of tenure has been subject to a long period of reform and ultimately abolition.

Under the system of subinfeudation, each time a new grant was created a new layer of ownership was added. Initially there was no limit on the number of tenures that could be created. However this changed in 1290 with the Statute of Westminster,[5] known as *Quia Emptores*. The main feature of this legislation was to prohibit any further subinfeudation. Rather than granting land by way of the creation of a new grant, land could now be substituted between 'Tenants' without the consent of the lord. This meant that the number of new estates being created was curtailed while at the same time allowing tenants more control over their land. This provides the basis for one of the most important principles in modern land law – the rule against inalienability. Under *Quia Emptores* the holder of a fee simple estate had the right to freely alienate that estate. Any attempt to restrict the transfer of land would be contrary to the rule against alienability and therefore void. Tenants were therefore free to sell their estate or to leave it to their successors in a will.

---

2   This could include both personal services to the King, which would have been restricted to the King's closest allies, and knight service under which the land was granted subject to the tenant providing a fixed number of knights or armed horsemen each year. See JCW Wylie, *Irish Land Law*, (4th edn, Bloomsbury Professional, 2010) paras [2.16]-[2.17]

3   This was known as Free and Common Socage and was the most prevalent tenure. Wylie (n 2) para [2.26]

4   Ibid para [2.08]. This meant that not only did the feudal system provide an income for the King and his lords, but it was also the means of subsistence for the bulk of the population; see para [2.35]

5   Quia Emptores 1290 (18 Edw 1 c 1)

After *Quia Emptores* the feudal system began to fall into decay. The system of tenures was abolished in England and Wales in 1660 by the Tenures Abolition Act, introduced in Ireland in 1662. The effect of these statutes was to do away with feudal incidences, and to convert all remaining feudal tenures into freehold tenure. This greatly simplified the system of landholding and forms the origin of the modern system of estates. One continuing reminder of the feudal system exists under the Administration of Estates Act (NI) whereby any real property left unclaimed following intestacy will revert to the Crown as *bona vacantia*.[6]

The recent report by the Northern Ireland Law Commission has proposed that the doctrine of tenure is "outmoded and is only of technical significance today".[7] It has therefore been recommended that tenure be abolished in Northern Ireland and that both the doctrine of tenure and estates be replaced with a "straightforward concept of ownership to align the law with public perception."[8] They view this move as dealing with a legal technicality that has little or no practical significance rather than a radical overhaul of the system of land law in Northern Ireland. These proposals are codified in the draft Land Law Reform Bill, Section 1(1) of which provides:

> "On or after the appointed day the concepts of tenure and estates in land are abolished and ownership of land relates to the physical entity of the land itself."[9]

However, the Law Commission proposals notwithstanding, while the creation and enforcement of feudal tenures has long since been abolished, the doctrine of estates remains.

1.3 The Doctrine of Estates

The doctrine of estates was an integral part of the feudal system of landholding. As land was not owned but simply held under a grant from another, the doctrine of estates determined how long the interest in land would last. The term 'estate' therefore has a very specific meaning in land law that differs from its contemporary common usage. An 'estate' in land law refers to the duration for which an interest in land is enjoyed. Therefore an estate denotes not the physical being of property, but the duration for which your interest or rights in property exist. The duration of your rights will be

---

6   See chapter 14
7   NILC *Land Law* (n 1) para 2.1
8   Ibid para 2.4
9   Draft Land Law Reform Bill (Northern Ireland) 201[], section 1(1). See NILC *Land Law* (n 1) 146

determined by the nature of the estate granted (or purchased). Estates can be limited in scope – for example a life estate ends when the person on whose life it is contingent dies; or it can last forever which is the case with the fee simple where the estate and the property rights can be passed on from generation to generation.

A complicating factor, however, is that a number of different estates or lesser interests in land can exist simultaneously. The Law Commission has proposed that even if the doctrines of tenure and estates are abolished, that it will remain possible to create 'sub interests' in the land.[10] It is therefore important to understand the nature of the different types of estates and interests that can be created. Examples of lesser estates may include life estates or leasehold estates that are carved out of an existing fee simple. Interests, on the other hand, refer to rights in relation to land that may be enforceable against successors in title of the person who first granted the interests. Examples of these include certain types of licence, covenants and easements. However, what is important to note is the idea that land can be subject to a whole range of lesser interests which also give the holder rights in the property.

1.4 Types of Estate

There are two types of legal estate: freehold and leasehold. In theory these are two completely distinct concepts. Freehold estates have evolved from the feudal system (the conversion of feudal tenures into free and common socage) and embody the principle that it is a bundle of rights that one enjoys in the property and not absolute ownership of land. As a general rule, when one owns a freehold estate there is no other person with a superior interest in the land except the Crown. Your rights to the land are limited only by the duration of the estate and the conditions attached to it. Leasehold is regarded as a lesser estate, partly because of its historical origins as a contractual arrangement rather than giving rise to an estate per se (until relatively recently land held under lease was deemed to be personal property rather than real property), but also because a leasehold estate is usually carved out of a greater, freehold, estate and the converse cannot be true – freehold cannot be granted out of a leasehold interest. Leasehold is today regarded as a form of legal estate, but this reflects its importance as a commercial commodity and the desirability of being able to sell or transfer leasehold property.

---

10 Northern Ireland Law Commission, *Land Law* (Law Com CP No 2, 2009) para 3.1

A. Freehold Estates

In Northern Ireland it is still possible to create all three of the legal freehold estates that existed under the feudal system – the fee simple, the fee tail and the life estate. This differs from England and Wales and indeed the Republic of Ireland in that those jurisdictions have restricted the number of freehold estates that can be created to one – the fee simple absolute in possession.[11] Nevertheless, Northern Ireland remains as something of a legal anomaly in that although the process of reform is underway, this is the only remaining jurisdiction in which all three feudal estates still exist.

i. Fee simple absolute

The fee simple is the greatest estate that it is possible to create in land. It is regarded as the closest thing to absolute ownership that exists under the doctrine of estates. In theory the fee simple estate can last forever. You are free to sell it to whomsoever you chose, or you can leave it to your heirs in your will. The fee simple will only end where the holder dies intestate with no identifiable heirs. There is nobody who enjoys a superior title to the land between the owner and the Crown. In its purest form this is an estate that you can use and enjoy how you please. The nature of the estate itself does not impose limitations on use or on alienation, but it may be subject to other lesser interests in land, depending on the terms of the transfer. The enjoyment of the estate may be limited by restrictions on the extent of ownership. Examples of restrictions might include the discovery of treasure,[12] or the discovery of valuable minerals below the surface to which the state may have a claim.[13] Restrictions may also be included in the terms of the conveyance.[14]

However, these are statutory restrictions on your enjoyment of the property and are not an inherent part of the definition of the estate itself. The fee simple should therefore be regarded as the greatest form of estate, one that is free from restrictions and which has the potential to last forever. This is also the only remaining legal freehold estate that can be created in England and Wales. Processes of reform over the last century have inscribed a preference for the fee simple into the fabric of land law. This is for the most part driven by the economic rationale that land is an important commercial commodity

---

11 Law of Property Act 1925 section 1(1); Land and Conveyancing Law Reform Act 2009 section 11(1)
12 Treasure Act 1996 section 4(1)
13 For example under the Mineral Development Act (NI) 1969, and the Petroleum (Production) Act (NI) 1964
14 See section 1.6

and that it should be kept freely marketable, reflecting the underlying importance of property to the capitalist system. As we will see, reforms have gradually moved away from allowing land to be tied up within families and towards a system where land is freely alienable – making interests in land something that can be bought and sold. The fee simple estate has been the predominant means of achieving this.

ii. Fee tail

The fee tail is the second category of freehold estate that exists. The fee tail estate was created in 1285 by the statute *De Donis Conditionalibus* – meaning, literally, a conditional gift. The gift or grant of land was made on the condition that it would not be sold or otherwise transferred away from the family.

Under a fee tail, the person in possession of the estate (the tenant in tail) enjoys all the same rights of use and possession as would be the case under a fee simple. However, where the fee tail differs is that the estate is not freely alienable. With a fee tail the class of persons to whom the estate may pass is restricted to the familial line, and usually the male branch of that line. The aim of this type of estate was to ensure that land would pass through successive generations of the same family, guaranteeing that power, wealth and status would remain within the family. This type of estate was the cornerstone of land law in England and Wales and also in Ireland for centuries. Its effect was to enable landowners to tie up or control land for generations, long after they themselves had died. The way this was achieved was to create a number of concurrent and successive interests in the property which meant that if the tenant in tail attempted to sell the property that there would be a number of other people within the family who had an interest in the estate and who had a legally enforceable right to it. So for example if the tenant in tail attempted to sell the estate, all that the purchaser would acquire would be an estate *per autre vie*.[15] The tenant in tail cannot transfer an inheritable estate. Thus when he/she dies, his/her heirs will become legally entitled to the estate, regardless of whether the person who bought it is still alive. The tenant had no power to alter succession to the estate by will. This meant that the land was virtually unmarketable because it would have been nearly impossible to establish clean title to the property.

The significance of the fee tail estate has gradually declined over the centuries. A number of statutory reforms were aimed at 'barring' the entail so as to allow the sale or transfer of these estates free from restriction. The first of these was the Fines

---

15 'For the life of another'

and Recoveries (Ireland) Act of 1834[16] which allowed the tenant in tail to execute a 'disentailing assurance', the effect of which was to give the tenant the power to transfer the fee simple.[17] More significant, perhaps, were the Settled Land Acts 1882-1890. These were passed in response to growing concern at the harmful effect of tying up land.[18] This legislation also had the effect of allowing the tenant in tail to convert the estate to fee simple, and to transfer clean title to property by overreaching family interests in land.[19] The effect of this legislation was that the fee tail was left with no practical significance. The fee tail was abolished in England and Wales in 1996 by the Trusts of Land and Appointment of Trustees Act, and in the Republic of Ireland in 2009 under the Land and Conveyancing Reform Act. The effect of both these pieces of legislation is to prohibit the creation of new fee tail estates, and to convert any existing or proposed fee tails into a fee simple.

While it still remains technically possible to create a fee tail estate in Northern Ireland, this type of estate unquestionably belongs to a different age, and is no longer likely to be created.[20] The draft Land Law Reform Bill proposed by the Law Commission recommends the abolition of the estate;[21]

6. (1) On or after the appointed day the creation of a fee tail of any kind at law or in equity is prohibited.

(2) Any instrument coming into operation on or after the appointed day which, but for this Act, would have created in favour of any person –

(a) a legal fee tail in possession in any land, renders that person the owner of the land; or

(b) any other fee tail, creates an equitable interest under a trust of land.

(3) Where, immediately before the appointed day, any person was entitled to –

(a) a legal fee tail in possession in any land not subject to a protectorship, that person becomes on that day the owner of the land; or

(b) any other fee tail, that person becomes entitled to an equitable interest under a trust of land.

---

16 Fines and Recoveries (Ireland) Act 1834 (4 & 5 Will 4 c 92)
17 This was subject to certain protections for other persons entitled under the Settlement, including the appointment of a protector and the requirement of consent. See Wylie (n 2) paras [4.128-4.130]
18 NILC *Land Law* (n 10) para 3.7
19 See chapter 5 for further discussion of overreaching
20 Wylie (n 2) para [4.117]
21 Draft Land Law Reform Bill (n 9) 149

Under this proposal any existing fee tail estates will be converted into ownership equivalent to a fee simple absolute in possession. This move will bring the law in Northern Ireland into line with that in England and Wales and in the Republic of Ireland. Although the fee tail therefore may be about to disappear from the legal landscape, it is nevertheless of historical interest.

iii. Life estate

The life estate is the third of the types of legal freehold estate that exists under the feudal system. This type of estate is exactly as described – an estate that is limited by the duration of a life. Often this will be the life of the person to whom the estate is granted. It is also possible to create a life estate *per autre vie* (for the life of another) – meaning that the duration of the estate is contingent upon the life of somebody else, like in the example of the tenant in tail who attempts to sell a fee tail estate. This estate grants all the same property rights as the fee simple, in terms of possession, with the only difference being the length of time for which those interests will last. As with the fee tail, a person holding property under a life estate also has the power to transfer the fee simple under the Settled Land Acts.

The Northern Ireland Law Commission has proposed to abolish the legal life estate, and to retain it as an equitable estate only.

iv. Legal rights of residence

A distinction should be drawn between a legal life estate and rights of residence for life that were traditionally used in Ireland as a means of providing for widows when farm land passed to eldest sons on the death of the father.[22] This type of arrangement remains common today not only among the farming community, but also with the practice of transferring title to the property of elderly parents to grown up children as a means of avoiding inheritance tax. In these situations it is necessary to protect a legal right of residence in the property for the life of the transferor. This can be achieved by creating a legal right of residence that can be registered against the property.[23] The Northern Ireland courts have confirmed that these rights are to be regarded as a

---

22 See B Harvey, 'Irish Rights of Residence – The Anatomy of a Hermaphrodite' (1970) 21 NILQ 389
23 Land Registration Act (NI) 1970 section 47

form of contractual licence.[24] They are therefore not the same as the legal life estate.[25] The right to reside in the property remains a personal right that will not run with the property, but the court may protect it through injunction or specific performance where appropriate.[26] The right will end when the life of the beneficiary ends. Therefore while it may retain the essential characteristics of a life estate in terms of exclusive possession of the property, the courts have recognised that it falls short of creating an estate that would give the beneficiaries any power to sell or transfer the estate under the Settled Land Acts.[27] However, given the similarity between the two, the court has cautioned that those seeking to create such interests need to be precise in their drafting in order to ensure that the intended interest is created.[28]

v. Fee farm grant

The fee farm grant is an estate peculiar to Ireland. It consists of the conveyance of the fee simple estate, but subject to a perpetual rent. In this way it combines the features of freehold and leasehold estates.[29]

The historical interest of these estates derives from the confiscation of Irish land in the 17th century and the desire of the English landlords to be able to make grants of land *non obstante quia emptores* – the statute that had forbidden further subinfeudation of land.[30] This type of arrangement whereby a grant was made by the crown to a loyal lord, subject to a rent payable to the crown – known as a quit rent – allowed the process to continue for much longer in Ireland than in England.[31] These types of grant were much more common in what is now Northern Ireland because of the grants made at the time of the plantation of Ulster.[32] While much of this land in rural areas has now been bought and converted into fee simple estates, in urban areas this link with the feudal system remains with residential land still subject to ground rents. This traditional feudal form of fee farm grant is regarded as a freehold estate in that the fee simple passes and

---

24 *Jones v Jones and Others* [2001] NI 244 (Ch) 255-256
25 *Re Walker's Application* [1999] NI 84 (QB) 90-92
26 *Jones* (n 24) 256
27 See chapter 5
28 *Walker* (n 25) 92
29 There are a number of different variations of the fee farm grant. These include feudal tenure, landlord and tenant conversion grants, 'Deasy's Act' grants and rentcharges. A detailed explanation of each of these different types of grant can be found in Wylie (n 2) Ch 4
30 See chapter 5
31 For a more detailed discussion see JCW Wylie, 'The 'Irishness' of Irish Land Law' (1995) 46 NILQ 332
32 Wylie (n 2) [1.30]

there is no reversion to the landlord as would be expected under a lease. The obligation of the rent service passes with the property rather than being a contractual arrangement between a landlord and tenant.

A second type of fee farm grant to note is that which creates a leasehold interest, effectively establishing the relationship of landlord and tenant between the parties. This is known as a Deasy's Act grant. The Northern Ireland case of *Re Courtney*[33] confirmed that a fee farm grant may come within the scope of the Landlord and Tenant Law (Amendment) Act 1860, known as Deasy's Act. This blurs the distinction between the old feudal system of estates and the more modern approach of landlord and tenant law.[34] However the significance of these types of estate is greatly diminished as a result of legislative intervention aimed at simplifying the law.

In Northern Ireland legislation is now in force to allow these rents to be bought out – in particular the Ground Rents Act (Northern Ireland) 2001. You can no longer create a fee farm grant in Northern Ireland by virtue of the Property (Northern Ireland) Order 1997. Any conveyance that purports to create a fee farm grant will instead have the effect of creating or transferring a fee simple absolute, free from any rent or other obligation.[35]

B. Words of Limitation

In order to properly create or transfer an estate in land, there are well established common law rules that require certain technical words and phrases to be used in the deed of conveyance. It is important to know what these words are, for failure to use to correct technical words of limitation can, in Northern Ireland, result in the wrong estate being passed. A freehold estate can only be created if the correct words of limitation appropriate to the particular estate are used.

The principle that correct words of limitation must be used was a result of the need for certainty in the construction of deeds of conveyance. When creating or transferring an estate, there are two types of words; words of purchase, and words of limitation. The words of purchase indicate to whom the estate is being passed; the words of limitation define the nature of the estate being created or transferred.

---

33 *Re Courtney* [1981] NI 58 (Ch) [8]
34 Wylie (n 2) paras [4.94]-[4.95]
35 Art 28(2)

i. Common law rules

The fee simple

> To A and his heirs

> To A = words of purchase – indicates that A is the person to whom the estate is to be transferred

> And His Heirs = words of limitation – indicates that the estate to be transferred is the fee simple

The fee tail

> To B and the Heirs of his body

> To B = words of purchase – indicates that B is the person to whom the estate is to be transferred

> And the Heirs of his body = words of limitation – indicates that the estate to be transferred is a fee tail (with all the restrictions that that implies)

Life estate

> To C for life

> To C = Words of Purchase

> For Life = words of limitation – indicates that the estate is a life estate that will last for the life of C

> To C for the life of D

> To C = words of purchase

> For the life of D = words of limitation – indicates a life estate *per autre vie*. The duration of the estate depends on the life of D. When D dies the estate will end.

Fee farm grant

> TO F, his heirs and assigns

So what happens if you fail to use the correct words of limitation? Can you convey a fee simple by simply stating that you transfer your property to A forever, for example?

The answer, under the common law rules, is no. If you fail to use the correct words of limitation under the common law rules what will be transferred is a life estate, regardless of what you intended to transfer.

There have, however, been a number of legislative changes that have mitigated this rule. The situation is also complicated by a number of other factors, including whether the land is registered or unregistered; or whether the transfer is made between living parties (*inter vivos*) or by will. The effect, by in large, of these statutory provisions, has been to reverse the common law rule that where the correct words of limitation are not used that the life estate passes.

The table opposite demonstrates the extent to which the common law rules on words of limitation have been amended by statute. The effect of most of this legislation has been to reverse the common law presumption that if the correct words of limitation were not used that the least estate would pass. There is now a strong presumption in favour of passing the fee simple. This simply reflects the preference more generally for the fee simple estate and the desire to abolish lesser estates such as the life estate.

Where land is registered or where it is left in a will, the presumption is now that the greatest estate is intended to pass. The only exception to this reversal of the common law presumption remains the *inter vivos* transfer of unregistered land. And this exception exists only in Northern Ireland. In England and Wales Section 60 of the Law of Property Act 1925 abolished the need for words of limitation. There is now a general presumption in English law that in the absence of technical words of limitation the fee simple will pass, unless there is evidence of intention otherwise. This Act repealed the 1881 Conveyancing and Law of Property Act[36] which remains in force in Northern Ireland. Under the Conveyancing Act the alternative formula of 'in fee simple' may be used in place of the traditional 'and his heirs' to transfer a fee simple estate. However there is still a requirement that the correct words be used, and this is subject to strict construction. Therefore Northern Ireland remains the only jurisdiction where correct words of limitation must still be used. But this is in limited circumstances – only for *inter vivos* transfers of unregistered land.

---

36 hereinafter 'Conveyancing Act'

	Unregistered Land	Registered Land
Inter Vivos	*Conveyancing Act 1881 Section 51(1)* "In a deed it shall be sufficient, in the limitation of an estate in fee simple, to use the words in fee simple, without the word heirs; and in the limitation of an estate in tail, to use the words in tail without the words heirs of the body; and in the limitation of an estate in tail male or in tail female, to use the words in tail male, or in tail female, as the case requires, without the words heirs male of the body, or heirs female of the body."	*Land Registration Act 1970 Section 35(a)* "A document of transfer of a registered freehold estate without words of limitation shall be construed as passing the fee simple, or other the whole estate, which the transferor had power to transfer, unless a contrary intention appears in the document of transfer."
By Will	*Wills Act 1837 Section 28* "Where any real estate shall be devised to any person without any words of limitation, such devise shall be construed to pass the fee simple, other the whole estate or interest which the testator had power to dispose of by will in such real estate, unless a contrary intention shall appear by the will."	*Wills Act 1837 Section 28* "Where any real estate shall be devised to any person without any words of limitation, such devise shall be construed to pass the fee simple, other the whole estate or interest which the testator had power to dispose of by will in such real estate, unless a contrary intention shall appear by the will."

C. Leasehold Estates

The lease is the second of the legal estates that are recognised in land law. While the lease was traditionally regarded as a contractual arrangement that created no property rights,[37] it is now a well established principle of land law that a lease creates a proprietary interest.

The law on leases is likely to undergo reform in Northern Ireland. This is due to lingering complexity caused by the range of different leasehold interests that can be created in Northern Ireland. However, under the draft Land Law Reform Bill it is confirmed that the lease constitutes a legal interest in land that may be created or transferred.

S 5(1) provides:

> The only legal interests in land to which the owner of land may be subject and which the owner may create out of the land or dispose of are –

> (a) a tenancy;

This provision clearly confirms the ongoing recognition of the lease as a legal estate. Under the terms of the proposal the term 'tenancy' will be used rather than 'lease'. This is to extend the application of the Bill to all situations where the relationship of landlord and tenant is created.

1.5 Future Interests

As previously noted, it is possible to create a number of different estates that exist simultaneously in respect of the same plot of land. In addition to the estate that is vested in possession, it is also possible to have future or contingent interests. These are interests that vest sometime in the future but nevertheless constitute legal interests in land.

A. Reversions

A reversion exists where a smaller estate is carved out of an already vested estate.

For example, if A transfers land 'To B, for life', A would be entitled to the estate in possession, and B would hold a fee simple in reversion. As the name suggests, the estate will 'revert' to the person who originally owned it.

---

37 Wylie (n 2) para [4.07]

B. Remainders

The second type of future interest is a remainder. This type of interest is created where the land is to be transferred to a third party at a point in the future rather than reverting to the original grantor.

For example, A transfers land 'to B, for life, remainder to C and his heirs'. B will be entitled to the life estate in possession, but instead of the fee simple reverting to A, who originally made the grant, the fee simple will pass to C on termination of the life estate. C is not entitled to possession of the property while B remains alive, but they nevertheless have a legally enforceable right in respect of the land. If, in either example, B tried to sell the property, the fee simple in reversion or remainder could be enforced against the purchaser. The holder of the life estate could not sell a greater estate than they owned. They could not, therefore, sell a fee simple, making the value of the land limited. This type of fragmentation is becoming less and less common with the abolition of the lesser types of estate and the presumption in favour of fee simple. With the proposal to abolish the doctrine of estates and move to a system of ownership, these future interests will cease to exist as legal interests. They will instead be converted to equitable interests only.[38]

1.6 Conditional and Modified Estates

When creating or transferring an estate, you can choose to attach conditions to the estate itself. It is necessary therefore to be able to determine the types of conditions that can be attached, the criteria for deciding whether such conditions are valid, and the consequences of a condition being held by the court to be invalid.

A. Determinable Fee

Where a determinable fee is created, this means that the person to whom the estate is being transferred enjoys only a limited estate. The deed in this case would specify the words of purchase 'To A' but the words of limitation would contain a condition, such as 'until...', 'while' or 'during' for example. In this situation A enjoys not the full fee simple, but a determinable fee – one that lasts only until the specified event occurs, if ever. It is therefore a limited type of estate. The important point to note is that the condition is regarded as part of the words of limitation.

---

38 NILC *Land Law* (n 1) 267

The person who creates such an estate – the grantor – retains what is known as the 'possibility of reverter'. This is a legal interest in the land, but is contingent upon the determining event occurring. If the event does occur, the fee simple will revert to the grantor or his successors. This happens automatically and does not require action on the part of the grantor. As the possibility of reverter exists as a legal interest in the land, it can be passed by will to the heirs of the grantor, but it cannot be sold as a commodity, as a future estate in land.

The determining event attached to the estate may or may not occur. In the situation where the condition becomes impossible, or does not occur within a certain length of time, the estate converts into a fee simple absolute.[39]

Wylie suggests that it is now the form rather than the substance that determines whether an estate will be regarded as determinable or on a condition. Broadly speaking, a condition whereby a certain state of affairs must persist or the estate will be determined is regarded as a determinable fee. For example, granting an estate to Smith so long as he remained an amateur golfer means that once Smith became professional the estate terminated; compared to granting an estate to Smith, but if he turns professional, to Jones – a condition subsequent. The intention is clearly the same, but the nature of the estate is interpreted differently. This is not a problem where the intention and the condition that will give rise to termination of the estate is clear, but could prove more problematic where there is ambiguity (for reasons to be discussed).

B. Conditional Fee

Whereas with the determinable fee a lesser interest is transferred until such times as a determining event occurs, with the conditional fee, the full estate is transferred, but this is subject to a specified condition. The condition is not part of the words of limitation – not an integral part of the estate – but rather a condition imposed upon the enjoyment of the estate.

The type of condition can be either condition precedent, or condition subsequent. It is very important to be able to distinguish between these two types of conditions, for the rules determining their validity, and ultimately the consequences for the beneficiary vary greatly depending on what type of condition is attached.

It can be difficult, however, to determine precisely which type of condition is attached. The court has developed rules to help with this determination, but as a general

---

39   Perpetuities Act (NI) 1966 section 13(3)(a). This period is set at 80 years.

rule a condition precedent is a 'so long as' clause, and a condition subsequent can be described as 'but if' clause. This simply reflects the nature of the conditions. A condition precedent, as the name suggests, is a condition which must be fulfilled *before* the gift can vest. Examples can include coming to reside in a property; paying a fixed sum of money or becoming a member of a particular church.

Where a condition subsequent is imposed, the gift will vest, but is liable to forfeiture either if a certain condition arises or is not met, depending on the terms of the grant.

In the case of *Re Porter*,[40] the court gave some general guidelines regarding how to distinguish between the two different types of conditions:

Setting a time limit for performance may show condition to be precedent; but where a specific time is mentioned for the performance of the condition but not for vesting then it may be subsequent. If the condition can be performed right away then it will be precedent; but, if time is required for its performance then it may be subsequent. If the nature of the interest is such to allow time for the performance of the act before the interest can be enjoyed, it will be precedent; but if it is reasonable to suppose that the estate must vest in possession before the condition can be complied with then it will be subsequent.

Being able to distinguish between these two types of condition is of more than pure theoretical significance. The nature of the condition attached will determine how the court approaches the question of the validity of the condition and consequently the effect of the condition on the grantee.

i. Condition precedent

Where a person receives an estate subject to a condition precedent, they may wish to challenge the validity of that condition. This can be done on two main grounds – that the condition conflicts with public policy or that it is void for uncertainty.

There is a well-established jurisprudence in the Northern Ireland courts suggesting that conditions that are contrary to public policy cannot be attached to grants. The two key areas of policy that have been focused on are the restriction on the right of a grantee to marry, and restrictions on the alienability of the property.

There is a strong presumption in favour of marriage evident in the case law. Clauses which seek to prohibit or prevent marriage altogether will be void on the grounds of public policy. This does not mean, however, that the type of person to whom the grantee may be married cannot be restricted. So for example in the case of *Re Tuck's Settlement*

---

40 *Re Porter* [1975] NI 157 (Ch) (Lowry LCJ)

Trust[41] the court upheld a condition that an approved wife must be of the 'Jewish Faith' and of 'Jewish blood' as a valid condition precedent. This means that such restrictions will not automatically fall foul of the rules on public policy, and must be decided on their own terms.

Similarly, conditions that interfere with family life – particularly in respect of minors, will be held to be invalid. This was seen in the case of *Re Johnston*[42] where a condition that would have required a 15 year old boy to move out of his family home and assume caring responsibilities for a disabled adult was held to be contrary to public policy.

The second key element of public policy is that land must remain freely alienable. This element, and indeed the factors the court will take into account, will be equally valid in the context of condition subsequent too. You cannot attach conditions to land which would have the effect of preventing land from being freely bought and sold as this would violate the long established Rule Against Inalienability.[43] So for example you cannot establish future legal interests that would affect the land, or you cannot unduly restrict the class of persons to whom the land may be transferred. Where such conditions are attached they will be held to be void on public policy grounds.

More common, however, is dispute over whether or not a condition is sufficiently certain. In the case of a condition precedent the test that court will apply is whether or not the condition can be given any ascertainable meaning. This is a relatively lenient test. If the court can give any sensible meaning to the condition then it will be upheld and must be met before the gift will vest. Common examples of where the question of certainty arises include the definition of a particular faith, for marriage purposes, as seen in *Re Allen*[44] where the court decided that 'member of the Church of England' was sufficiently certain. Similarly in *McCausland v Young*[45] the definition of 'Roman Catholic' was held to be a question of fact capable of being understood with certainty and being ascertained with precision.

They also include conditions upon residency which are quite common in such cases. Often testators will leave property with the intention that the beneficiary will come and reside in that property. The way in which this intention is worded can be problematic.

---

41 [1977] EWCA Civ 11, [1978] 2 WLR 411
42 [1986] NI 229 (Ch)
43 This rule dates back to Quia Emptores and provides that land may not be transferred subject to conditions that prohibits the grantee from freely disposing of the land.
44 *Re Allen (Deceased) (No 1)* [1953] 3 war 637 (CA), [1953] 2 All ER 898
45 [1949] NI 49 (CA) (Andrews LCJ)

For example, in *Re Doherty*[46] a condition that the beneficiary come to live at the property within 12 months of the testator was held to be a valid condition precedent. This can be contrasted, however, with the case of *Re Waring's Will Trusts*,[47] where the word 'reside' was held to be insufficiently clear to be given ascertainable meaning.

Finally, where there is ambiguity in the wording of the condition, such as in *Re Porter* where a condition that 'satisfactory arrangements' be made was held to be insufficiently certain.

If, however, the court cannot give any ascertainable meaning to the condition, the condition itself will be held to be void for uncertainty and the gift will fail – meaning that the beneficiary receives nothing. Where a condition precedent is held to be void for uncertainty it is generally because of evidential uncertainty – namely how could it be established what was intended by the condition, and whether or not that had been met.

The severity of the consequences for the beneficiary in such cases is the reason behind the relative leniency of the test for certainty of a condition precedent.

ii. Condition subsequent

The rules are slightly different for a condition subsequent. Where the court determines that a particular condition is subsequent rather than precedent, its validity will be subject to the same considerations of public policy and uncertainty just discussed. However the way in which these criteria are interpreted varies from that for condition precedent. This is particularly the case with regard to uncertainty.

Where a condition subsequent is attached, the court will apply what is known as the *Rule in Clavering and Ellison*[48] to determine whether or not it is sufficiently certain. This rule states that a condition subsequent will only be void for uncertainty if the court cannot see precisely and distinctly from the beginning what events will give rise to forfeiture.

The standard is much higher with the case of condition subsequent than with condition precedent. The reason for this is that whereas with a condition precedent the condition has to be met before the gift can vest, where a condition subsequent is attached the gift will vest in the beneficiary, but this is subject to forfeiture in the event that the condition occurs or is not met, depending on the nature of the condition. Therefore before the court will allow the gift to vest, there must be absolute conceptual certainty as to the conditions that will result in forfeiture. If the court cannot say with any certainty from the outset what circumstances will lead to forfeiture then they will declare the condition to be void for uncertainty.

---

46 *Re Doherty, Quinn v Clarke and Another* [1950] NI 83
47 [1985] NI 105 (CA) (Hutton J)
48 *Aloysius Clavering v PG Ellison and Others* (1859) 7 HLC 707, 11 ER 282

Here again the rules on condition subsequent differ from those on condition precedent. Whereas if a condition precedent is held to be void for uncertainty the entire gift fails and the beneficiary gets nothing, where a condition subsequent is held to be void for uncertainty it is only the condition that fails. The result is that the beneficiary will take the gift free from the condition. This is clearly a more satisfactory outcome, because it results in the successful demise of the property.

While these rules may appear relatively straightforward in theory, it is not always easy to determine whether a condition is precedent or subsequent. Therefore much of the dispute that ends up before the courts in these cases centres around the nature of the condition itself – whether it should properly be regarded as condition precedent or subsequent. This matters to parties because of the consequences of a finding that the condition is either valid or void for uncertainty.

Where there is ambiguity the court will lean towards the construction that holds a condition to be condition subsequent rather than condition precedent. This is clear from the decision of the court in *Re Porter*[49] where the court stated:

> "Where it is doubtful whether a condition is precedent or subsequent, the court leans towards a construction which will hold it to be a condition subsequent, for that construction will lead to the early vesting of the gift and there is a presumption in favour of early vesting."

Therefore as can be seen from this statement, the preference for condition subsequent is not based on a desire for the beneficiary to take the gift, nor to defeat the intentions of a testator, but rather is based on a preference for early vesting. Where a valid condition precedent is attached the gift cannot vest until such times as the condition is met. This means that there can be delay in administering the estate. However where a valid condition subsequent is attached the gift will vest, but may be forfeit at a later date. This is the preferred option of the courts.

A preference for early vesting also favours the beneficiary in cases where the condition is held to be void for uncertainty. Rather than the entire gift failing, the beneficiary will take the gift free from the condition. This has the effect of confirming the estate as a fee simple absolute.

This is evidenced in the case of *Re Johnston,*[50] where the court interprets what at first glance look like two separate conditions – that the beneficiary come to live in the property, and continue to live there to care for a disabled sister – as one single condition

---

49 *Re Porter* (n 40) (Lowry LCJ)
50 *Re Johnston* (n 42)

subsequent which is subsequently found to be void on both grounds of public policy and uncertainty.

Finally, what happens if a valid condition subsequent is not met, giving rise to forfeiture?

Whereas with the determinable fee the possibility of reverter operated automatically in respect of the grantor or his heirs, the right of re-entry is a different type of interest. It must be actively exercised by the person who is entitled to the land under the grant. The estate remains vested in the beneficiary until such times as the right is exercised.

These estates are subject to the Rule Against Perpetuities. This rule arose as a result of attempts to tie land up into the future and provides that legal estates may not be created that will vest outside the perpetuity period. This helps to ensure that there is reasonable certainty as to future ownership of property. In Northern Ireland the rule is placed on statutory footing in the Perpetuities Act (NI) 1966. The perpetuity period is specified in the legislation as not exceeding 80 years. The Law Commission propose extending this to a period of 125 years. Therefore any right of re-entry or possibility of reverter that arises after the perpetuity period has expired will not be exercisable.[51]

However, modified and conditional fees are becoming increasingly rare in Northern Ireland. As a result the Northern Ireland Law Commission has recommended that existing modified fees be converted into fee simple absolute in possession. This would allow them to be treated the same way as the fee simple in terms of holding legal title and being able to dispose of the property. The right of re-entry and possibility of reverter will remain as recognised legal interests under Section 5(1) of the Land Law Reform Bill. However the Lands Tribunal will be given the power to modify or extinguish such interests upon the application of the owner of the modified estate. It is hoped that by making this provision modified estates will cease to exist in law.

1.7 Conclusion

While many of these technicalities have ceased to be of importance in England and Wales by virtue of the 1925 LPA, they remain an integral part of land law in Northern Ireland. It is therefore important to be aware of the technical rules that exist in this jurisdiction for the creation and transfer of estates in land.

---

51 Perpetuities Act (NI) 1966 section 13(1)

CHAPTER 2

The Extent of Property

2.1 Introduction

A key distinction to be drawn in property law is that between real property and personal property. Real property is property in respect of which a right of action exists. This relates to your rights of 'ownership' over your property and the way in which they can be enforced against third parties. An essential characteristic of property law, and that which distinguishes it from other areas of private law such as contract law, is the extent to which your legal rights are enforceable against not only a person or persons with whom you have an agreement such as a contract, but are enforceable against the whole world. Although property is generally understood to refer to a physical entity, such as a house, the concept of property refers more accurately to the bundle of rights that you enjoy in that house. These include the right to exclusive possession of your property; the right to freely alienate (to sell or transfer) the property; and the right to exclude all others from it. Where one or more of these rights is violated the law will recognise your right to take action to remedy the breach. So for example if a squatter moves into your property, as the owner of that property you have the right to take legal action to remove that squatter and to regain possession. This is because the law recognises you as having a better claim to the property than the squatter.

In Northern Ireland we do not have a system of absolute ownership of property. All title to, and rights over, property are relative in that they will be determined with reference to the rights of other people. Any number of different interests may exist in the land either at the same time or consecutively. These different rights and interests can be divided into corporeal and incorporeal hereditaments. Corporeal hereditaments exist in respect of a physical entity. If you purchase a house, what you purchase is a bundle of rights in respect of that house. You can live there and you have the right to exclude anyone else from entering the property. While you do not technically own the property itself under our current feudal system of landholding,[1] it is easy to see the extent of your 'property' in that case. Incorporeal hereditaments, on the other hand, are rights that exist without any physical form. They are generally rights that you enjoy over the land of someone else.[2] So for example you may enjoy a right of way to cross another person's land. Your rights are not equal to those of the person who holds the estate in the land (the person we think of as the owner), and they may not be visibly apparent if you were to inspect the property, but they are nevertheless rights over land that you are entitled to have enforced by the courts. The crucial distinction is that there is no physical form to these rights. The 'property' exists in purely abstract form.

Because a number of different interests can exist at the same time in the same property, it is impossible to establish absolute ownership of land. Our system of ownership is therefore relative. It depends on being able to establish that you have a better claim to the land than anyone else. With the purchase of a house, for example, this is achieved through the production and exchange of title deeds that are held to be proof of title.[3] However it is impossible for title deeds to record every specific detail of each property. How then are we to establish the extent of property and our rights to it? If there is disagreement over who owns the property, or who has an interest in it, how is this to be resolved?

This is an area in which there has been very little statutory intervention, and almost no judicial consideration in Northern Ireland. Our system continues to be governed by common law principles that have arisen in English case law. Yet it is an area of law that is of increasing relevance in Northern Ireland. For example, being able to establish rights of ownership below the surface of the land may yield significant benefit if natural resources such as gas are found there. Less happily, with many homeowners facing repossession of their homes, being able to ascertain the extent of ownership over the contents of the property is increasingly important. These issues are also important when property is being sold or otherwise transferred. Therefore while the principles remain rooted in old authority they nevertheless provide an important backdrop to most property transactions.

---

1   See chapter 1
2   See chapter 11
3   See chapter 4

2.2 Common Law Maxims

The extent of property is said to be governed by two maxims:

> '*Cuius est solum eius est usqe ad coleum et ad infernos*'

and

> '*Quicquid planatur solo, solo cedit*'.

Taken together these two maxims are said to define the extent of real property.

A. *Ciuis est solum eius est usqe ad coleum et ad infernos*

The first maxim means 'He who owns the soil owns everything up to the sky and down to the centre of the earth'. This provides us with the basic principle of property law that if you own land, then your rights in that property extend vertically up from that land and also directly below the surface of the land.

However, case law reveals that far from being a cast iron definition of property, the maxim simply provides a general principle that has been modified by the courts.

i. Down to the Centre of the Earth

The principle that the owner of land owns everything to the centre of the earth is relatively easily established. While ownership to the centre of the earth may present certain practical difficulties in terms of exercising rights of ownership, the principle is more readily applicable to ownership of the soil directly below the surface. This principle has been invoked in respect of items found below the surface of land.

The key authority in this regard is the case of *Elwes v Brigg Gas Co.*[4] In this case a prehistoric boat was found below the surface of land forming part of the estate of Elwes. The land had been leased to Briggs Gas Co., who claimed that they were entitled to the boat. Elwes replied that the boat itself had not been included in the terms of the demise (ie in the lease) and that therefore the boat remained his property. In determining who should be entitled to the boat, the court confirmed the principle that the person who is in lawful possession of the ground was entitled to everything that lay beneath the surface 'down to the centre of the earth'. In this case because the lease permitted *only* possession and profits from the land, the court held that ownership of the boat had not passed to the Gas Co. and remained vested in Elwes.

---

4   [1886-90] All ER Rep 559

The principle has recently been confirmed by the Supreme Court in the case of *Bocardo SA v Star Energy*. In this case the issue was whether a company had trespassed by laying pipes under the plaintiff's land. The court confirmed the principle that:

> "The owner of the surface is the owner of the strata beneath it, including the minerals that are found there, unless there has been an alienation of it by a conveyance, at common law, by statute or to someone else."[5]

While this remains the general principle in land law, there are a number of statutory exceptions to this rule. These exist primarily in respect of valuable minerals found below the surface of the land that the state may reserve for itself.[6] The current interest in the process of 'fracking' to exploit natural gas in Co Fermanagh may lead to interesting legal questions over ownership of and access to minerals under the ground in that context.

ii. Up to the Sky

The second part of the maxim refers to ownership of the air above land. As with ownership below the surface, the maxim provides that the owner entitled to possession of land will also be entitled to exercise proprietary rights over the air above it. This principle was established by the courts in the case of *Kelsen v Imperial Tobacco Co*.[7] In this case the plaintiffs had leased a shop adjacent to premises owned by the defendant. The shop leased had a flat roof, and signs affixed to the side of the defendant's premises protruded into the airspace above the plaintiff's shop. Following dispute between the parties, the plaintiffs asked the defendants to remove the sign. When they failed to do so the plaintiffs brought an action for trespass. In order to rule on the question of trespass, the court had to address the question of whether the plaintiffs were entitled to exercise proprietary rights over the airspace above the shop. Finding in favour of the plaintiffs, the court determined that the lease of the property also included the airspace above that property. Similarly in the case of *Anchor Brewhouse Developments*[8] the court held that booms of cranes overhanging the plaintiff's land at a height that did not affect his use of the land nevertheless constituted trespass.

What both these cases demonstrate is that the courts have accepted in principle that

5   *Bocardo SA v Star Energy Ltd and Another (Secretary of State for Energy and Climate Change Intervening)* [2010] UKSC 35; [2011] 1 AC 380, 399
6   See Mineral Development Act (Northern Ireland) 1969; section 11(3) of the Land Registration Act (NI) 1970 also confirms that registration of title to land does not guarantee title to mines and minerals found beneath the surface.
7   [1957] 2 All ER 343
8   *Anchor Brewhouse Developments Ltd v Berkley House (Docklands Developments)* [1987] 2 EGLR 173

ownership of land also entails ownership of the airspace above that land. However, this is not an absolute and unrestricted right. In the case of *Bernstein v Skyview* the defendant was a company who sold aerial view photography.[9] They had taken photographs of the plaintiff's property and offered them to him for sale. The plaintiff tried to sue the company for trespass, alleging they had no right to fly over his property for such purposes.

The court found in favour of the defendants. It was confirmed that although in principle the owner of the land also owns the airspace above that land, that the rights of the landowner must be balanced with those of the general public. To do this, the rights of a landowner in the airspace above his/her land will be restricted to such a height as is necessary for the ordinary use and enjoyment of the land. Beyond this the landowner has no greater rights than any other member of the public. Therefore although the maxim is accurate in principle, in practice it may be restricted on grounds of public interest.

One further issue to note is that while the *Bernstein* case was concerned with the question of property rights above land, the introduction of the Regulatory and Investigatory Powers Act (2000) (RIPA), applicable in Northern Ireland, has created a statutory framework for the protection of individuals from intrusion such as that at issue in *Bernstein*.[10] Where this intersects with property law is the recognition that one's property, including the airspace above it, can be the subject of trespass or unwanted intrusion. It also demonstrates the increasing influence of principles of human rights on property law.[11]

iii. Rebuttable Presumptions

In addition to regulating the ownership above and below the ground, a number of legal presumptions have also evolved that help to determine where the boundaries between property should lie. These presumptions are known as 'rebuttable' presumptions, because they apply only in the absence of evidence to the contrary. Some examples include:

- **The Hedge and Ditch Presumption**

---

9   *Lord Bernstein v Skyviews & General Ltd* [1977] EWHC QB 1, [1978] QB 479

10 This legislation is intended to regulate intrusion in the context of investigation, whether criminal or civil, and only indirectly speaks to the question of property rights.

11 In particular article 8 of the European Convention on Human Rights protects the privacy of the home. RIPA came into force one year after the Human Rights Act 1998 gave effect to the provisions of the ECHR in UK law.

Where separate parcels of agricultural land are separated by a hedge and a ditch, the law presumes that the landowner stood on the boundary of his/her property, facing his/her own land to dig the ditch. The earth removed from the ditch will be deposited on his/her side of the ditch and a hedge planted on top. This makes the edge of the ditch and not the hedge the boundary. However this presumption applies *only* where no evidence to the contrary can be produced. The existence of land registry maps, for example, would serve to render the presumption inapplicable.[12]

• Roads

Although the surface of the road will be vested in the local authority, in the absence of evidence to the contrary, the boundary between properties adjoining the road will be presumed to run along the centre of the road, beneath the surface.

• Rivers

As with roads, where properties adjoin a river the law will presume that the boundary lies in the middle of the river.

• Party Walls

A party wall is the wall that divides two adjoining properties. This wall forms the boundary between the properties and ordinarily belongs to both parties.

B. *Quicquid planatur solo, solo cedit*

The second maxim of property law is '*Quicquid planatur solo, solo cedit*'. Translated, this means 'That which is attached to the land becomes part of the land'. It is this maxim that gives rise to the distinction between fixtures and fittings in property law.

In general terms an object brought onto land can be classified in one of three ways:

- • A chattel
- • A fixture
- • Part and Parcel of the land[13]

The categorisation of property is important because of the consequences of determining that an item is a fixture, and therefore part of the property, and a fitting,

---

12 *Hayes v McGuigan and Others* [2011] NICh 25, 288 (Deeny J)
13 *Elitestone Ltd v Morris and Another* [1997] UKHL 15, [1997] 2 All ER 513

which remains personal property. The origins of this distinction arise in an early series of cases in which the court was asked to determine whether items could or could not be removed from properties when the estate passed to a new owner.

The first of these cases was *D'Eyncourt v Gregory*.[14] This was a complex dispute over the succession of an estate. One party had elected not to fulfil the conditions imposed on him in the will and would therefore forfeit his entitlement to the estate. However he wished to take certain valuable items with him. These included tapestries that were hung on the walls and ornamental statues that decorated the front of the property. The plaintiff in the case was the trustee of the estate and he asked the court to determine what items were fixtures, and thus belonged with the estate, and which were fittings and could therefore be removed. The court stated that "the question is not whether the thing itself is easily removable, but whether it is essentially part of the building itself." In this case the items in question were tapestries. They were hung on the walls as decoration in a similar manner to wallpaper. This means that they had become a part of the building. As a general rule, the maxim suggests that an item must be physically attached to the land in order to become a fixture. However there are exceptions to this rule. Items that are not attached to the land but simply rest on their own weight may in some cases be held to be part of the building itself where they contribute to an overall architectural design of the property. In this case statues that rested on their own weight fell into this category because they were part of an overall landscape rather than simply ornamental.

In the later case of *Holland v Hodgson*[15] the court provided a two part test to help determine the distinction between fixtures and fittings that remains applicable today. The court stated that when determining whether an item is a fixture or a fitting it is necessary to consider both the degree of annexation and the purpose of annexation of the item in question.

The degree of annexation refers to the manner in which the items are attached to the property. If they are attached in such a way that to remove them is likely to cause damage to the property then they are more likely to be fixtures. However if they can be easily removed then they will remain fittings.

The purpose of annexation refers to the reasons for which the items were brought onto the property. If an item is intended to improve the value of the property then it is more likely to be a fixture. If it is there for ornamental purposes, simply to be enjoyed

---

14 (1866) LR 3 Eq 382 (Ch)
15 (1871-1872) LR 7 CP 328 (Exch)

as an item, then it is more likely to be a fitting. These are only general guidelines, and whether an item is a fixture or fitting will depend on the circumstances of the case.

The final case in this series was *Leigh v Taylor*.[16] In this case tapestries were also at issue. The court, applying the two part test set out in *Holland v Hodgson*, considered whether they were fixtures or fittings. Whereas in *D'Eyncourt v Gregory* the tapestries had been attached to the wall in a manner similar to wallpaper, in *Leigh v Taylor* they were hung on frames and as such could be more easily removed. Therefore the degree of annexation was less in this case. Similarly the purpose for which the tapestries were hung was held to be ornamental. What is interesting about this case is that while it applies the same legal principles as were applied in *D'Eyncourt*, to the same items, the decision reached is different. In *Leigh v Taylor* the tapestries were deemed to be fittings that could be removed. This demonstrates how the facts and circumstances of the case will be relevant. In the time between *D'Eyncourt v Gregory* and *Leigh v Taylor* fashions had changed. By the time *Leigh v Taylor* was decided they were used as ornamental decoration rather than as wallpaper.

The judge commented:

> "something has changed very much … I suspect that it is not the law or any principle of law … but it is a change in the mode of life."

This means that although the legal test remains the same, the decision may be different as fashions change. In recent years the practice of property development has provided interesting examples of this. Whereas in the past it would have been unusual for items such as carpets to be considered as fixtures sold as part of a house,[17] the expectation of purchasers today is that the fresh neutral carpets are part and parcel of the deal. In these cases carpets are sold as fixtures that constitute an essential feature of the property. This does not mean that the legal test for distinguishing between fixtures and fittings has changed, but rather what we understand the 'purpose' of annexation of the items to be. If neutral carpets are introduced to the property in an attempt to raise the value of the property, they are likely to be deemed to be fixtures rather than fittings. A carpet with a pattern that is unfashionable but to the taste of the owner of the property is much more likely to be regarded as a fitting, as the purpose of introducing the carpet is to enjoy the carpet itself rather than to improve the value of the property.

However these are just guidelines. As a general rule the burden of proof when establishing whether an item was a fixture or a fitting would lie with the person making

---

16 *Leigh v Taylor* [1902] AC 157
17 See *Botham and Others v TSB Bank Plc* [1997] 73 P & CR D1 (CA)

the claim. Therefore if a purchaser wants to establish that carpets were fixtures that should have been sold with the property they will need to demonstrate that the purpose of the carpets was to improve the property so as to raise its value and facilitate its sale.

The starting point for applying the test, however, was the degree of annexation. The purpose of annexation became relevant where there was ambiguity as to the extent of the degree of annexation.[18] This approach has evolved a little in recent years and the purpose now appears to carry more weight. This is seen in the more recent decision on the distinction between fixtures and fittings is the case of *Botham v TSB Bank*.[19] In this case the test set out in *Holland v Hodgson* was applied to modern living.

2.3 Fixtures and Fittings: The Modern Context

In *Botham* the plaintiff had failed to keep up with the repayments on his mortgage. As a result the bank sought to repossess his property, a flat in Chelsea. However the value of the property was not enough to discharge the mortgage. What was at issue was whether the contents of the flat retained their character as personal property, for which he should receive credit from the bank, or whether they had become part of the property and therefore belonged to the bank as a result of the repossession of the property. When deciding the case the court divided the contents of the flat into a number of classes of goods. These included items such as fitted carpets and light fittings as well as more substantial items such as sanitary ware in the bathroom, and kitchen appliances.

The important thing about this case is the guidance it provides on how the degree of annexation and purpose of annexation tests are to be applied. While it does give specific examples of items that may and may not be considered to be fixtures, it is important to remember that this calculation will be made in light of the circumstances of the case, and that the degree and purpose are what are important. The court emphasised that the purpose of annexation is the key issue for the court to address, the degree test "serving merely as a reminder that there must be some physical annexation before a chattel can become part of the land."[20]

The court in Botham offered guidance on how the purpose of annexation may be approached. In particular they offered four issues to consider. The first was the nature of

---

18   *Berkley v Poulett* [1977] 1 EGLR 86, 88-89 (Scarman LJ)
19   *Botham* (n 17)
20   Ibid

the object itself. If it is ornamental and the attachment is simply to allow the item to be enjoyed then it is more likely to be a fitting. However, this may be qualified by the second criteria. Where the item can be removed without damaging the fabric of the building then it is likely to be a chattel. The example the court uses to distinguish between the two is ornamental tiles. Although these are added to a house to be enjoyed, removing them will cause damage to the fabric of the property. This demonstrates how the tests must be applied in light of the relevant facts. The third consideration is whether the land is owner occupied or is rented. There will be a stronger presumption that items brought into rented property are intended to remain as fittings (and therefore personal property) than if the property is owner occupied. This is because the court does not presume that a tenant intends to improve the property in the same way that an owner would. Finally, the court may take into account the way in which the items are attached. In particular items that require a builder or plumber to install them are much more likely to be fixtures and therefore become part of the land than items such as carpets or curtains.

The overarching aim of the 'purpose of annexation' test is to determine the extent to which an item was intended to permanently improve the property. Good examples of this reasoning are provided by the installation of kitchens or bathrooms, commonly understood to be essential to selling property. The installation of a new kitchen is likely to significantly improve the value of a property. Removal of the kitchen would adversely impact the property. It is therefore more then likely that kitchen units are fixtures. Appliances may be a little more complicated. In *Botham* the court referred to 'white goods', such as a fridge or a cooker, as the electrical appliances that can simply be unplugged and removed from a kitchen or utility room. In these circumstances the appliances will remain fittings. However where integrated appliances such as an oven or a dishwasher are included as part of the design of the kitchen it is much more likely that they will be deemed to be fixtures as they form part of an overall design that improves the property. Similarly with bathroom furniture, the removal of a bathtub or sink will diminish the value of the property and will render the room useless as a bathroom. Therefore the purpose of annexation of these items is most likely to improve the property, making them fixtures rather than fittings.

The rise and fall of the property market demonstrates why it is important to be able to distinguish between fixtures and fittings. When house prices are rising, money spent improving property by adding items such as cookers and integrated fridges can easily be recouped. However, when prices are falling or people are facing repossession proceedings, it is important to be able to distinguish what items have become part of the property, and can therefore be re-possessed with the property, and what items remain personal property and can be removed by the owner.

A. Expanding the Definition

The two part distinction between fixtures and fittings dominated the reasoning of the courts in this area of law. However, a more difficult issue was presented in the case of *Elitestone v Morris*.[21] In this case the items in question were not objects that had been attached to land, but were bungalows that rested on their own weight. The question was whether these bungalows should be considered to be fittings, because they were not physically annexed to the land, or whether they were in fact fixtures. This raised questions over the interpretation of the requirement that a fixture be 'attached to' the land.

On the facts of the case the court decided that the bungalows were to be considered as part and parcel of the land. The judgment of the House of Lords confirmed that each case will be decided on its own merits, but that the two part test of degree of annexation and purpose of annexation will be significant. In the case in question the bungalows could not be removed without being destroyed. Therefore on the degree of annexation test they were more likely to be held to have become part of the land. On this matter the House of Lords overruled the Court of Appeal, who had decided that the bungalows were to be considered as fittings because they rested on their own weight. This confirms the principle that absence of attachment does not automatically prevent an item from becoming part of realty. Where the item is constructed in such a way that it cannot be removed without destruction, the House of Lords held that it cannot have been intended to remain as a chattel, but rather it was intended to form part of the realty (ie part and parcel of the land).

The case also clarifies how the purpose of annexation is to be determined. It had been suggested that the parties had agreed that the bungalows would remain fittings and that this agreed intention should be taken into account. In *Elitestone* it was clarified that the purpose of annexation was to be determined objectively. Therefore the court has the power to define, according to objective criteria, what the purpose of annexation was. The subjective intention of the parties cannot affect the question of whether the chattel has, in law, become part of the freehold.

What is most legally significant is the introduction of a new three part test for determining the extent of real property. The introduction of the criteria of 'part and

---

21 *Elitestone* (n 13)

parcel of the land' reflects the reality that items such as chalet bungalows cannot properly be considered in the same category as smaller items that are physically attached to the land.[22] It also addresses the ambiguity that arose in *D'Eyncourt v Gregory* that items resting on their own weight may nevertheless be considered fixtures, notwithstanding the absence of physical attachment.

Therefore it can be seen that while the maxim of 'that which is attached to the land becomes part of the land' provides a general statement of a principle in property law, its interpretation is subject to a number of different factors and cases must ultimately be decided on their own facts, in light of the three part test set out in *Elitestone*.

2.4 Finders Keepers?

The previous discussion on the distinction between fixtures and fittings aimed to demonstrate the physical limits of real property. However, when it comes to ownership of personal property the emphasis shifts away from defining the limits of that property and towards the question of possession – namely who is entitled to property.

Nowhere are the issues surrounding possession and ownership better illustrated than in the law relating to lost property. Land law in Northern Ireland, as in the rest of the United Kingdom and Ireland, is based on a system of relative title to property. We do not have any recognised concept of absolute ownership, therefore determining who is entitled to property is done on a relative basis – namely who has the best title. To establish that you are entitled to property you must be able to show that there is nobody with a better claim than you to the property. Therefore the question of lost property raises interesting legal issues.

The (non-legal) maxim of 'finders keepers' sums up the idea of ownership based on possession. If property rights were determined solely on the basis of possession the owner of a lost item would have no claim against a person who had found it. However the law does not recognise this to be the case. In order to establish who has a better claim to the property there are a number of different considerations. Because ownership is relative, there may be any number of people with competing claims. The rules explained here outline how to determine who has the best claim. Despite a recommendation that the law in this area be codified, legislation has not been passed. The ownership of lost

---

22 See Heather Conway, 'Case Comment: Elitestone v Morris [1997] 1 WLR 867' (1998) *Conveyancer* 418

property therefore continues to be governed by common law rules.[23]

A. The True Owner v The Finder

It is accepted law that if the true owner of lost property can be identified that they are entitled to the property. However, if the true owner cannot be identified then the finder will have to establish that they have a better claim than anyone else to the property.

The case of *Armory v Delamirie*[24] is widely cited as authority that a finder has better title than anyone else to the property. In this case a young chimney sweep had found a ring. He handed it to a jeweller's apprentice to have it valued, and when it was returned to him the gem from the ring was gone. It was decided:

> "That the finder of a jewel, though he does not by such finding acquire an absolute property or ownership, yet he has such a property as will enable him to keep it against all but the rightful owner, and consequently may maintain trover."

Therefore in principle it appears that the finder of property should have the best claim to that property against anyone except the original owner.[25] However the principle has not been as widely interpreted as this in practice.

B. Finder v Landowner

Where lost property is found, the owner of the land on which it is found may make a claim to that property. This is possible because of the maxim discussed previously that 'he who owns the earth owns everything up to the heavens and down to the centre of the earth'. There are two distinct potential scenarios to consider here.

i. The property is found under the ground

The application of the maxim in the context of lost property was confirmed in *Elwes v Brigg Gas Co*. In addition to demonstrating the application of the maxim, this case also sheds light on the priority of claims to lost property. Because the remains of the boat had been found underground, attached to and therefore part of the land itself, the court ruled that the owner of the land had a better claim to the property than to the finder. Therefore in principle the two maxims outlined provide useful guidance in these

---

23 *Parker v British Airways Board* [1982] 1 AU ER 834
24 (1722) 1 Strange 505, 93 ER 664
25 This principle was also confirmed in *Parker* (n 23)

circumstances. As a general statement of law, the possessor of land is entitled, as against the finder, to chattels found on the land.[26] This principle was established in the case of *South Staffordshire Water Co. v Sharman*, in which a ring had been found in a pool of water on private property. The defendant had been employed by the plaintiff to clean the pool, during the course of which he found the ring. The question that arose was who, as between the landowner and the finder, had the better claim to the rings. In its judgment the court drew a distinction between public and private property, demonstrating how a claim to entitlement to lost property is integrally linked to possession of the land. It was confirmed that "legal possession rests on a real de facto possession constituted by the occupier's general power and intent to exclude unauthorised interference." Therefore possession is an inherent right of property ownership. The owner of the land will therefore have a better title to the object than the finder.

One notable exception to this principle arises in the case of treasure. If the items found under the land are of particular historic value they may come within the terms of the Treasure Act 1966. This legislation applies to Northern Ireland as well as to England and Wales and provides that treasure, within the definition of the Act, belongs to the Crown. The meaning of treasure is defined with reference to both the age of the objects and the content of valuable metals.[27]

In Northern Ireland searching for such treasure on historic or archaeological sites is prohibited.[28] However, if you do find treasure you should hand it in to the Northern Ireland Environment Agency, the Ulster Museum or to the Police Service of Northern Ireland.

The situation is more complicated where a lost item is found on the surface of the land.

ii. Items found on the surface of land

Where items are found on the surface of the land the maxims are less clearly applicable. While in *Sharman* the court confirmed that the inherent right to restrict access to the land was enough to ground a claim for possession, recent cases have tended to qualify this principle. Where items of lost property are not attached to the land, then the owner will have to demonstrate that he/she exercised 'manifest control' over the land so as to indicate an intention to control the land and anything found on it. The leading regard in this case is *Parker v British Airways Board*.[29] In this case the plaintiff had found a

---

26 *South Staffordshire Water Co v Sharman* [1896] 2 QB 44
27 Treasure Act 1966 section 1
28 Historical Monuments and Archaeological Objects (Northern Ireland) Order 1995
29 *Parker* (n 23)

valuable bracelet in a passenger lounge at Heathrow Airport. He handed it to the airline staff, but asked that it be returned to him if the true owner did not return to claim it. He later discovered that British Airways had sold the bracelet and kept the proceeds. The question that arose was who had a better claim to the property in the absence of a claim by the true owner?

In a judgment that provides a comprehensive re-statement of the law of lost property, the court outlined the principles to be applied when deciding who, as between a finder and the landowner, has better claim to the item. It was emphasised that:

> "a finder of a chattel, whilst not acquiring any absolute property or ownership in the chattel, acquires a right to keep it against all but the true owner or those in a position to claim through the true owner or one who can assert a prior right to keep the chattel which was subsisting at the time when the finder took the chattel into his care and control."

This confirms that the finder will lose their claim against a landowner who can demonstrate the existing interest in the land, such as was the case in *Sharman*. However, these rights are qualified by the requirement that the owner or occupier of the land on which the lost property is found must demonstrate a 'manifest intention' to exercise control over that land. The manifestation of intention may be express or implied from the circumstances.[30] For example, signs that indicate ownership or restricted access to the property may fulfil this requirement. The publicised existence of a lost property policy may also suffice. However where such intention is not evident the landowner may lose a claim against a finder. This was the case in *Parker*, where the court decided that the degree of control was not sufficient. The court pointed to the fact that although access to the airline lounge was restricted to a certain class of passengers, there was no evidence that British Airways had any intention of controlling items lost in the lounge. This confirmed the principle from the earlier case of *Bridges v Hawkesworth* that where an item is found on property to which the public has free access the finder may establish a better claim than the landowner.[31]

It can therefore be seen that the claim of a landowner to lost property can be determined according to two separate criteria. The first is that the property is an integral part of the real property. The second is that the degree of control exercised over the property demonstrated an intention to exercise rights of property ownership in respect of all items found on the land.

---

30   *Parker* (n 23) 843 (Donaldson LJ)
31   *Bridges v Hawkesworth* [1843-60] All ER Rep 122 (QB) 124 (Patteson J)

There are other criteria that may also be taken into account. In *Parker* it was emphasised that the conduct of the finder and the circumstance in which they come to be in possession of the lost property will be relevant.

iii. The conduct of the finder

Where the finder of lost property has acquired the property as a result of trespass or other illegal conduct then they are less likely to be able to make a successful claim. In *Parker* it was confirmed that the finder of a chattel acquires very limited rights over it if he/she takes it into his/her care and control with dishonest intent or in the course of trespassing.[32] This was first established in the case of *Hibbert v McKiernan*.[33] In this case a young boy was accused of stealing golf balls from a golf course. It was argued that the golf balls did not belong to the club as they were merely lying on the surface of the land and there had been no effort to assert ownership of them. The key question to be addressed was therefore to what extent was the golf club 'in possession' of the golf balls at the time they were taken?

This raised a bigger question over the meaning of possession that would have significant implications for the decision in this case but also for the concept of property and the law of finding. The court decided that ownership of property entails an intention to exclude wrongdoers from that property. This is enough to support a claim for possession of items found on the land. However the conduct of the finder was also deemed relevant. Because the balls had been found as a result of trespass, the court did not deem it necessary to consider the rules that would have applied had he been an 'honest' finder. This suggests that the courts will not look favourably upon a claim to possession of lost property where it is found as a result of trespass. The rights of landowner in these cases will most likely prevail. This principle was considered and ultimately confirmed in the later case of *Waverly Borough Council v Fletcher*.[34] This case raised an interesting legal question because the land on which the lost property was found was a park that was, unlike the golf club, open to the public. The case was therefore described by the judge as a "collision of two familiar concepts of English law: finders keepers, and that an owner or lawful possessor of land owns all that is in or attached to it."[35]

In this case a brooch had been found beneath the surface of the land. This brought it within the scope of the rule that such property is an integral part of the real property and therefore belongs to the landowner. However because the land was open to the public

---

32 *Parker* (n 23) 837 (Donaldson LJ)
33 [1948] 2 KB 142
34 [1995] 3 WLR 772 (CA)
35 Ibid 338 (Auld LJ)

the court was asked to consider the relative merits of the arguments of the parties. The court confirmed that different principles will apply depending on whether the property is found under the ground or on the surface. However in this case the determining factor was the conduct of the defendant. He had found the brooch while using a metal detector in the park. This activity was prohibited by the Council, although signs to this effect were not clearly visible. The court therefore accepted the argument of the Council that the use of the metal detector had constituted trespass. This meant that he did not have a valid claim to the property.

In this case the reasons for finding in favour of the Council were straightforward as the item had been found below the surface of the ground, making it part and parcel of the land. Nevertheless the principle remains that a trespasser will not be able to establish good title to lost property.

iv. Finder v Employer

Where property is found by an employee in the course of his/her employment, the employer will have a better claim to the property. This was demonstrated in the pre-partition Irish case of *McDowell v Ulster Bank Ltd* in which a caretaker who found money while working at the bank was deemed not to have full possession of it, but rather to be holding it for his employer.[36] This can be justified on the basis that the finder in these circumstance would not have had access to the land on which the lost property was found but for their employer. A similar line of argument was also seen in *Sharman*, and the principle was confirmed in *Parker v British Airways Board* where the court stated that the employee take the item into his care and control on behalf of his employer. As a result it is the employer who acquires any finder's rights rather than the actual finder.[37]

The law of lost property, as governed by the common law rules, therefore demonstrates the concept of relativity of title. In order to make a claim to property it must be established that there is no other person who has a prior or superior claim to the finder. Each case will be decided on its own facts, applying the general principles outlined. The concept of possession will be a crucial determining feature – whether the possession of the person who finds the item, or the possession of the landowner which grounds a superior claim to it.

---

36   (1899) 13 ILT 96, 33 ILT Jo 225
37   *Parker* (n 23) 1018 (Donaldson LJ)

This is an area of law where the same common law principles apply in Northern Ireland as apply in England and Wales. There has been no specific statutory reform of this area, nor has case law amended or developed the law in this jurisdiction.

CHAPTER 3

Law and Equity

3.1 Introduction

One of the key distinctions that exists in property law is that between law and equity. This distinction underlies many of the key principles of property law and determines the extent of rights and interests in land and property. Interests in land can be either legal or equitable. The status of the interest will determine the extent of the interest and the ways in which it can be protected. It is therefore important to be familiar not only with the relationship between the two, but also with the way in which the different rules operate to regulate property ownership.

As discussed in chapter 5 the origins of modern day equity lie in land law and the regulation of the use of land. It is therefore unsurprising that equity exerts a considerable influence on land law. It is not the intention of this chapter to provide a detailed explanation of equity per se, but rather to introduce key concepts of equity as they are relevant to the study of land law.

It is commonly understood that equity arose as a result of the need to mitigate the harshness of the common law. Equity will intervene where to allow one party to insist on their strict legal rights will cause unfairness to another party. This reflects the origins of equity in the office of the chancellor and his 'court of conscience'.[1]

---

1   JE Penner, *The Law of Trusts* (8th ed, OUP, 2012) 3; see chapter 5 on the evolution of equity in the context of land law

3.2 Key Principles of Equity (Maxims)

Equity rests on a number of rules or 'maxims'. These are general principles that provide guidance on the application of equity to legal disputes. Detailed discussion of all of these maxims is beyond the scope of this book. However, a number of these maxims are directly relevant to property law and will appear throughout the course of this book. It is therefore worth outlining these maxims and explaining their application in the context of property.

A. Equity Follows the Law

This maxim reflects the fact that equity and law are not entirely separate systems of rules. While they initially developed through two different court systems, since the Judicature Acts 1873-1875 the two systems have been fused. This means that legal and equitable arguments can both be raised in any court. Equity also depends on the common law for its existence. Arising as a reaction to hard cases at common law, equity exists to rectify injustice caused by the common law, not to replace it as a system of adjudication. Therefore in the first instance it is common law that will be applied to a legal dispute. Equity will presume that the correct position is the legal position unless it is shown to be otherwise.[2] However, where allowing one person to insist on their strict legal rights will cause unfairness, equity may intervene and the outcome of a decision based on equity will be different from that under the common law.

B. Where the Equities are Equal the Law Prevails

Equity can intervene where application of the common law will cause injustice to one party. However, where both parties rely on equitable arguments and the court determines that both equitable arguments are of equal merit, the decision will be made in accordance with the law. This is because there is no reason for equity to intervene where the position between the parties is equal.[3]

C. Where the Equities are Equal the First in Time Prevails

This maxim refers to the rules of priority that govern equitable interests in land. This is discussed in more detail in section 3.5.

---

2   See for example *The Law Society of Northern Ireland* v B [2011] NICh 21
3   See *Northern Bank Ltd v Rush and Davidson* [2009] NICh 6 [15] (Deeny J)

D. Equity Regards as Done that which Ought to be Done

This is another maxim with particular application in land law. The creation or transfer of estates usually requires execution by deed. Where the formalities for the transfer of an interest are not met then the interest will not take effect in law. However because of the maxim that 'equity regards as done that which ought to be done', agreements to create or transfer interests in land that are improperly executed may still take effect in equity.[4] This was the case in the famous Rule in *Walsh v Lonsdale* whereby it was held that a contract for a lease was as good as a lease.[5] The interests created in these circumstances will be equitable rather than legal. The basis for this intervention is the promise made in the contract and allows equity to enforce the obligations that have been undertaken.

E. Equity Acts *in Personam*

This maxim is important because it reflects the importance of conscience to the exercise of equitable jurisdiction. Equitable remedies are granted where the conscience of one party is so affected as to make it unfair to allow them to insist on their strict legal rights. This means that the equitable remedy is directed against a specific person. Its remedies will not necessarily be of general application.[6]

Although this is not the full extent of the equitable maxims, these are the maxims most likely to be encountered in the study of the principles of land law. There are other maxims that arise in specific contexts and these will be highlighted where they are relevant.

The two principle areas in which equity has intervened in property law are the creation of the trust, and the provision of equitable remedies.

3.3 The Trust

The origin of the modern day trust lies in the 'use' of land discussed in chapter 5.[7] The purpose of the use was to separate the legal and the beneficial ownership of property, creating a system whereby one person legally owns the property, and is entitled to deal with it as the owner, but must do so on behalf of another person. The person who

---

4   There are also two related maxims that 'Equity presumes an intention to fulfil an obligation' and 'Equity looks to intent rather than form' which further support this intervention.
5   (1882) 21 Ch D 9 (CA)
6   See for example the intervention of equity in relation to contractual licences – chapter 9.2.C.ii
7   See section 5.3

holds the legal estate is the trustee, and the person who is entitled to the benefit is the beneficiary. Trusts arise in a number of different situations.[8]

A. Express Trusts

It may be the intention of one person to create a trust of property for another. For example, property may be left in a will on trust for the benefit of minor children. The legal title to the estate will vest in the trustees, who will have legal powers to deal with the property, but they will do this on behalf of the minor children, who are entitled to the benefit of the property. Similarly where property is left in a will to a number of beneficiaries, it may be stipulated that the property should be sold and the proceeds of sale divided between the beneficiaries. This is known as a trust for sale. The legal estate will vest in a trustee who will be responsible for selling the property and ensuring that the proceeds are divided according to the terms of the will. The rights of those entitled to the proceeds of the property are equitable rights only.

Trust may also arise more indirectly than this. In the law of property two particular types of trust feature prominently. These are the resulting trust and the constructive trust.

B. Resulting Trusts

Resulting trusts arise where equity presumes that the property is held on trust by one person for the benefit of another by virtue of the circumstances in which the property was acquired. For example, where two people have contributed equally to the purchase price of a property but only one person is named as the legal owner, equity will presume that the intention of the parties was that both parties would have equal beneficial ownership of the property. The party named as the legal owner will be deemed to hold the property on trust for the other contributing party. The trust therefore arises 'as a result of' the contribution to the purchase of the property. In these situations the extent of the beneficial interest under the trust will be commensurate with the extent of the contribution made to the purchase price.

C. Constructive Trusts

Recent decisions in land law, particularly in the area of family property, have seen an increasing use of the constructive trust to protect the equitable interests of spouses in

---

8   For an introduction to the range of trusts available see Penner (n 1)

occupation of property. The constructive trust is said to arise by operation of law. This means that it is not expressly created by the parties, and does not arise naturally as a result of the property transaction, but is imposed on the parties as an equitable remedy in appropriate circumstances. In the context of family property, for example, when determining if the imposition of a constructive trust is appropriate in the circumstances the court will take into account the course of dealings between the parties to try and infer whether there was a common intention that the beneficial ownership of the property should be shared, even where only one party is named as the legal owner.[9] In these circumstances the common intention constructive trust identifies the true beneficial owner and the extent of their beneficial interest.[10]

The use of constructive trusts is also seen in relation to the revocation of contractual licences.[11] In these cases the court is concerned with the conscience of the licensee. Where it would be unfair to allow one party to revoke a contractual licence the court may impose a constructive trust to protect the licencee.[12]

The law of trusts is a wide area of law in and of itself. These are just basic examples of where trusts arise in relation to property law. There are two key points to bear in mind when considering the relationship between law and equity. The first is that equity may intervene to protect (or in some cases create) rights in property where necessary. The second is that the nature of these rights will be equitable and subject to the rules on equitable interests discussed in section 3.4.

3.4 Nature of Equitable Remedies

The most important feature to note about equitable remedies is that they are discretionary. They are not an entitlement but something granted by the court as a result of the facts of the case. The remedy extends only to what is necessary to do equity.[13] The extent of the remedy will therefore be commensurate with the injustice of the case. This means that the nature of the remedy will vary from case to case.

---

9   See *Law Society* (n 2); *Bank of Scotland plc v Brogan and Another* [2012] NICh 21 for discussion of the use of constructive trusts in the context of family property in Northern Ireland.

10 *Stack v Dowden* [2007] UKHL 17, [2007] 2 AC 432 (Walker LJ)

11 This is discussed in detail in chapter 9

12 See most famously the English decision of *Binions v Evans* [1972] EWCA Civ 6, 1972 Ch 359

13 *Mulholland v Kane and Kane* [2009] NICh 9 [21] (Deeny J)

Equitable remedies may involve relief as basic as declaratory relief – a ruling that a person has a proprietary interest that can be protected by the court.[14] Where necessary an equitable right to possession may also be protected by injunction.[15] Another available remedy involves the enforcement of the terms of a contract, on the basis that equity regards as done that which ought to be done. The existence of a specifically enforceable contract will be regarded in equity as evidence of intention to fulfil the obligations therein. In the context of property law this often entails the creation of a proprietary interest, for example an agreement to enter into a lease or a mortgage.[16] Where the formalities are not completed equity will not allow one party to evade their obligations on the basis of a technicality where it would unfair to the other party to do so. Where specific performance of the terms of the contract is not appropriate damages may be ordered.[17]

The most far reaching effect of an equitable remedy can be the creation or recognition of a proprietary interest. This arises in the context of proprietary estoppel,[18] and also in relation to trusts of the family home.[19] In both these circumstances the courts may decide, on the basis of the course of dealings between the parties, that a proprietary interest has arisen. Equity therefore plays an important function in ensuring that rights are recognised even where they cannot be established in common law.

All of these remedies will be discussed at various points throughout this book.

3.5 Legal and Equitable Interests

In property law there are two different types of interest that can exist. These are legal interests and equitable interests. The distinction arises as a result of the historical division of law and equity. Traditionally all interests in land would have been legal. As discussed in chapter 1, property refers not to the physical being of land, but rather to the bundle of rights that property entails. These include the right to possession of the property, the right to freely sell or transfer the property, and the right to exclude

---

14 *Jones v Jones and Others* [2001] NI 244 (Ch) 255 (Girvan J)

15 Ibid

16 *Russell v Russell* (1783) 1 Bro CC 269, 28 ER 1121

17 *Tanner v Tanner* [1975] EWCA Civ 4, [1975] 3 All ER 776

18 *Johnston v Johnston and McKee* [2008] NICh 11; *McLaughlin v Murphy* [2007] NICh 5 (Deeny J); see chapter 9

19 *Bank of Scotland* (n 9); *Law Society* (n 2); see chapter 1

all others from it. Where a legal estate or interest in property exists the owner of that estate can freely exercise all these rights. The most significant aspect of this is the ability of the owner of the legal estate to exclude others from the property. Where a property right exists is it said that the right is enforceable against all the world. This is what distinguishes a property right from other rights such as rights arising under a contract. A right under a contract will only be enforceable against the parties to the agreement. A property right, by contrast, is enforceable against all third parties. This gives rise to the right to take court action to recover property, or to sue for trespass, for example. A legal interest will always be binding on third parties, subject to the rules of priority and registration discussed in section 3.6. This means that where a legal interest exists it will burden the land and will pass with the land to anyone who subsequently purchases it.

An equitable interest, on the other hand, is more limited in scope than a legal interest. Where an equitable interest exists the owner does not enjoy the full powers of ownership. Rather they are simply entitled to some benefit from the property. This may be a benefit in terms of possession or use of the property, or it may be entitlement to an income or share of the proceeds of sale of a property. The difference between legal and equitable interests is that equitable interests are not automatically binding on third parties. They are subject to rules of priority and notice that will determine whether the equitable interest will pass with the land and as a result be binding on third parties.

3.6 Rules of Priority

Because an inherent feature of a property right is that it is exercisable against all the world, there are some categories of rights that will burden the land itself. These are generally legal interests. Where this type of right exists or is created it is said to 'run with the land'. This means that anybody who buys that land will take it subject to that interest. An example might include a right of way across one piece of land to access another. If this is a legal interest then it will be binding on whoever owns the land, not just on the person who created it. In this way it will *take priority* over the subsequent legal interest. It is therefore vitally important for a prospective purchaser of the land to be able to determine what interests burden the land itself, and which do not. If an interest burdens the land then the purchaser will take the land subject to that interest, irrespective of the fact that he/she was not party to its creation. In these circumstances, where a property right exists, it is common to speak of it being binding on successors in title. This means that it will pass to whoever owns the land. Because of the existence of these types of rights and interests in land rules are required that will determine when interests will run with the land in a way that binds successors in title and when they will not. Where the estate or interest in question is legal the position is straightforward. A legal estate will bind third parties, including successors in title. As a general rule where there are two legal interests the first in time will prevail. That is why it is important to ensure that no other legal estates in the land exist other than the one being sold. In the event that another legal estate is discovered the purchaser will have acquired bad title, regardless if he/she knew about the prior estate.

The position is more complicated when it comes to the priority of equitable interests. An equitable interest will not automatically be binding on successors in title. Binding third parties depends on whether or not it can be shown that they knew of the existence of the equitable interest before they bought the property. This is known as the doctrine of notice. The essence of this doctrine is that a purchaser will only be bound by those equitable interests of which he/she was aware. However this is interpreted more broadly than actual subjective knowledge of the interest. There are three types of notice: actual notice, constructive notice and imputed notice.

A. Actual Notice

This arises where it can be shown that the purchaser did in fact know of the existence of the equitable interest. This is a subjective test and would arise, for example, where a purchaser knew of a spouse in actual occupation of a property who would have an equitable interest in the property but disregarded that fact. In this case the purchaser will take the property subject to the equitable interest.

B. Constructive Notice

This arises where the person did not know about the interest, but should have known. The best example of this is where an equitable interest is registered in the registry of deeds. It is the responsibility of the purchaser or their solicitor to make all necessary inquiries as to the interests that exist in the property. Had the purchaser consulted the register they would have discovered the existence of the interest. In these circumstances the purchaser cannot plead ignorance as a means of avoiding the interest. They will be deemed to have constructive notice of the interest because reasonable inquiries would have revealed the existence of the interest. The result of this is that the purchaser will take the property subject to the equitable interest.

C. Imputed Notice

Imputed notice is similar to constructive notice in that although the purchaser themselves may not have been aware of the interest their agent was. So for example if the solicitor carries out the necessary searches and discovers the existence of an equitable interest in the property but fails to pass this information on to the purchaser, the knowledge of the solicitor, acting as agent for the purchaser, will be imputed to the purchaser him/herself. In these circumstances the purchaser may have a cause of action against the solicitor, but they will still be bound by the equitable interest.

It is therefore reasonably difficult for a purchaser to establish that they were unaware of the existence of an equitable interest. However where they do succeed they will take the property free from the equitable interest. This applies only to what is known as a

'Bona fide purchaser for value of the legal estate without notice'

All of these elements must be present to allow the estate to be taken free from existing equitable interests.

i. Bona fide

This means that the purchaser must have acted in good faith. Any evidence of fraud or deception will prevent the purchaser from evading the existing interest.

ii. Purchaser for value

This rule also only applies to someone who pays valuable consideration for the property. It will not apply where the estate is inherited, for example, or where it is acquired through adverse possession.

iii. Without notice

As discussed, if the purchaser had notice, either actual, constructive or imputed of the existence of the interest they cannot take the land free from it.

The most likely scenario in which a purchaser can successfully claim to be a bona fide purchaser for value of the legal estate without notice is where the equitable interest has not been registered in the Registry of Deeds.[20] In these circumstances, where the interest could have been registered but was not, the purchaser may take the land free from the interest and the interest will be lost.

Where interests are registered, either in the Registry of Deeds or in the Land Registry then priority will be determined according to the rules of registration rather than the common law rules of priority.

---

20 See chapter 4

CHAPTER 4

Registration

4.1 Introduction

In order to sell or otherwise transfer land, it is necessary to be able to establish that you own the legal estate that you are purporting to sell. The purchaser must be confident that there is no other person who has a claim to the land. This is known as being able to establish title to the property. If good title cannot be proved then a purchaser risks buying land to which someone else has a claim. If this happens they will potentially either lose the land or take it subject to an existing interest.[1] It is therefore vitally important to be able to establish title.

A key distinction in land law that will govern the rules applicable to dealing with land is whether the land in question is registered or unregistered. There are two separate systems of registration that operate in Northern Ireland – registration of deeds, and registration of title. Both continue to apply today, although law and practice are steadily moving towards a complete system of registration of title.

The distinction arises from the practice of registration of title to land. As discussed in section 4.3, this is a process whereby title to land is guaranteed by its registration in the Land Registry. Where land is registered in this way it is known as 'registered land'. This is to be contrasted with unregistered land. Where land is unregistered it does not appear in the land registry. It is therefore more difficult to establish who owns the land and what other interests may be attached to it. Although title to this land is not registered, transactions relating to the land may be registered in the Registry of Deeds. While this register does not guarantee title to the property it nevertheless plays an important role in unregistered conveyancing.

---

1   This might include, for example, an easement or a mortgage that continues to burden the land.

4.2 Registration of Deeds

The purchase of land had traditionally been problematic. The relative system of ownership introduced under the feudal system meant that ownership was often fragmented amongst different persons. This included the existence of successive interests in property, as well as the existence of lesser interests that would be part and parcel of the property.[2] Added to this, possession of land did not necessarily imply ownership of an estate. For example, in Ireland a tenant farmer may have been in possession of the land but did not own the freehold. Physical inspection of the land would not be enough to determine the nature of the estate held or the range of different interests that might also exist in the same piece of land. Ownership of interests in land was therefore difficult to discern or to guarantee.

Yet in order to successfully sell or transfer property it is necessary to be able to establish good title – meaning that the vendor is entitled to sell the property and that no other parties will be able to establish that they have a legal interest that overrides the interest of the purchaser. This gives rise to the practice of searches to ensure that the purchaser takes clean title.

In order to prove lawful possession of an estate, the vendor is required to produce relevant documents and deeds (root of title) that demonstrate how he/she came to hold the estate.[3] In this way the purchaser could be reasonably sure that the vendor's title was good, but did not guarantee it. For example, although the legal title may look good, transactions may have taken place that were not recorded on the deeds; Easements,[4] covenants[5] or mortgages[6] may have been created – giving another person an interest in the land. The question would then arise as to what extent would a purchaser be bound by such matters, particularly if they were unaware of their existence? It is for this reason that the registration of deeds plays an important role in unregistered conveyancing. This system commenced with the Registration of Deeds (Ireland) Act 1707, but was more recently restated in the Registration of Deeds Act (NI) 1970.

---

2   See chapters 1 and 11
3   Under the Vendor and Purchaser Act 1874 (37 & 38 Vict c 78) the time period set for establishing title was 40 years.
4   See chapter 11
5   See chapter 10
6   See chapter 13

A. Registration of Deeds – Key Principles

Most transactions involving land must be executed by deed. This provides a record of transactions and provides 'root of title' – proof of the sale or transfer of the interest in the land. Under the system of registration of deeds a memorial of documents relating to land may be registered in a central registry.[7] This allows a prospective purchaser of land to see what transactions have taken place within the past number of years.

The registration of deeds serves to secure the interest by guaranteeing its effect in law.

Section 3 of the 1970 Act provides:

> "every document which is registered shall be deemed and taken as good and effectual both in law and equity according to the priority of time of registering it…"

There are two aspects to this. This first is that the document itself is taken as good and effectual in law and equity. This provision guarantees the interest against a potential purchaser. The registration of the interest in the central register means that a purchaser cannot claim that they did not have notice of it. Even where the purchaser or their agent fails to consult the register they will be deemed to have had notice of the interest by virtue of the fact that it is registered. This means that if the land is sold the interest will continue to burden the land.

Conversely, however, where such an interest is not registered, then it will not be binding on a purchaser. In this way the system protects both purchasers and those who have lesser interests in land that could be lost as a result of sale. Where the deed creating the interest is registered in the Registry of Deeds the purchaser should be aware of its existence and can therefore reasonably be expected to take the land subject to the interest. Where the opportunity existed to protect the interest but was not availed of, then it is reasonable that the purchaser should take the land free from an interest of which he/she could not be expected to be aware.

The second aspect of Section 3 is that it provides for priority of interests in order of registration rather than order of creation. This avoids the common law rules of priority and allows for certainty in relation to the protection of interests.[8]

---

7   Registration of Deeds (NI) Act 1970 section 1(1). The exceptions to this rule are leases of under 21 years duration and documents relating to registered land.

8   A similar function is performed in England and Wales by the Land Charges Register established by the Land Charges Act 1925 and replaced by the Land Charges Act 1972.

B. Registration of Deeds – Practicalities

The form of a deed is subject to the general rules on the execution of deeds. For deeds created before 2005 they must be signed, sealed and delivered in order to be valid.[9] Since the entering into force of the Law Reform (Miscellaneous Provisions) (Northern Ireland) Order 2005, deeds executed need not be sealed,[10] but must be expressed to be a deed in a way that conveys the intention to create a deed or conveyance.[11] It must also be signed and the signature witnessed.[12]

The form of the Deed will not be uniform. This is because it is the lodgement of an existing document rather than the creation of a new 'folio', as is the case when the land is registered. There are, however, some quite detailed rules on the way in which such documents should be prepared and submitted. While the technical details are of little concern to the undergraduate student, suffice to note that Section 4 of the Registration of Deeds Regulations (Northern Ireland) 1997 provides detailed instructions on the presentation of deeds for registration.

When deeds are submitted to the Registry they are allocated an individual serial number. These numbers are allocated according to the calendar year in which they are received[13] and in order or receipt by the registry.[14]

C. Validity of Deeds

Where an error appears in the deed this may cause the deed to be invalid. For example, an incorrect spelling of a name will mean that a deed will not appear in a search of the register. This is an invalid registration of the deed. Where a deed is invalid in this way there is a risk that it will lose priority over subsequently registered interests. This will not automatically be the case, but will depend on the facts of the case.[15]

The system of registration of deeds provides some certainty in land transactions by maintaining a record of dealings with land. However it does not provide a guarantee of the validity of those transactions. Difficulties therefore remain in tracing the extent of legal and equitable interests that exist. The system of registration of title goes much further towards providing certainty in respect of ownership of land.

---

9   See *Santander UK Plc v Parker (No 2)* [2012] NICh 20 [5]-[8] (Deeny J)
10 Law Reform (Miscellaneous Provisions) (Northern Ireland) Order 2005 article 3(1)
11 Ibid article 3(2)(a)
12 Ibid article 3(2)(b)
13 Registration of Deeds Regulations (Northern Ireland) 1997 section 5(1)(a)
14 Ibid section 5(3). Where two or more deeds are received together they will be allocated serial numbers as directed by the person making the lodgment.
15 *Northern Bank Ltd v Rush and Davidson* [2009] NICh 6

4.3 Registration of Title

In order to address some of the difficulties of establishing ownership of land, a system of land registration has developed that aims to provide conclusive evidence of ownership. This is a system of registration of title. Where title to land is registered it is possible to determine who owns the land by consulting the register. Subject to certain exceptions, the register will provide conclusive evidence of rights and interests in that land.

This is an area of land law where legislative developments in Ireland advanced ahead of those in England and Wales.[16] The onset of registration of title in Ireland was hastened as a result of the Land Purchase Acts passed in the late nineteenth century allowing Irish tenant farmers to purchase the fee simple estate of the land that they worked.[17] A condition of accessing finance to buy land under this scheme was that the land would be registered in a central registry. The operation of these Acts meant that a large percentage of rural agricultural land in Ireland, North and South, was registered. This has created a distinction that continues to exist today between rural and urban land in Northern Ireland. While much of the rural land is registered, land in urban areas tended to remain unregistered. There are practical reasons for this. First, for the most part the Land Purchase Acts did not apply to land in urban areas. Therefore compulsory registration of title did not apply to this land. Second, the feudal structure of land holding meant that urban land was often subject to complex pyramid titles which made it very difficult to establish what interests existed in the land. In order to register the land these titles would have to be investigated and unravelled, making it a time consuming process that was not ultimately necessary. The result of this is that urban land remains largely unregistered and therefore subject to the rules on unregistered conveyancing.[18]

The rules on registration introduced as a condition of the Land Purchase Acts laid the foundation for the system of land registration that continues in force in Northern Ireland today.

There are three key principles that underpin the system of land registration. These are the mirror principle, the curtain principle and the insurance principle. Each of these principles is demonstrated in the provisions of the Local Registration of Title (Ireland) Act 1891 which provided the basis for the compulsory registration of land in Ireland.

---

16 See generally A Dowling 'Of Ships and Sealing Wax: The Introduction of Land Registration in Ireland' (1993) 44 NILQ 360
17 See chapter 5
18 See section 4.2

A. The Mirror Principle

It is a core principle of land registration that the register should 'mirror' the interests that exist in the registered land. The purpose of maintaining such a register is so that a prospective purchaser of land can discover the nature and extent of the burdens affecting the land.[19] This is important because the effect of registration of such interests in the land will be to make them binding on the purchaser. Conversely, however, failure to register an interest will make it void against a purchaser.[20] The register therefore reflects the practical reality of ownership of the land and provides conclusive evidence of that ownership.

B. The Curtain Principle

While the underlying purpose of land registration is to provide an accurate record of interests that exist in land, there are nevertheless some interests that will not appear on the register. These are equitable interests such as interests arising under a trust. Under the 1891 Act land could be registered 'subject to equities'. This meant that the register provided conclusive evidence of title to the land – to ownership of the estate – but that equitable interests may exist in the land that did not appear on the register. These interests are said to exist behind the curtain. Where such interests existed they would continue to bind the purchaser. It would therefore be necessary for the purchaser to carry out the necessary inquiries and inspections to determine what such equities might exist.

C. The Insurance Principle

The final principle of land registration is that where land is registered the state guarantees the title to that land. A purchaser can rely on the register as conclusive evidence of ownership of the property. Where a defect in the title is subsequently discovered the state will indemnify the purchaser against any loss suffered as a result. Under the 1891 Act an Insurance Fund was established for this purpose.[21] Where loss is suffered as a result of a defect in title today compensation may be paid by the Department of the Environment.[22]

---

19 DB Murray 'The Statutory Charges Register Act (Northern Ireland) 1951' (1950-1952) 9 NILQ 90, 91
20 Local Registration of Title (Ireland) Act 1891 (54 & 55 Vict c 66) section 45
21 Ibid section 92. This fund was continued under Land Registration (NI) Act 1970 section 70(1) but was wound up under the Registration (Land and Deeds) (Northern Ireland) Order 1992 section 30
22 Registration (Land and Deeds) (n 21) section 31

These principles are reflected in the current Land Registration Act (NI) (1970) and continue to underpin the system of land registration as it operates today. This is an area of land law where the law in England and Wales is developing in a different direction to that in Northern Ireland. Central to the system of registration of title as it applies in Northern Ireland is that it simply reflects existing interests in land. An estate or interest is created by deed or other transfer and the interest that this creates is then registered in the Land Registry. The process of registration itself is not an integral part of the creation of that interest.[23] However in England the recent reforms introduced under the Land Registration Act 2002 have moved away from this system whereby registration reflects title to a system whereby title is created by virtue of registration. The 2002 Act provides that in many instances an interest will not take effect in law unless it is registered. Registration itself therefore becomes a precondition to the creation or transfer of an interest. This aligns closely with a preference for registration as a means of ensuring that land remains in commerce, subject to simple rules for transfer that facilitate its character as a commercial commodity. The law in Northern Ireland has not taken this approach and it appears unlikely that this will be the case in the near future. Therefore it is to be borne in mind that the law on land registration in England and Wales is more technical than that which applies in Northern Ireland.

4.4 Land Registration in Northern Ireland

A. Key Principles

Land Registration is an area of law that rests on one key piece of legislation. The Land Registration Act (NI) 1970 provides the statutory framework for registration of title in Northern Ireland. The system of land registration is known as a 'positive' system of land registration in that it provides an authoritative system that allows purchaser to rely on registered title as proof of legal ownership.[24] Where title to land is registered the state guarantees that title, even if it turns out to have been procured by defective means. The

---

23 It should be noted however that where a person is entitled to register the land this should be done as expeditiously as possible because under the 1970 Act only the registered owner of the property is entitled to deal with it. Failure to register the interest will therefore restrict the exercise of property rights. LRA (n 21) section 32(1)

24 *Swift 1st Limited v McCourt and Another* [2012] NICh 33 [11] (Horner J)

exception to this in Northern Ireland is that registered title obtained by actual fraud will not be guaranteed.[25]

Section 11(1) of the Act incorporates the mirror principle by providing that the register shall provide conclusive evidence of the interests shown on that register. The effect of this provision is to create a register that reflects the existing rights and interests that affect a specified piece of land. In Northern Ireland any of the existing legal estates may be registered. The owner of a fee simple estate or of a leasehold estate can be registered as full ownership. Persons currently entitled to possession of a fee tail estate or other limited form of estate may also apply to be registered as owners of a limited estate.[26] In addition to legal estates, lesser interests that benefit the land, known as appurtenant rights, may also be entered on the register.[27] There are two ways in which this operates. Where the benefit of a right is enjoyed, it may be noted against the title to the property. Similarly where a property is burdened by an interest the burden may also be noted on the title of the burdened property. For example, if an easement of access is created to allow the owners of property A access to their property across the land of property B, the benefit of the easement may be noted on the title to property A, and the burden of the easement may be registered against the title to property B.

However, while the register is intended to provide conclusive evidence of the interests that exist in land, the curtain principle continues to apply under the 1970 legislation. Section 38 of the Act provides for burdens that will continue to bind the land without the need for registration.[28] These are lesser interests in the land that are capable of being registered, but that will continue to exist 'behind the curtain' even if they are not registered. Section 38 sets out the basic principle that these interests will continue to bind and replaces the idea of land being registered subject to equities. The interests to which this section applies are set out in schedule 5 of the Act. They include express or implied leasehold covenants,[29] easements not created by deed,[30] leases for less than 21 years,[31] and equitable rights of those in actual occupation of the property.[32] The effect of this section is to make these interests binding on any purchaser of the land, even

---

25 Ibid [11]
26 LRA (n 21) section 12-14; see chapter 1
27 Ibid section 51
28 This is equivalent to the category of 'overriding' interests under the Land Registration Act 2002 in England and Wales.
29 LRA (n 21) schedule 5 section 6
30 Ibid schedule 5 section 9
31 Ibid schedule 5 section 12
32 Ibid schedule 5 section 15

if they could not have discovered their existence through inspection of the register. This is a limitation to the key principle of registration of title that the register provides conclusive evidence of the interests that exist in the land. It also means that although the register can provide a conclusive record of ownership of the estate, it does not altogether remove the need to conduct detailed searches of the title to the property.[33]

For example, John and Sara own a house in Belfast. John falls into debt and creates a mortgage on the family home to pay off his creditors. At the time the mortgage is created the title deeds to the property are in John's name, but Sara is also resident in the property. If the solicitor for the lending bank consults the register they will discover that John does in fact have legal title to the property and is therefore entitled to create a charge against it. They will not, however, be able to discover from inspection of the register alone that Sara lives there. Sara may have an equitable interest in the property by virtue of being in actual occupation.[34] This is an interest that burdens the land without registration. The bank will therefore accept the mortgage security subject to Sara's interest, even though it does not appear on the register.[35] Although Sara may register her interest in the property against the title, this is not a precondition to it being protected. In order to discover whether such interests exist it remains necessary to carry out a physical inspection of the property that would alert the lender to the possible existence of such interests.

Section 39 makes provision for further interests that may be registered as a burden against a property. These differ from the interests protected under Section 38 in that they must be registered to be binding on a purchaser. In the case of *Armstrong v Shields*,[36] Lord Justice Girvan confirmed that because the purpose of registration is to simplify the investigation of title, the register will be deemed to be conclusive of the extent of interests. This will be the case even where the interest has been incorrectly registered or there is a divergence between the details contained in the deed creating an interest and the registration of that interest.[37] This is because the purchaser in these circumstances is entitled to rely on what is apparent on the face of the register.[38] This

---

33 *Swift Advances Plc v McGuire and McManus* [2011] NIQB 55 [7] (Deeny J)

34 Actual occupation is determined at the time the charge is created. *Northern Bank Limited v Doyle and Others* (NICh, 26 June 1995), citing with approval the English authority of *Abbey National Building Society v Cann* [1991] 1 AC 56 (HL), [1990] 1 All ER 1085

35 See *Bank of Scotland v Brogan and Another* [2012] NICh 21 (Deeny J)

36 *Karl Armstrong and Margaret Elaine Armstrong v Phelim Bernard Shields and Rosaleen Shields* [2010] NICh 10 (Girvan LJ)

37 *Northern Bank Ltd v Rush and Davidson* [2009] NICh 6 (Deeny J)

38 Ibid [23]

also suggests that where such interests are not registered at all they will not be binding on any subsequent purchaser who cannot discover their existence through inspection of the register. These interests are listed in schedule 6 of the legislation and include primarily financial interests, including charges on the land or liens for unpaid monies.[39] Under Section 41 of the Act the registered owner of a property is entitled to charge the land. Such charges will be registered against the land, thereby reflecting the lender's interest on the register. Registrable burdens under schedule 6 also include rights of way or profits à prendre created by deed. In these cases the interest can be registered against the title to the burdened land.

Once such interests are registered they will take priority according to the time at which they were registered, not the time at which they were created.[40] This is provided for under Section 40 of the Land Registration Act, which provides that registered interests shall rank in priority according to the order in which they are entered, or are deemed to have been entered, on the register.

Although in the past land registration was only compulsory for land transferred under the Land Purchase Acts and other categories of estate listed in the 1970 Act,[41] all land in Northern Ireland is now subject to compulsory first registration.[42] This means that as unregistered land is transferred, whether through an *inter vivos* transaction or by will, a condition of that transfer will be the registration of title to the land. This must be done within a timely fashion or the interest may be lost.[43] The aim of this policy is to bring all of the land in the jurisdiction within the scope of the land registration system, transferring registration from the Registry of Deeds, to the Land Registry, thereby enormously simplifying conveyancing and ultimately allowing for a more streamlined system of electronic conveyancing.[44]

These rules mean that it is important to be aware of the rules of registration. Although this is a technical area of land law, more suited to the practitioner than the student, a brief outline of the process of registration can help to understand the basic principles and the rules governing priority of interests in registered land.

---

39 LRA (n 21) schedule 6 section 6
40 Registration (Land and Deeds) (n 21) article 20
41 Including land within a specified area, land that was subject to compulsory purchase, and certain leasehold interests. LRA (n 21) Part 1 schedule 2
42 This process was completed with the 'Compulsory Registration of Title (No 2) Order (Northern Ireland) 2002' which brought all of Northern Ireland within the scope of the compulsory first registration legislation.
43 LRA (n 21) section 4 (1); *Northern Bank Ltd v Rush and Davidson* (n 37)
44 Electronic Registration (Northern Ireland) Order 2011; Land Registration (Amendment) Rules (Northern Ireland) 2011

B. Practicalities

As outlined, land registration involves maintenance of a central register by the government which records who owns what interests in any piece of land at any given time. This system is operated by the Land Registry, which is overseen by the Registrar of titles.[45] The scope of the functions of the Land Registry is set out in the Land Registration Act.[46] The Registrar is the person responsible for overseeing the register. This entails a number of duties, including determining whether or not a person is entitled to register an interest in land.[47]

There are three different types of interest that can be registered. These are freehold estates, leasehold estates and other lesser interests in land, such as incorporeal hereditaments. These interests are all entered on one single register,[48] making it easier to determine the different interests that exist in a single piece of land.

For each piece of land purchased a separate folio is created. Each new folio is allocated its own individual number that will be used to identify the land. Where registered land is sold the purchaser will apply to the land registry to have the title transferred. In these circumstances the folio number remains the same. Where the land is sub-divided, or a lesser estate such as a lease is created, a new folio will be created for the sub-divided land. Upon registration this land will be allocated its own folio number that distinguishes it from the estate from which it was created. Lesser interests will be registered against the folio of the burdened land.

A folio consists of three parts:[49]

i. Description of the land

This includes maps that identify the land in question. It will record the date of registration and also set out details of any other folio that is related. For example, if a piece of land is sub-divided with one portion sold and one retained, the folio will reference the folio number of the land from which the new estate is being created. This helps to record the history of title to the property. Similarly if a lease is created from an existing freehold

---

45 For a detailed examination of the operation of the Land Registry see Arthur H Moir & Emily K Moir, *Moir on Land Registration: A Guide to Land Registration Law and Practice in Northern Ireland* (SLS Legal Publications (NI), 2011)

46 LRA (n 21) Part 1

47 Ibid section 33

48 Registration (Land and Deeds) (n 21) article 6

49 Land Registration Rules (Northern Ireland) 1977 section 5

estate then the lease will also be recorded. This section also details all existing interests in or rights appurtenant to the land.

ii. Name of title holders

This includes the name and address of the owner and the nature of the estate or interest that is being registered.

iii. Any burdens that affect the property

This includes lesser interests that exist in the property as well as charges that are to be registered against it. These interests will not be allocated their own folio number, but will instead be registered against the existing folio. This means that they are apparent from inspection of the title to the property. This plays an important role in ensuring that lesser interests are protected where land is sold or otherwise transferred.

The register therefore fulfils an important function by alerting a potential purchaser of land to the existence of other interests in that land. This has the effect of protecting the purchaser from buying land subject to burdens of which he/she was not aware. It also protects the beneficiaries of these lesser interests. If these interests, for example mortgages, are properly registered then they will continue to burden the land even if it is sold. The register is available to search, and it is the role of a conveyancing solicitor to carry out all the necessary searches to ensure that good title can be established to a property their client wishes to purchase.

The Registrar is ultimately responsible for ensuring that the person who applies to register land is entitled to do so. He/she must therefore approve applications for registration,[50] and has the power to decline such applications where appropriate.[51]

C. Rectification

If it turns out that a mistake has been made during the registration process the Registrar also has the power to rectify the register. Mistake in this context may be either a mistake that occurs within the Land Registry in the course of the registration process, or a mistake on the part of the person registering the interests. Rectification is a discretionary power that arises under Section 69 of the Land Registration Act. Rectification may occur on three grounds:

---

50 LRA (n 21) section 14 (5)
51 See for example *Donnelly v Hegarty* [2011] NICh 22

i. Error

Where there has been an error that has resulted in an interest being incorrectly registered the Registrar may order rectification of the register. This may be because of mistake, or omission, or simply because the registered folio does not accurately reflect the extent of the estate or interest.[52] However this discretion cannot be exercised too widely. Under Section 69(3) of the Act the register shall not be rectified so as to affect the title of a registered owner unless it can be done without loss or damage. This provision protects innocent parties who have paid valuable consideration and acted in good faith, relying on the register. In these circumstances, where the error has been made prior to a purchase for value the register may not be rectified if it will cause loss or damage.

ii. Fraud

Under Section 69(4) the register may be rectified where the transfer of an estate has been brought about by fraud.

iii. Mistake

Where there has been a mistake as to the interest to be registered the register may be rectified to reflect this. This can be either a mistake common to both parties or unilateral mistake.

D. Compensation

Where rectification is necessary under any of these headings the injured party may be entitled to compensation.[53] Provided the parties can show that they were not party to the mistake that has led to the need for rectification they may be able to claim for compensation on the basis that the register erroneously reflected their entitlement in respect of the land.[54] Compensation will be calculated on the basis of loss.

In *Armstrong v Shields*, Girvan LJ summarised the purpose of registration of title as being to "simplify investigation of title and give successor in title protections arising out of the simplified registration system."

---

52 See *Armstrong* (n 36); *Hayes v McGuigan and Others* [2011] NICh 6; For a detailed discussion of the scope of rectification see A Dowling 'Rectification of the Title Register' (1993) 44 NILQ 133
53 Registration (Land and Deeds) (n 21) article 31
54 *Armstrong* (n 36)

While the register works reasonably well in terms of providing a repository for information on the interests that exist in land, the limitations outlined mean that it remains a long way from providing conclusive evidence. This simply means that for the time being the system of registration of title and registration of deeds continue to operate alongside each other for property in Northern Ireland.

4.5 The Statutory Charges Register

The final register to be aware of is the Statutory Charges Register. This register was created in 1951 and exists to record burdens that are imposed on property as a result of statutory provisions.[55] These burdens are not created by the owner of the property but may nevertheless significantly impede enjoyment of the property. It is therefore important to be able to ascertain whether any such charges affect land before it is purchased.

Although the register is known as the statutory charges register, it also includes notices and burdens that do not charge the land with debt.[56] Some common examples include public rights of way that burden the land;[57] the listing of buildings that will restrict development of the property;[58] or planning restrictions in the area.

This register operates alongside the Registry of Deeds and the Land Registry, and operates on the same principles. It is designed to ensure that any potential purchaser of land that is affected by a statutory scheme will be able to discover the burden imposed on the property, removing the risk that the land would be purchased without notice of the restriction. Similarly where the statutory charge is not registered the effect will be that a purchaser will take the property free from the charge.

---

55 Statutory Charges Register Act (Northern Ireland) 1951
56 See Murray (n 19)
57 Access to Countryside (Northern Ireland) Order 1983 Part II
58 Planning (Northern Ireland) Order 1991

CHAPTER 5

Land Law in Historical Context

5.1 Introduction

"Land law can best be understood if its essentially historical and evolving nature is always remembered."[1]

Although the focus of this book is the modern system of land law that applies in Northern Ireland, central to understanding some of the core concepts of land law is an appreciation of its place within a broader history of political, economic and social development. Placing land law in context helps to illustrate why laws were passed, what function they played in the evolution of society, and ultimately demonstrates just how connected land law is to politics. This is particularly true in Ireland, both North and South. The land question has been inextricably entwined with political campaigns for centuries. Land, politics and conflict are inseparable in the history of Ireland, and appreciating this relationship can help to put modern land law into perspective and explain some of the more complex features of the law.

This chapter provides an overview of the historical development of land law in Great Britain and Ireland, considering how political, economic and social factors helped to shape the law and the lingering influence of these factors on land law today. The chapter presents a necessarily potted history of land law, as the topic would be too vast to cover in any meaningful detail. What it highlights, however, are key historical factors that have shaped the development of land law that will place the content of this book into context and provide a better overall understanding of the place of land law within history and

1   JCW Wylie, *Irish Land Law* (3rd edn) (Dublin, Bloomsbury Professional, 1997) [1.09]

society more generally. In particular the chapter provides an introduction to the shared heritage of land law in Northern Ireland with that in England and Wales, as well as explaining some of the key differences between the two jurisdictions.

The first thing to note is that before 1920 Ireland was one jurisdiction. Land law therefore has a common history in Northern Ireland and the Republic of Ireland. It is only after partition that the laws start to diverge. Similarly, the history of land law in Ireland shares common origins with that in England and Wales, having been subject to British rule for much of its history. The divergence of the systems of land law between the two jurisdictions has come about as a result of the differing social and political contexts which pertained in each state.

5.2 Medieval Land Law

The period between the 12th and 17th centuries is the period in which the foundations for a common system of landowning were laid. The Normans brought to Ireland a new centralised system of government known as feudalism. Under this system all authority was vested in the Crown, and the Crown was deemed to own all of the land. In England and parts of Ireland this new centralised system supplanted traditional systems of law that had existed prior to the Norman conquest. The feudal system was introduced in England in 1066 and brought to Ireland over 100 years later in 1172. The feudal system operated on a pyramid basis. The King would make a grant of land to Lords loyal to him. These grants were subject to 'feudal incidences' that were an early form of taxation that raised revenue for the Crown. They might, for example, have included providing knights for the King's army, or providing agricultural services. These Lords were known as 'Tenants' and could in turn make smaller grants. In this way the land became subdivided between an ever increasing number of people. This process was known as subinfeudation. However the Irish were hostile to the imposition of this new system of government. Whereas in England land was granted to local citizens, in Ireland most superior tenants (the tenants in chief at the top of the feudal pyramid) were not Irish but English or Welsh lords who were loyal to the King.[2] This created hostility towards feudalism in Ireland, resulting in the incomplete imposition of the system. The feudal relationship of landlord and tenant (not to be confused with the

---

2   See FH Newark, 'The Bringing of English Law to Ireland' (1972) 23 NILQ 3 for an overview of the arrival of the common law.

modern day relationship) was based on a system of loyalty. The tenant professed loyalty to the landlord, and in return the landlord was under an obligation towards his tenants.[3] No such relationship of loyalty existed in Ireland. As a result feudalism was never fully implemented beyond the 'pale' – the area surrounding Dublin and down the East coast of Ireland. Most areas of Leinster and Munster were successfully subjected to the new land law. Ulster and Connaught, however, remained under the control of Irish Chiefs.

At this time there was extensive subinfeudation of the land in both England and Wales and in Ireland. Most English legislation was also imported into Ireland during this period, including foundational statutes such as *Magna Carta*, *De Donis Conditionalibus*, and *Quia Emptores*.[4] However by the 16th century the influence of feudalism in Ireland had begun to wane. Many of those who were initially granted land by the King had been living in Ireland for generations, and had begun to adopt native practices and indeed follow the traditional Irish laws. In fact the number of English Lords 'going native' had grown so great that in 1366 the Statute of Kilkenny was passed to forbid the English from using native Irish law.[5]

Therefore in this period the development of land law in the two jurisdictions follows a similar trajectory. Both are in theory operating under the same system of law (that which would continue to dominate land law for centuries to come) and common legislation was applicable (in some instances legislation was not specifically passed for Ireland, but was applied regardless). This demonstrates the common origins of land law in England and in Ireland, and why a number of the core concepts, rules and principles of land law remain the same in both jurisdictions.[6]

5.3 The 17th–18th Centuries

In the 17th century the history of land law begins to diverge, although a number of similarities remain. This period in the history of land law is interesting in England because it is here that the origins of the modern system of equity can be seen. One of the key differences between the two jurisdictions since 1925 is the extent to which equity plays a role in land law. There is a much higher use of equitable doctrines in England and Wales, partly as a result of the differing nature of land use in England and Wales

---

3   For detailed discussion of the concept of tenure see AWB Simpson *A History of the Land Law* (2nd edn) (Clarendon Press, 1986)
4   See chapter 1
5   Wylie (n 1)[1.26]
6   See JCW Wylie 'Developments in Northern Ireland Law since 1921: Land Law' (1972) 23 NILQ 107

compared to in Ireland and the reforms undertaken to address this.[7]

However, in the early years these developments occurred equally in England and in Ireland, but are to a certain extent obscured in the history of Ireland because of the ongoing uprisings against the English. Nevertheless, in this period the history of land law remains linked.

As noted, the grant of land by subinfeudation carried with it certain feudal incidences which the tenant owed to the lord. These services were a vital source of wealth for the lord and indeed for the Crown, and represented the closest equivalent to taxation that existed in the day. The statute *Magna Carta* was the result of tensions between land owners and the Crown, demanding fair taxation, rather than variable taxation at the whim of the King. The burden imposed by these feudal incidences led to some ingenious methods of avoiding payment. The most significant for our purposes is the development of the idea of the 'use'. What happened was that the person who wished to either create or transfer an estate would transfer the legal title in the estate to one person, for the use of another, who was said to have the beneficial interest. The person to whom the estate was transferred was known as the *feoffee to uses*, and the person for whose benefit it was transferred was known as the *cestui que use*. The legal ownership was therefore separated from the beneficial ownership of the property, effectively allowing one person to own property on another person's behalf. There were several reasons why this might be done. This was a time of military adventure, and in particular the time of the Crusades. Where a Knight was under an obligation to provide military service, he would transfer his property to a friend, to the use of himself, in order to ensure that there was someone who could look after and deal with the property in his absence. The use could also be used as a means of creating a settlement of land and ensuring it remained within a particular family. This is the origin of the modern day doctrine of equity.

However, the separation of the legal title from the beneficiary (the *cestui que use*) left the beneficiary vulnerable to fraud. Because the legal title to the property was vested in the *feoffee to uses*, they were legally entitled to dispose of the property. The risk was that they would sell the title to the property and disappear, leaving the *cestui que use* with nothing. Because the legal title was vested in the *feoffee*, they had the legal right to do this. Common law could provide no remedy for the *cestui que use*. Circumstances such as this gave rise to intervention by the Chancellor in the name of good conscience. Gradually as appeals were made to the Chancellor against fraudulent actions taken by

---

7   In particular the introduction of the 1925 'Birkenhead' legislation in England and Wales has resulted in significant difference in the law between the two jurisdictions.

feoffee to uses, a species of protected interest began to emerge, and be recognised as giving rise to rights in property (equitable interests). Such interests were recognised as creating rights over property which could be transferred with the land. Thus if the *feoffee to uses* attempted to dispose of the property and keep the proceeds for himself, the purchaser could find themselves bound by the terms of the use because of the equitable interest enjoyed by the *cestui que use*. This in turn gave rise to the doctrine of notice that still operates in respect of land law today. Effectively what this means is that an equitable interest in property will bind all outsiders, including a purchaser for value if they either knew about or should have known about the interest. This acts as a disincentive for a *feoffee to uses* to act fraudulently in respect of a property and also gives rise to the practice of searches in conveyancing, to ensure that the person who is selling the title is entitled to do so, and also that there are no encumbrances over the land that will affect its value.[8]

However, the prevalence of uses in respect of land and the resulting avoidance of feudal duties had a severe impact on the income to the Crown. In 1536 legislation known as the Statute of Uses was passed to outlaw this practice. The equivalent legislation was passed in Ireland in 1634.[9] The effect of this statute was to treat the legal estate as vested in the *cestui que use*, thus 'executing' the use. By vesting the legal estate in the *cestui que use*, the *feoffee to uses* no longer had any power to deal with the land, and the *cestui que use* gained the power to dispose of something which in strict law he did not have. This also resulted in the unification of the legal and equitable interest in *the cestui que use*.

It is the idea of a use, and in particular the separation of the legal and equitable interests in the property, that gives rise to the modern day doctrine of the trust, which plays a central role in property law.[10]

The influence of these struggles between King and Parliament can also be seen in Ireland. The 17th and 18th centuries were the period of the greatest incidence of confiscation and re-settlement of Irish land by the English. These were centuries dominated by war, the central factor for most being struggles over the ownership and control of land. This period represents a more determined effort by the English to complete the conquest of Ireland that had begun in 1172 but had never been fully successful. This conquest happened both militarily and in the Courts. In this period the courts ruled a number of traditional Irish practices of land law as unlawful.[11]

---

8   See chapter 4
9   This legislation remains in force in Northern Ireland today.
10 See chapter 4
11 Case of Tanistry (1607) Dav 28; See generally Newark FH, 'The Case of Tanistry' (1952) 9 NILQ 215

The early 17th century witnessed a comprehensive policy of confiscation and re-settlement introduced in Ireland. The Flight of the Earls in 1607, following an unsuccessful rebellion marked the beginning of the transfer of land to loyal English lords which was continued most prominently with the Plantation of Ulster from 1609-1641. Whereas the original conquest had failed because of the failure to earn the loyalty of the Irish tenants and the policy of allowing the two to live alongside each other, the aim of the plantation was to replace the rebellious Irish with landowners who were loyal to the crown altogether. This required integration of the new landowners into all aspects of society, ensuring loyalty to the crown and leaving no room for those who were disloyal. In the years between 1649 and 1654 Oliver Cromwell undertook large scale confiscation and re-settlement of the lands of the rebellious Irish, including those who would have originally been granted land by the king under the feudal system. This policy gave rise to the famous battlecry of 'To Hell or To Connaught' whereby landowners who had taken part in uprisings against Cromwell's forces were offered the choice of death or re-settlement on land west of the Shannon, widely regarded as poor land and thus tantamount to death anyway.

The plantations and the policy of re-settlement were put on a legal footing by the Act of Settlement in 1662. The land question in this period was therefore linked closely with the religious struggles that were occurring at the time. However, despite these efforts to establish control of Ireland and subject it to the feudal system of government, the influence of the feudal system itself was declining in this period. This is in part related to struggles for power, and in particular the conflict between monarch and Parliament that led to the English Civil War in the 17th century. Again the development of land law in this period should be seen in broader social and political context. The rules emerge in the context of what is essentially a struggle over powers of taxation – with the King claiming feudal dues, and Parliament attempting to reserve the right of taxation to itself – linked to the idea of representation. Eventually Parliament prevailed, and the doctrine of tenure was abolished by the Tenures Abolition Act (1660). This legislation also converted all remaining feudal tenures into freehold estates, thus releasing the hold of the Crown over land ownership.

The decline of feudalism gave way in Ireland to a system of leasehold tenure. Grants of land in Ireland continued to be made '*non obstante Quia Emptores*'[12] to lords loyal to the Crown, and within these grants there was extensive subdivision by way of lease.[13]

---

12 This means literally 'notwithstanding Quia Emptores'. This was a statute that had banned the practice of subinfeudation of land and the division of land into an ever increasing number of lesser estates.

13 See Wylie JCW 'The 'Irishness' of Irish Land Law' (1995) 46 NILQ 332, 337

Leasehold land was subject to rent, and the aim in this period was to extract as much income as possible for the landowner from the land. Therefore it was not land per se that was valuable, as was the case in England, but rather the income that could be generated from it. The result of this policy was the rapid growth in the incidence of leasehold land that was never seen in England. This also resulted in the division of the land into smaller and smaller parcels of land, the effect of which continues to influence land law today.

Because of the extent of leasehold land, and the power imbalances that it embodied, the landlord tenant relationship in Ireland was subject to constant physical, political and legal battles. These battles precipitated the legislative codification of land law, and in particular the landlord and tenant relationship. As had been the case under the feudal system, the majority of landlords in Ireland were English. Because of ongoing political disturbances, however, most preferred to live in England, appointing an agent to run the estate in Ireland. This class of landowner came to be known as an absentee landlord, on account of their absence from Ireland. The exception to this phenomenon was Ulster, where the plantations had more successfully integrated the landlords into Ulster life.

The role of the land agents was to extract as much income as possible from the land. This resulted in the widespread subdivision of land, conferring estates and interests less than freehold on a number of different people. Most common was leasehold conveyancing, with leases made subject to recurrent rents and profits. This led to the evolution of leases particular to Ireland, which were never used in England and Wales.[14] These included long leases of up to 999 years, and also the lease for lives renewable forever.[15]

At this time a number of factors combined to create discontent in respect of the land laws. The effect of discriminatory legislation,[16] the sub-division of land into smaller and smaller plots, and the imbalance of powers between the landlord and tenant combined to create a volatile situation in Ireland. Agrarian disturbances dominated the political landscape, and ultimately ushered in a period of profound change in land law. This commenced with the passing of the Act of Union in 1800 which brought Ireland under the control of the Parliament at Westminster. The effect of this unpopular piece of legislation was to give the Irish direct representation at Westminster for the first time. This enabled them to campaign for change directly in London. There were two key political issues of the day; resolution of the land problem, and Home Rule for Ireland.

---

14 Wylie (n 1) [1.35]
15 For more detailed discussion of these types of lease see JCW Wylie 'The 'Irishness' of Irish Land Law (1995) 46 NILQ 332
16 The Penal Laws prevented Catholics from owning land or entering into long leases.

However, the state of the land by the turn of the 19th century was poor. The fact that the land was leased rather than owned by the tenant farmer gave no incentive to improve the land, and much was falling into poor condition. Estates had been sub-divided to such an extent that most small holdings could not produce enough to feed the tenant farmer and his family. The effect of this poorly managed agrarian economy was that much of the population relied on the potato for basic sustenance. So when the famines came, most famously in 1845-1847, the effect was catastrophic. These events served to highlight the plight of the Irish farmers. A Commission of Inquiry was formed to investigate the causes of famine. They travelled around the country witnessing its effects first hand. The result of its report was the famous Landlord and Tenant Law Amendment Act of 1860, known as Deasy's Act after the Attorney General who guided it through Parliament. This Act continues to form the cornerstone of landlord and tenant law in both jurisdictions of Ireland today.[17] However at the time it brought about very little change. It was viewed as simply consolidating existing landlord and tenant legislation that favoured landlords. Deasy's Act places the landlord tenant relationship on a contractual footing, effectively increasing the power of the landlord to set the terms of the agreement and providing very little protection for a tenant.[18]

At this point in history the story of Ireland again merges with that of England and Wales. Both have reached the same precarious position in respect of land law, but by different routes. In England there had never been the phenomenon of leasehold land to the same extent as in Ireland. Land in England until the 19th century remained a key source of wealth and status. Therefore rather than subdividing the land to maximise profits, the central concern of landowning families and conveyancing lawyers at the time was to ensure that the estate remained intact and remained in the family for generations to come. Settlements existed where the land was subject to successive estates less than a fee simple,[19] or where it was held in trust.[20] There were therefore two different purposes of a settlement. A settlement whereby land was subject to successive estates was known as a strict settlement. The aim of this type of settlement was to prevent land from being sold outside a particular family. This was achieved through the use of limited estates such as the life estate and contingent remainders, such as the fee tail that

---

17 See chapter 8
18 Wylie (n 1) [1.41]
19 Settled Land Acts 1882-1890 section 2(3)(a)
20 Settled Land Acts section 2(3). Trusts for sale of land allowed land to be sold and the proceeds used to provide an income for the beneficiaries.

allowed the creator of the settlement to control the use of the land into the future.[21] The aim of the settler in these circumstances was to ensure that no person could achieve an unencumbered estate which they could then freely alienate. This was achieved by creating successive estates and interests in the land that meant that at any one time several family members would have a legally enforceable interest in the land and could prevent its alienation outside the family. Where a settlement was created the person currently entitled to possession of the estate was known as the tenant for life.[22] They would typically have owned a limited estate such as a fee tail or a life estate.[23] Upon the death of the landowner the estate would traditionally pass to the eldest son of a family, making him the tenant for life. Because of the limited nature of the estate the widow of the tenant for life would not inherit the estate but it would pass instead to the eldest son. However financial provision would also have to be made for female family members, such as the widow, and for younger sons. There were therefore significant financial obligations to be discharged from the land. These rights to a share from the estate were legal rights, and attached to the land. This was equally true of the rights of those who would for example be entitled to the estate in remainder when the life estate of the current tenant for life expired.[24] This meant that much of the land was tied up with a large number of cumbersome concurrent and consecutive legal interests, making it almost impossible to sell. Add to this the fact that all estates were of limited duration, removing any right to exploit the land to discharge financial obligations such as portions, and also providing little incentive to improve the land.

The combination of these factors meant that by the 19th century land was in very poor condition in England as well as in Ireland.

Therefore the underlying need for reform was the same as in Ireland – to ensure effective use of the land – but it was needed for different reasons. Whereas in Ireland the reforms were precipitated by famine, in England it was more closely tied to economic change in the 19th century. The development of land law was integrally linked to the maintenance of status and privilege. Ownership of land had been closely linked to economic and political power, for example only landowners had the right to vote. The rules of land law developed in response to a desire by the wealthy to maintain their position. However in the 19th century the political influence of the landowning class was diminishing. A belief in the value of a free market economy had taken over, and

---

21 See chapter 1
22 Settled Land Acts 1882-1890 section 2(5)
23 Settled Land Acts 1882-1890 section 58
24 See chapter 1 on future legal interests, including remainders.

to include land within this, market reform would be needed to cheapen and facilitate the transfer of landed property.[25] A newly enriched mercantile class were keen to buy land as an indicator of status, and this required that land come onto the market. A Real Property Commission was appointed to investigate the possibilities of simplifying land law in general, and conveyancing more specifically. The Commission report drew a distinction between the mechanisms for the transfer and creation of rights on one hand, and the substance of what could be created on the other. Effectively they saw no need to abolish foundational concepts such as tenure, but rather to establish a system of private conveyancing based on a scheme of registration of deeds and instruments.[26]

This report led to a number of piecemeal legislative responses in both Ireland and England in the mid 19th century. These include many pieces of legislation that remain in force in Northern Ireland today, including the Fines and Recoveries Act 1834;[27] the Wills Act 1837;[28] the Conveyancing Act 1881; and these reforms culminated in the Settled Land Acts of 1882-1890 which also continue to govern settled land in Northern Ireland. Rather than abolishing outright legal institutions such as entails and settlements, the effect of the legislation was a gradual and progressive increase in the powers of the tenant for life (the family member currently entitled to possession). The aim of the legislation was to assimilate the position of the tenant for life with that of the owner of a fee simple. This would occur in legal terms only, however. So for example given the limited nature of the estate owned by the tenant for life, and the extensive other legal interests that existed in the property, the tenant would be entitled to an income from the estate but not to the capital value. The tenant would also remain bound by any existing beneficial provisions, and those duties would still have to be discharged. The ultimate effect of the Settled Land Acts was to make it impossible to ensure that estates were kept within a family compulsorily. They achieved this by converting the rights of beneficiaries under the settlement by operation of law from rights in land to rights in a shifting fund. Thus the land could be sold if desired, and the obligations would attach to the proceeds of sale rather than to the land itself, allowing good and unencumbered title to be transferred to the purchaser. Its aim was to facilitate conveyancing by providing a determinative list of interests that existed in respect of the property through the registration of deeds to the property.

---

25 See generally Simpson AWB *A History of the Land Law* (1986)
26 For a detailed discussion of the work of the commission see Sokol M 'Jeremy Bentham and the Real Property Commission of 1828' (1992) 4(2) Utilitas 225
27 This legislation gave the tenant for life of a fee tail estate the power to bar the entail, allowing him to sell a fee simple in the property. Fines and Recoveries Act 1833 section 15
28 This legislation simplified the rules on passing estates by will. See chapter 1

Therefore this was a period of significant reform of land law in both Ireland and in England. In Ireland, however, reform was to be more radical.

5.4 The 19th Century

In 1800 the Act of Union was passed. The effect of this legislation was to give Irish politicians direct representation in the Westminster Parliament. Once the Irish achieved this representation at Westminster they set about campaigning for land reform. The most significant of these campaigns were the Irish Land Leagues under the leadership of Charles Stewart Parnell. The aim of this campaign was to secure the right of Irish tenant farmers to purchase the freehold of the land which they worked. This campaign began as one of civil disturbance, and in particular of the ostracisation of any tenant who co-operated with the landlord. The first estate to fall victim to this tactic was run by a Captain Boycott, and it is this event which gave rise to the idea of a 'boycott'. The Land Leagues had three fundamental demands, known as the three Fs:

- Fair rent
- Free sale
- Fixity of Tenure

These three Fs existed at the time in Ulster only, and for this reason were known as the Ulster Tenant Right. The Land Leagues campaigned to extend their application to the rest of Ireland. These demands were given statutory recognition in the Land Law (Ireland) Act of 1881. While this legislation did bring about initial improvement in the position of tenants, such as a significant reduction in rents, it was later superceded by more radical demands. As the Home Rule campaign gathered momentum, the British Government adopted a policy of killing Home Rule with kindness, trying to prevent rebellion by granting concessions on the land issue. This commenced with the Purchase of Land (Ireland) Act 1885. This legislation marked the beginning of a process whereby Irish tenant farmers could access finance from the State to buy the freehold of the land that they worked. This was further consolidated by the Irish Land Law Act of 1903, under which 220,000 holdings were bought out by tenants.[29] As a result of these policies almost all rural land in Ireland was converted to freehold land, free from complex pyramid titles found in urban areas.

---

29 Wylie (n 1) [1.56]

Despite the widespread conversion of leasehold estates into freehold estates, the lease continues to cast a long shadow over land law in Northern Ireland. Much urban land is held on long leases of up to 999 years, and the lease remains a popular method of landholding in areas of high density housing such as housing developments and apartment blocks.[30]

Thus it can be seen that the history of land law in Ireland is intertwined with that in England. The most often cited reason for divergence between the two jurisdictions in the modern day is the process of reform that took place in England and Wales in 1925 but was never introduced in Northern Ireland. The Land Purchase Acts provided the last systematic overhaul of land law in Ireland. Despite four major reports on land law reform since the creation of the state of Northern Ireland,[31] there has to date been no systematic reform of the law in this jurisdiction. This means that the law remains a combination of pre-1925 English law mixed with legislation passed in or specifically for Northern Ireland.

With the passage of time, however, the divergence between the two jurisdictions caused by the 1925 legislation has decreased in significance. A number of the key reforms were eventually introduced into Northern Ireland law, with some significant exceptions.

5.5 The 1925 Legislation

Many of the difficulties raised as a result of the fragmentation of ownership of land were addressed in the 1925 legislation, known as the Birkenhead Legislation.

In England the Land Registration Act of 1925 was a vital step in the same direction as that taken in Ireland under the 1891 Local Registration of Title Act. In 1925 the vast majority of land in England remained unregistered and in the absence of a scheme such as the land purchase scheme in Ireland, large scale registration was not possible. The need to address the problems associated with unregistered conveyancing was thus a major policy imperative in England and Wales where it was not in Northern Ireland.

The additional fact that by 1922 Northern Ireland was a separate jurisdiction that had already addressed its particular land concerns meant that there was no appetite for

---

30 See chapter 8
31 Committee on the Registration of Title to Land, Registration of Title to Land in Northern Ireland (1967) ('The Lowry Report'). Working Party of the Faculty of Law, QUB, Survey of the Land Law of Northern Ireland (1971). Office of Law Reform, Department of Finance & Personnel, Belfast, Final Report of the land Law Working Group (1990); Northern Ireland Law Commission, *Land Law* (NI Law Com No 8, 2010) para 3.1

the 1925 scheme in Northern Ireland. In 1925, rather than simply introducing a Land Registration Act in England and Wales, the Government also introduced the Settled Land Act; the Trustee Act; the Administration of Estates Act; the Land Charges Act, and perhaps most significantly, the Law of Property Act. This was a fundamental overhaul of the whole of land law in England and Wales. One feature was the repeal of a host of old legislation (such as the Conveyancing Acts and the Settled Land Acts which continue in force in Northern Ireland) repackaging only the elements that were deemed useful – discarding the more technical, artificial and obsolete aspects of previous provisions – a mixture of consolidation and reform. The old legislation still applies in Northern Ireland, so this explains some of the deviations in law between the two jurisdictions. In particular because the Law of Property Act was never introduced into Northern Ireland the number of legal estates remains higher in Northern Ireland than in England and Wales. Subsequent amendments to the law in both jurisdictions have led to further differences, however these tend to be differences of detail, leaving the broad substance of the law much the same in most areas of land law.

This 1925 tidying up exercise was natural in the context of a process of a fundamental reform/consolidation programme. It is more important to examine the reform in question and to examine the fundamental differences that emerged between the two jurisdictions as a result. The key theme is to make land more readily transferable, particularly unregistered land.

Land was to be treated as an asset, and if it was to be such, it was necessary that it could easily be traded and converted into another form without affecting property rights. This was a radical re-think as up until that point a significant concern of property law had been tying land up in detailed settlements. A purchaser of land would be automatically bound by legal estates or by legal interests such as easements, charges or mortgages. In addition a purchaser would also be bound by equitable rights such as a trust if he/she was deemed to have notice of it. Thus being able to ascertain if an estate is legal or equitable was of vital significance, because an innocent purchaser may find themselves bound by legal interests of which he/she was completely unaware, while the owner of an equitable right may lose it to a purchaser without notice. Neither outcome is desirable. In respect of any proprietary interest, it is important to ask; firstly if the right is capable of existing as a legal or an equitable right; and if so, whether they actually exist as a legal or equitable right.

5.6 Legal Estates and the Significance of Equity

To facilitate such inquiry, the 1925 Law of Property Act provides that the only legal freehold estate that will be recognised is the fee simple absolute in possession.[32] Leases remain legal because they are an important source of income from the land rather than a burden on it. All other estates exist in equity only.[33] Similarly the number of legal interests was significantly reduced to easements, rights and privileges (profits) and mortgages. The result is that the number of estates and interests that would automatically bind a purchaser (ie legal estates and interests) is dramatically reduced, and the number of equitable estates and interests (those who bind only a purchaser with notice) was significantly increased. The resulting dramatic increase in the number of equitable interests that would not automatically burden the land meant that detailed rules were required to protect the beneficiaries of such interests in the event of a sale or transfer of the property. The Land Charges Act therefore provided for the registration of such interests as a means of protecting them.[34]

The primary concern of the legislation, however, was to free land from interests that could take effect in possession, thereby restricting the value of the property. For example, under the rules of succession estates would pass to the eldest son of the family. It would have been traditional for the widow of the deceased tenant to receive a life estate in the property. While the life estate was a legal interest this was enforceable against any purchaser of the estate, meaning that the widow would have a right to continue to reside in the property. However, under the Law of Property Act the life estate became an equitable estate only. This meant that it could potentially be lost if a purchaser bought the property without knowledge of it. While the Land Charges Act meant that a purchaser would have knowledge of the interest, and therefore take the property subject to it, it remains inconvenient for a purchaser to acquire a property in which another person has a right to reside. This would have a significant detrimental impact on the value of the property. A way needed to be found to protect the equitable interest of the widow but at the same time allow a purchaser to take the property free from a right in possession. The solution was the doctrine of overreaching.

---

32 LPA section 1(1)
33 LPA section 1(3)
34 See further chapter 4

5.7 Overreaching of Family Interests

The 1925 legislation draws a fundamental distinction between 'family' and 'commercial' interests. The creation of successive interests in land using life estates or entails is indicative of a family arrangement. To return to the example:

If land is left in a will to A – the widow – for life, remainder to B in fee simple, under Section 1 of the LPA 1925 neither has a legal estate – both are equitable. This is because the life estate is no longer recognised as a legal estate, and a fee simple in remainder is a future legal estate, not an estate in possession, and therefore is also not recognised under Section 1. However, as a legal estate is necessary to transfer the land, the Settled Land Act of 1925 vests the land in A, who holds the land on trust for B. Therefore A is allowed to sell the fee simple in the property, but may not keep the proceeds of the sale. In such a case two trustees (the modern day equivalent of the *feoffee* to uses) are appointed and the money from the purchase is transferred to them. The purchaser is thereby able to take the fee simple free from the life estate. The trustees would invest the money and A would be entitled to any profit from it during his lifetime, and on A's death B becomes entitled to the fund.

Thus the fundamental principle here is that 'family interests' in property are overreached by the sale of property – the purchaser need not be concerned about them. The owners of such estates instead have an interest in the purchase money. This also applies under the provisions of the Settled Land Acts, which apply in Northern Ireland. Under this legislation where the legal title to property is transferred to at least two trustees the equitable interest will be overreached, allowing a purchaser to take clean title to the property.

There is current debate in Northern Ireland and in England and Wales over the extent to which overreaching should apply to all equitable interests. This arises from the situation where a spouse in occupation of a residential property has an equitable interest in the property that may prevent sale or enforcement of a judgment against the property. In these circumstances where money is likely to be transferred to only one trustee (the legal owner of the property) the equitable interest cannot be over-reached and the spouse retains an equitable interest that burdens the property. There does not appear to be consensus on the way forward with this issue.[35]

The most significant element of difference between the land law in England and in Northern Ireland has been the shift in balance between law and equity that has occurred in England, and the use of the trust as a means of regulating this.

---

35 Northern Ireland Law Commission, *Land Law* (NI Law Com No 2, 2009) para 3.45

The key role played by trusts as a result of Section 1 of the LPA 1925 together with the role of the LPA 1925 as the core statute (although not a codification of the law) is probably the key distinguishing factor between Northern Ireland and England and Wales. The reform project in 1925 has produced many minor deviations. Overall, Northern Ireland legislation has tended to follow subsequent developments in England and Wales, though some divergence is inevitable. For example, the Land Registration Act (Northern Ireland) 1970 reflects much of the equivalent 1925 legislation in England and Wales. Similarly the Registration of Deeds (Northern Ireland) Act 1970 fulfils the same function as the Land Charges Act. The outstanding difference that underlies the different approach between the two jurisdictions has been the emphasis placed on the reduction of the number of interests that will burden land per se, and the emphasis on keeping land marketable through ease of conveyancing. The greater connectedness to land and the importance placed on land as a place rather than as a commercial commodity is reflected in many of the decisions of the Northern Ireland courts and in the recent report on land law reform produced by the Northern Ireland Law Commission. Therefore while there may be differences of substance between the two jurisdictions, the more fundamental difference probably lies in the underlying value placed on land in Northern Ireland and the way in which this is reflected in law. When considering land law in Northern Ireland the historical context should not be forgotten. The similarities and the difference in the law tell their own story.

CHAPTER 6

Adverse Possession: The Common Law Doctrine

6.1 Introduction

Adverse possession is a doctrine that has arisen in property law whereby a person other than the owner of land can acquire a proprietary interest in that land through use that is inconsistent with the rights of the owner. What this means in practical terms is that where a squatter has been using land for a certain period of time without the consent of the landowner, the rights of the owner will eventually be extinguished, leaving no other person with better title to the land than the squatter. It doesn't have to be a squatter in the common sense of the word, but can arise as a result of a boundary dispute, or where a person simply starts to use land adjoining their own and the owner does nothing about it. It is a divisive feature of land law. Some people view adverse possession as legalised land theft, while others regard it as necessary to ensure that land remains in use.

Adverse possession currently operates under the provisions of the Limitation (Northern Ireland) Order 1989, but the rules relating to adverse possession of unregistered land have been developed by case law since the late 19th century. It is part of the law of limitations and its practical effect is not to positively give land to a squatter, but rather to extinguish the title of the landowner through barring their right to recover the land in the courts.[1]

---

1   Limitation (Northern Ireland) Order 1989; Interesting to note, however, the proposals of the Northern Ireland Law Commission to replace reference to the extinguishment of title with provision for title to "vest … in the person in whose favour the limitation period has run" section 110. See Draft Land Law Reform Bill (Northern Ireland) 201[], section 110(1). See Northern Ireland Law Commission, *Land Law* (NI Law Com No 8, 2010) 209

There are different regimes applicable in respect of unregistered and registered land. In Northern Ireland unregistered land is subject only to the provisions of the Limitation Order, while registered land is also covered by the Land Registration Act (1970). In England and Wales the 2002 Land Registration Act introduced extensive changes to the law as it applies to registered land. However, the difference between unregistered and registered land only becomes important once it has been established that the owner has in fact been dispossessed and the limitation period has expired.

In 1998 a Consultative Document on Land Registration prepared by the Law Commission for England and Wales summarised the four most cogent reasons often given in favour of adverse possession.[2] These were:

- That it prevents defendants from stale claims being made against them and encourages land owners not to sleep on their rights. This is part of a broader rationale for limitations in any context, but applies with equal force in the context of land law. Essentially what it aims to prevent are claims being brought years later which may be difficult to defend.

- If land and its ownership are out of kilter the land may become unmarketable. Where the registered owner has disappeared and cannot be traced, and a squatter takes possession, the doctrine of adverse possession ensures that in such cases the land remains in commerce and is not rendered sterile. This reflects the importance of the free alienability of land in English land law.

- Because in cases of mistake the innocent but mistaken squatter may have incurred expenditure, adverse possession can be justified on grounds of hardship (drawing parallels with the principle of proprietary estoppel).

- Because it facilitates and cheapens investigation of title to land.

Adverse possession is therefore a well-established feature of land law across many jurisdictions. It has played a key role in ensuring that land remained marketable and that possession and title were, as far as possible, coincident. In Northern Ireland it also continues to play an important role in relation to doubtful titles, the estates of deceased persons, particularly farmers, and cases of boundary mistake.[3]

There are two aspects to the law of adverse possession. First, it is necessary to determine whether the requisite elements of adverse possession have been established.

---

2 Law Commission, *Land Registration for the Twenty First Century: A Conveyancing Revolution* (Law Com No 271, 2001) 30-32
3 NILC (n 1) para 2.23-2.33

Only then is it necessary to consider the effect that a period of adverse possession will have on the title to land. Therefore while significant reforms have been undertaken in recent years, it remains necessary to understand the common law rules as the basis of any claim of adverse possession.

6.2 General Principles of Adverse Possession

The current statutory basis for the doctrine of adverse possession in Northern Ireland is the Limitation (Northern Ireland) Order (1989). This gives effect in Northern Ireland to the Limitation Act (1980) in force in England and Wales. Technically the way in which the doctrine operates is not to grant property rights to the squatter, but to place a statutory limitation on the time after which the owner may assert his/her rights to the property. This means that after the specified time has elapsed, the rights of the owner will be extinguished.[4]

This will happen after a period of 12 years of adverse possession of the land in question,[5] unless it belongs to the Crown, in which case the limitation period is 30 years, or 60 years if it is foreshore. However, the general presumption of the law is that possession follows title. It is therefore up to the squatter to demonstrate that they have been in adverse possession of the property for the requisite period.[6] There are three elements that must be demonstrated:

A. Dispossession

According to schedule 1 of the Limitation (Northern Ireland) Order, there are three necessary criteria which must be fulfilled before a right of action accrues and time can begin to run against the landowner:

- The true owner (ie the person who owns the land on paper) has, while entitled to the land, been dispossessed or has discontinued his/her possession[7]

- A trespasser (squatter) has gone into possession[8]

---

4   Limitation Order (n 1) section 26
5   Ibid section 21
6   *Morris v Newell and Newell* [2007] NICh 2 [3]
7   Limitation Order (n 1) schedule 1 para 1(1)(b). The right of action in respect of the land will be treated as having accrued on the date of the dispossession or discontinuance.
8   Ibid schedule 1 para (8)(1) "[n]o right of action to recover land is to be treated as accruing unless the land is in the possession of some person in whose favour the period of limitation can run..."

- The possession of the squatter is adverse[9]

The first requirement, that the true owner must have been dispossessed, or have discontinued their possession simply means that the squatter is using the land rather than the owner. There is no requirement of a physical act of removal of the owner. The recent decision of *Norbrook Laboratories Ltd v Maguire and Another*[10] demonstrates that the actions of the paper owner themselves may be deemed to be acts of discontinuance. Whether or not the owner has been dispossessed is judged according to the degree of possession that the squatter is exercising over the land, and to this extent, determining dispossession is tied up with the question of what acts will be held to constitute physical possession of the land by the squatter. Not all use of land by a squatter will be held to be possession for the purposes of the Limitation Order.

In the case of *Pye v Graham* the House of Lords stated that:

> "The question is simply whether the defendant has dispossessed the paper owner by going into ordinary possession of the land for the requisite period without the consent of the owner."[11]

The requirement of dispossession does not therefore connote an element of aggression, hostility or subterfuge, but refers primarily to the existence of a person who is in ordinary possession of the land and in whose favour the limitation period can run.[12]

But what sort of actions may constitute 'ordinary possession'? This is a question which the court has addressed in a number of cases.

B. Possession

The second requirement for adverse possession is that the squatter must have gone into possession. The burden of establishing possession will rest with the squatter, who must establish on the balance of probabilities that he/she has gone into possession.[13] There are two elements in determining the extent of possession for the purposes of adverse possession:

i.   Physical control

ii. Intention to possess or *Animus possidendi*[14]

---

9   Ibid schedule 1 para 8(2)(b) "[t]he right of adverse possession is not to be treated as accruing unless and until adverse possession is taken of the land."
10 *Norbrook Laboratories Ltd v Maguire and Another* [2012] NICh 32 [5]-[9]
11 *JA Pye (Oxford) Ltd and Another v Graham and Another* [2002] UKHL 30, [2003] 1 AC 419
12 *The Official Receiver for Northern Ireland v McAnulty* [2010] NICA 38 [23]
13 *Re Faulkner* [2003] NICA 5 [29]
14 *Powell v McFarlane* (1979) 38 P & CR 452, 470-471; *Pye* (n 11) 432-433

i. Physical Control

In the 1979 case of *Powell v McFarlane*, Lord Justice Slade provided a re-statement of the basic principles relating to the concept of possession as it relates to physical control. These include:

- Factual possession signifies an appropriate degree of physical control. It must be single and conclusive possession – meaning that there cannot be possession by the owner and the squatter at the same time.

- The question of what acts constitute a sufficient degree of exclusive physical control must depend on the circumstances, in particular the nature of the land and the manner in which land of that nature is commonly used or enjoyed.

- It is impossible to generalise with any precision as to what acts will or will not suffice to evidence factual possession – but broadly what must be shown is that the alleged possessor has been dealing with the land in question as an occupying owner might have been expected to deal with it.

What is clear, is that there is no clear answer to what constitutes possession. What constitutes a sufficient degree of factual control will depend on the nature of the land and the manner in which land of its kind is commonly put.[15] Case law does, however, provide some guidance. The case law demonstrates that there are a number of factors that will be taken into account when considering whether a squatter has gone into possession.

Using the land in a manner inconsistent with the future use of the owner

• *Building on the land*

In the case of *Treloar v Nute*[16] the court decided that the levelling of the surface of the land to prepare it for building was sufficient to establish that the squatter had gone into possession of the land, thus dispossessing the owner, and causing time to run in his favour.

• *Agricultural use*

In the landmark case of *Powell v McFarlane*, the question of the use of land for agricultural purposes was raised. In this case the Plaintiff had, as a 14 year old boy, begun to use a

---

15   *McAnulty* (n 12) [23]
16   *Treloar v Nute* [1977] 1 All ER 230 (CA), [1976] 1 WLR 1295

piece of land for his own purposes without the consent of the owner. The owner of the land was a civil servant who had been posted abroad, and who had left the land lying unused. The plaintiff had initially requested his grandmother to write to the owner to request permission to use the land, but no reply had been received. He then decided to go ahead and use the land without permission. This was in 1956. Initially his actions in respect of the land consisted of cutting and taking a hay crop; some widespread repairs to the boundary fence, to the extent required to make them stock proof; he cut back a fair quantity of brambles and other growth to increase the hay area; he put his cow to pasture on the land; he connected a water supply and also engaged in some occasional shooting on the land. The question before the Court was whether or not these actions constituted possession. If it was found that they did then the period of limitation would start running from 1956 when he first started using the land.

Where there is doubt, the court will presume in favour of the paper owner. In *Powell v McFarlane* therefore it could be inferred that the plaintiff had not dispossessed the owner as he was simply using the land while they were abroad. The test applied by the court was an objective one – whether or not "any objective informed observer might probably have inferred that the plaintiff was using the land simply for the benefit of his family's cow…, during such periods as the absent owner took no steps to stop him." These actions were contrasted with those which were more unequivocally associated with possession, such as the ploughing and cultivation of agricultural land; the enclosure of land by a newly constructed fence or blocking the only means of access. The court stated that "in any case there the acts of an intruder, however continuous and far reaching, do not substantially interfere with any present or future plans which the owners may have for the use of unbuilt land, the court will not treat the intruder as having dispossessed the owner for the purpose of the Limitation Act." The plaintiff's action failed.

Although the action failed on the grounds that the plaintiff had not gone into possession in 1956, beyond the limitation period, his later actions, such as storing lorries on the land and erecting the advertising billboards were held to constitute acts of possession.

That grazing remains an equivocal act of possession and most likely insufficient in and of itself to support a claim of factual possession was recently confirmed in Northern Ireland in *Gallagher v Northern Ireland Housing Executive*.[17]

---

17 *Gallagher v Northern Ireland Housing Executive* [2009] NICA 50 [19]

• Excluding all others

It is a fundamental principle of adverse possession that the possession of the squatter must be exclusive. For a claim to be successful, only one part can be in possession of the relevant premises.[18] It is therefore necessary to be able to demonstrate some element of exclusive control of the land.

• Fencing/gates

An 1877 case called *Seddon v Smith* described erecting fencing around a piece of land constituted the strongest possible evidence of possession. The existence of fences and gates that physically demarcate the land is thought to be strong evidence of physical control, particularly where gates have been locked so that only the squatter has access to the land. In the Northern Ireland case of *Re Faulkner*[19] the court considered that fencing off land and erecting a gate was sufficient evidence of control, notwithstanding the fact that the gate was rarely secured.[20] This point was considered again in the recent case of *Morris v Newell and Newell* where the existence of a lock on the gates was the subject of dispute.[21]

It used to be the case that fencing and gates alone would not be determinative. For example, in *Powell v McFarlane* although the plaintiff had done work to ensure that the boundaries of the field were secure, this was done for the purposes of keeping the cow in, and not exclusively as a means of asserting exclusive possession of the land. There has also been a tendency, where there is a possible alternative motive for the actions of the squatter, for the court to resist finding that the owner has been dispossessed.[22] However it does seem that there has been some relaxation of the rules in recent years and English case law now suggests that alternative motives will not necessarily prevent a claim of possession from being successful.[23]

Using the land as the owner might

The court has asserted that the question of possession must be determined in the particular circumstances of each case. This will include looking at the use to which the land would ordinarily be put. If the intruder is treating the land as the owner would be

---

18 *McAnulty* (n 12) [23]
19 *Re Faulkner* (n 13) [7]
20 Ibid [7]
21 *Newell* (n 6) [10]-[15]; *Foxwell and Another v Ballyedmond and Others* [2005] NICh 3 [10] [26] [33]
22 *Littledale v Liverpool College* [1900] 1 Ch 19 (CA) 22-23
23 *Chambers v Havering LBC* [2011] EWCA Civ 1576, [2012] 1 P & CR 17 [59] (Lord Justice Lewison). Therein it did not matter that fences were repaired to keep cows in rather than to keep the owner out.

expected to then it is possible that they will be held to have taken possession.[24] This was demonstrated in *Re Faulkner* where acts such as storing boats and using the land to access the shore, while seasonal, were held to be sufficient to constitute possession in light of the nature of the land itself. More recently the nature of the use of land was considered in *Norbrook Laboratories Ltd v Maguire and Another*.[25] In this case the land in question was a small strip of rough land adjoining the defendant's garden. The court confirmed that while the act of possession were modest (cutting the grass and tethering a dog), they were nevertheless acts of possession that were appropriate on the land in question.

Because of the benefit that will accrue to the squatter if he/she is found to be in possession, the courts have taken a strict approach to the question of possession. This is also true of the question of intent, which is the second requirement of possession. If there is not clear evidence of intention on the part of the squatter, the courts will not infer it, even where the acts relied on could have sufficed to constitute factual possession.

ii. *Animus possidendi*

In addition to being in physical control of the land, if a squatter wishes to assert title to the land he/she must be able to establish that he/she had the requisite intention to possess. This is what's known as the *animus possidendi*. Again while intent is required by statute, the precise scope of its meaning is not apparent from the words of the Order, but has been developed through case law. In some cases it can be deduced from the objective acts of physical possession.[26] In other cases further evidence may be required. In these circumstances there are a number of factors that will be taken into consideration.

The earliest statement made on the subject of intent was in *Littledale v Liverpool College* in which the court stated that *animus possidendi* is the intention to exclude all others, including the owner. This re-affirms the principle that shared possession is not enough to establish adverse possession. If the owner continues to use the land at the same time as the squatter this implies that the squatter intends simply to use the land but not to claim title to it.

The definition was considered again, and in much greater detail, in *Powell v McFarlane*. This case demonstrates the extent to which the two elements of possession are linked, intent being a factor in determining whether the squatter has gone into physical possession or not.

---

24   *Re Faulkner* (n 13) [25]
25   *Norbrook* (n 10) [23]
26   *McAnulty* (n 12)

In *Powell v McFarlane* the question was whether or not the plaintiff had gone into possession of the land in 1956, as he claimed. At this time he was already grazing his cow on the land, cutting hay and had made secure the boundary of the field. The court, however, found that this was not sufficient to constitute possession, and this was partly due to uncertainty as to the extent of his intent in relation to the land at this time. The court, in re-stating what would be required to establish intent, stated that "the *animus possidendi* involves the intention, in one's own name, and on one's own behalf, to exclude the world at large, including the owner … so far as is reasonably practicable and so far as the processes of law will allow." This being the law, the court then went on to interpret this requirement in light of the facts in Powell. The Court stated that what was required was "clear and affirmative evidence that the trespasser, claiming that he has acquired possession, not only had the requisite intention to possess, but made such intention clear to the world." This is quite a high burden of proof to place on a squatter. The court continued that "if his acts are open to more than one interpretation and he has not made it perfectly plain to the world by his actions or words that he has intended to exclude the owner as best he can, the courts will treat him as not having had the requisite *animus possidendi* and consequently as not having dispossessed the owner."

What the court is emphasising is that it is for the trespasser to prove his intent in relation to the land. In the Powell case the court held that there was ambiguity as to whether or not the plaintiff had intended to possess the land – that is to exclude the owner. Previous authorities had provided that where someone uses land simply while the owner is not making use of it, this is not sufficient to amount to an intention to possess. This is how the facts were interpreted in relation to Mr Powell in 1956 – that it could reasonably have been inferred that he simply wished to use the land without having any intention to appropriate it as his own. The court did note, however, that the position had changed by 1962, when the plaintiff was older and was making greater proprietary use of the land. The Court held that by this time the plaintiff's intention towards the land had probably hardened, along with the increasing use of the land, so as to become more clearly those of a person asserting ownership. But 1962 was too late for the plaintiff, as taking possession only then, rather than in 1956, meant that the limitation period had not yet run in his favour and time was now stopped.

The next question that arises in relation to intention relates to circumstances where the squatter knows that the paper owner of the land has future plans for it, but that it is not currently in use. The earlier authority of *Leigh v Jack* suggested that where this was the case, a person using the land until such times as the true owner did put it to use could not be held to have established possession.[27] This was later distinguished in the case of *Buckinghamshire CC v Moran*,[28] which considered the extent of the intention required. The court in this case considered that the rule in *Leigh v Jack*[29] had been amended by statute,[30] and that what was relevant was not the intention to *own* the land, but the intention to *possess* it. This was decided on the basis of the judgment that it was "too broad a proposition to suggest that an owner who retains a piece of land with a view to its utilisation for a specific purpose in the future can never be treated as dispossessed…"

The Court considered that enclosure (by fencing) by itself would indicate *prima facie* the requisite *animus possidendi*. It was held that the placing of the new lock and chain on the gate did amount to a "final unequivocal demonstration of the defendant's intention to possess the land."

This provides a good example of the relationship between physical possession and intention, and the fact that intention may be deduced from the objective act of possession.

This represented a significant change in direction of the law. Whereas the court in *Powell* had decided that the plaintiff was merely using the land for his own benefit so long as no-one stopped him, and that this meant that he did not display the necessary intention to appropriate the land as his own, in *Buckinghamshire CC*, the court decided that it did not matter whether the defendant knew of the Council's future plans for the plot, but that "what is required for this purpose if not an intention to own or even an intention to acquire ownership but an intention to possess – that is to say, an intention for the time being to possess the land to the exclusion of all other persons, including the owner of the paper title." So even where the squatter knows of the future intent of the owner, if they are held to have had the necessary intent to possess the land in the meantime, and a period of 12 years elapses, then they may be successful in a claim of adverse possession.

This was taken even further recently in the case of *JA Pye Ltd (Oxford) v Graham*.[31]

In Pye the disputed land consisted of four fields. This land was separated from the adjoining land by hedges. There was also a gate that led from the public highway onto the land, but this was kept locked, and the defendant, who was the party making the

---

27   *Leigh v Jack* (1879) 5 Ex D 264 (CA)
28   [1990] Ch 623 (CA) 646 (Nourse LJ)
29   *Leigh* (n 27)
30   Limitation Act 1980 schedule 1 para 8(4)
31   *JA Pye* (n 11)

claim of adverse possession, kept the key. Pye had no other right of access. The facts that led to the case were that Mr Graham had acquired a property adjoining that of Pye. At the time of the sale Mr Graham was aware that the disputed land had been used, by agreement, for grazing, although he also knew that Pye's intention was to apply for planning permission to develop the land. Graham initially entered into a grazing agreement with Pye, which allowed him to graze animals on the land for one year. After the expiry of the agreement Pye permitted Graham to cut hay from the land, but no further agreement was granted in respect of grazing. This was because Pye had been advised that if he wanted to apply for planning permission in respect of the land that it would be better for him to have it in hand – unencumbered. Despite the refusal of a new grazing agreement, Graham continued to use the land, maintaining it as he did the rest of his property (so things like harrowing, rolling and fertilising the ground). This remained the situation for 12 years. Mr Graham admitted in court that he would have been willing to pay Pye for the grazing or the hay had he so requested, but no such demand was ever made. When it came to the attention of Pye that Graham intended to assert a proprietary claim over the land, he tried to have this prevented. The main question surrounded the implications of the fact that first Mr Graham knew of Pye's intended use of the property; and second that he would have been willing to pay for the land, or to enter into a formal agreement had it been requested.

On the first point, the court took care to overrule a line of authorities which had suggested that it was the intention of the owner in relation to the land that would determine intention rather than that of the squatter – meaning that the squatter would have to put the land to a use that was inconsistent with the intended use of the owner. In other words the court confirmed that it doesn't matter if the owner has an intended future use for the land which the squatter is aware of. If the squatter intends to possess the land then this will be sufficient to ground a claim.

Regarding the second question, that of willingness to pay, the court followed the precedent set in *Buckinghamshire CC v Moran* and confirmed that what is relevant is not the intention to own the land but the intention to possess it. This is necessary because of the conceptual difficulty of a requirement that means that a squatter must intend to own the land, thereby excluding the owner, when they know that the owner may lawfully recover the land from him. To address this the court cited Powell, where the intention was held to be an intention to exclude the world at large, including the owner, "so far as is reasonably practical and so far as the process of the law will allow". The Court concluded that although Mr Graham would have been willing to pay for the use of the disputed land if asked, such willingness is not inconsistent with them intending to possess the land in the meantime. This loosens the requirement in relation to intent, in that it recognises that a squatter may be willing to enter into a formal agreement with the landowner. This would previously have been interpreted as negating the intention to possess, because such intention would require the squatter to intend to exclude the landowner as well. Following Pye, what is required is simply an objective intention to possess the land; intention to exclude the true owner of the land is not necessary.

It is not necessary to establish that the squatter deliberately intended to exclude the true owner, but where acts of physical possession are clear and unequivocal the courts in Northern Ireland have held that they will generally constitute sufficient manifestation of the intention to possess.[32] This will vary according to the facts of the case.

Having established whether or not the squatter has gone into possession, the final element to consider is whether or not the squatter's possession is adverse to the owner.

C. Possession Must Be Adverse

What is meant by adverse is that the squatter is there without the consent of the landowner. According to the House of Lords in Pye, "it is clearly established in law that the taking or continuation of possession by a squatter with the actual consent of the paper title owner does not constitute dispossession or possession by the squatter for the purposes of the act."[33]

This requirement is related to the definition of intent, and has undergone radical revision over the years. Initially the position, as laid out in the 1879 case of Leigh v Jack was that in order to defeat a title by dispossessing the former owner, acts must be done which are inconsistent with his enjoyment of the land for the purposes for which he intended to use it.[34] If a squatter came to court claiming adverse possession, and the owner could demonstrate that they had a future use for the land of which the squatter was aware, the squatter would be held to have used the land under an implied licence from the owner, thus preventing time from running against him. The only way to get around this was to put the land to a use that was actually inconsistent with the owner's intended use.[35] This sets the bar quite high in relation to the actions that a squatter must take to satisfy the court that his/her possession is adverse to that of the owner. This

---

32 McAnulty (n 12) [23]
33 Pye (n 11) 434
34 Leigh (n 27)
35 Wallis' Clayton Bay Holiday Camp Ltd v Shell-Mex and BP Ltd [1975] QB 94 (CA), [1974] 3 All ER 575

position was however amended by statute in 1980, where the Limitation Act abolished the doctrine of implied licence and relaxed the definition of adverse. This was effectively a means of remedying an increasingly complex body of case law that was emerging in relation to adverse possession, driven essentially by the reluctance of the Courts to grant proprietary title to a squatter at the expense of the landowner.

The new act, and the corresponding NI Order, therefore provides:

> "For the purpose of determining whether a person occupying land is in adverse possession of the land it shall not be assumed by implication of law that his occupation is by permission of the person entitled to the land merely by virtue of the fact that his occupation is not inconsistent with the latter's present or future enjoyment of the land."[36]

This has clarified the position, and cleared the way for decisions such as that in *Buckinghamshire CC v Moran* and *Pye* whereby it is the intention to possess the land in the meantime that is relevant, rather than any physical ouster or the owner in order to put the land to a contrary purpose.

The most recent statement in this regard is to be found in the *Pye* case. The House of Lords in this case questioned the reasoning behind such a stringent requirement in relation to adverse possession, stating that it was difficult to see how the intentions of the paper title owner (unless known to the squatter) could affect the intention of the squatter to possess the land. Now the question exists in terms of dispossession rather than of adverse possession, and the conclusion reached by the House of Lords is that where there is possession of the land by a squatter without the consent of the paper owner then that possession will be adverse and the owner will consequently be held to have been dispossessed. The regime is therefore much more favourable to the squatter than before – it requires neither a physical ouster of the owner nor a use inconsistent with the intention of the owner.

While these elements of adverse possession have evolved primarily through the English Courts, a number of recent cases in Northern Ireland have confirmed their applicability in this jurisdiction.[37]

Once it has been established that the squatter is in fact in adverse possession of the land, the consequences will depend on the nature of the land. This will vary according to whether the land is registered or unregistered; whether it is freehold or leasehold land; and whether the land is in Northern Ireland or in England or Wales.

---

36 Limitation Order (n 1) schedule 1 para 8(5)
37 In particular see *Re Faulkner* (n 13), *McAnulty* (n 12), *Norbrook* (n 10)

6.3 The Effect of the Limitation Order

By law, if a squatter or his/her successors can remain in possession of the disputed land for a period of 12 years then, in the case of unregistered land, the Limitation (Northern Ireland) Order 1989 provides that the 'true owner' loses the right to ever take action against the squatter;[38] and that the owner's title to the land is extinguished.[39] The same provision is made in the Limitation Act, under articles 15 and 17.

The practical effect of this is that because the previous landowner is barred from bringing any action to recover the land after the expiration of the 12 year period, no-one can establish better title to the land than the squatter and he/she can use the land as if it were his/her own, including selling it. This will happen automatically, by operation of law, upon the expiration of the 12 year limitation period. There is no need for the squatter to take action; the title of the owner will simply be extinguished, leaving the squatter with the greatest claim to the land.

If the landowner wants to prevent a squatter from extinguishing his/her title he/she must take action within the 12 year limitation period.

6.4 Stopping Time Running

Within the limitation period there are a number of options available to the landlord to prevent a squatter from gaining title by adverse possession.

A. Granting Permission

The first, of most concern to landowners, is the granting of permission. As possession is only adverse if it is without the consent of the owner, anyone occupying land with the landowner's permission cannot establish title through adverse possession. This was the case in *BP Properties v Buckler*.[40]

In *BP Properties* the defendants had taken court action to prevent their eviction from the house in which they had been living for a number of years without paying rent. Faced with a high profile publicity campaign in relation to this eviction of an elderly woman by a multi-national corporation, *BP Properties* issued a letter to the

---

38 Limitation Order (n 1) section 21(1)
39 Ibid section 26
40 [1987] EWCA Civ 2, (1988) 55 P & CR 337

Buckler's solicitor stating that they were withdrawing the Order of Possession which had been issued in respect of the property, and allowing the defendant to remain living in the property rent free for the remainder of her lifetime, thereby essentially granting a licence for her to occupy the property. The defendant never replied to the letter, but continued to live in the property until her death. Upon her death her successors attempted to claim ownership of the property on the basis of adverse possession. This claim was rejected by the Court because from the date of the letter she had been living there with the consent of the owner, and her possession had therefore ceased to be adverse.

B. Acknowledging Title

The decision may have been different, however, if the defendant had replied to BP Properties rejecting the offer and continuing in possession without consent. This is because it is not simply enough for the landowner to write to the squatter asserting proprietary title. The squatter will be aware that someone else owns the land, but they intend to continue in possession. This was seen in the case of *Wallis v Shell Mex*,[41] and also arose in the case of *Mount Carmel Investments v Thurlow*.[42] In the latter case a number of written notices to quit had been issued to squatters in a residential property in South Kensington. It had been argued that the issue of these notices would have the effect of stopping time running in favour of the squatter, but this was rejected by the Court. Lord Nichols stated:

> "Unless the squatter vacates or gives a written acknowledgement to the owner, the owner has to issue his writ within the prescribed time limit."

This means that if a squatter provides *written* acknowledgement of the title of the owner then time will stop running.[43] Otherwise the owner must issue legal proceedings against the squatter in order to have them removed. If a judgment is received in favour of the owner this must be enforced against the squatter within the 12 year time period. It is not enough either to threaten legal action, or to obtain a judgment and then fail to enforce it. This alone will not stop time from running.

---

41 [1974] 3 AU ER 575
42 [1988] 3 AU ER 129
43 See also *McGuckan v McGuckan and Another* [1990] NI 1 (Ch) where written acknowledgement of no claim to adverse possession was provided.

C. Interrupted Possession

The final way that time can be stopped from running is if the possession of the land in question is interrupted. This is an uncommon occurrence, but the case of *Generay v The Containerised Storage Co.* affirmed that interruption of the period of possession could mean that the limitation period began again.[44] In *Generay* the reason for the interrupted possession was that the piece of land in question had previously been the subject of a civil action against Generay for trespass. To try and defend this claim, a fence had been erected around the disputed land as if to prove that it was not being trespassed upon. This temporary self exclusion from the land, described by the judge as rather unusual, was held to have interrupted the possession of Generay and this caused time to start running anew.

This is the doctrine that operates in respect of freehold unregistered land in Northern Ireland. Even where the land is registered these common law principles continue to regulate the operation of adverse possession in both Northern Ireland and England and Wales.

6.5 Registered Land

Where the land in question is registered a different set of rules apply. In Northern Ireland the applicable legislation is the Land Registration (Northern Ireland) Act 1970, Section 53 of which provides that the Limitation Order shall apply to registered land in the same way it applies to unregistered land. Where a squatter remains in adverse possession of registered land for a period of 12 years, the squatter can apply to the land registry to be registered as the owner of the land.[45] As with unregistered land, the title of the true owner is extinguished automatically by operation of law because the Limitation Order applies to registered land in Northern Ireland. Where there is a gap in time between the title of the true owner being extinguished and the squatter applying to be registered, the paper owner will be deemed to hold the land on trust for the squatter. Therefore while there has been no formal change in title, the paper owner can only deal with the land for the squatter's benefit. The onus therefore remains on the owner to stop time from running before the limitation period expires. If an application for registration is successful then the registrar will rectify the register to reflect the change in title.[46]

---

44 *Generay v The Containerised Storage Co* [2005] EWCA Civ 478, [2005] 2 EGLR 7
45 Land Registration (NI) Act 1970 section 53(2)
46 Ibid section 53(4); For the most recent example of this in Northern Ireland see *Hayes v McGuigan and Others* [2011] NICh 25 [22]

The position in Northern Ireland is now significantly different from that which applies in England and Wales. The Land Registration Act 2002 has brought in significant reforms to the law in respect of registered land in England and Wales.

6.6 Adverse Possession of Leasehold Land

The other variable which exists is that of adverse possession where the land in question is held under a lease. Here the legal relationship between the squatter and the landowner is not direct, and so the position is less favourable to the squatter than is the case with freehold land. While a squatter will have to satisfy the same requirements of adverse possession in respect of leasehold land as of freehold land, the outcome will be less favourable.

Consider the following scenario:

> X, the owner of a fee simple, grants Y a lease for 20 years. If, in the third year of the tenancy a squatter, S, takes adverse possession of the land and remains in adverse possession until the 15th year, the right of the lessee (Y) to recover possession will have been statute barred, and his/her title to the land under the lease will be extinguished under the Limitation Act.

IMPORTANTLY: the rights of the Lessor (X) will be unaffected, because at no point during the 20 year term of the lease will he/she have any right to act against the squatter, unless a covenant of the lease has been breached by the lessee (Y) providing the lessor (X) with a right of forfeiture. This is because adverse possession operates against the current legal estate in possession – the lease. From the end of the 20 year term of the lease the lessor will have 6 years in which to regain possession before the squatter can claim the fee simple by adverse possession.[47] The reason that the lessor (X) can take no action against the squatter during the period of the lease is that the squatter is not bound by the terms of the lease – never having entered into a contractual agreement with the owner. This arises because of the 'no parliamentary conveyance' rule. It had, in the past, been argued that the occupation of land for the requisite 12 year limitation period by a squatter effected a 'parliamentary conveyance' of the title of the leaseholder to the squatter (as if the leaseholder had assigned his/her title). This was known as a parliamentary conveyance because it would be brought about by statute. In the case of

---

47 Limitation Order (n 1)

Y, the squatter would take the lease as an assignee and therefore be liable for all of the covenants of the lease.

But it has been decided in the House of Lords that this is not the case and that there can be no parliamentary conveyance when a squatter takes land by adverse possession. This means that the squatter does not take the existing title but will acquire a new title, independent of the one that has been dispossessed. This places the squatter in a very precarious position, as illustrated in the leading case of *Fairweather v St. Marylebone Property Co.*[48]

In *Fairweather* a man, seeing his neighbour's shed lying in a state of disrepair, took it over and treated it as his own for over 40 years, even subletting it as part of his own property. After 12 years the neighbour's right of action was barred. The whole of the neighbour's property was, however, subject to a 99 year lease, with 33 years remaining. He might therefore have thought that he would retain the use of the shed until such times as the lease expired. Before this time, however, the neighbour surrendered the remainder of the lease to the freeholder. The lease was thus terminated and the freeholder claimed an instant right to evict. Lord Denning considered that the title of the leaseholder to the shed was extinguished against the squatter, but remained good against the freeholder. The effect of dispossession of a lease is to extinguish the title of the dispossessed lessee, but not to extinguish the estate altogether. The lease would therefore remain in being and the squatter could remain in occupation for the duration of the lease, independent of the leaseholder or freeholder. However, Lord Denning found that the consequence of this was that although the leaseholder had lost his title relative to the squatter, he retained his rights as against the freeholder. Equally although the leaseholder had been dispossessed of the shed, the freeholder retained his remedy against the leaseholder for breach of covenants. This means that although the leaseholder had lost possession of the property, he remains liable for the covenants. The squatter is not liable to pay rent or perform the covenants contained in the lease, except to the extent that breach of covenant may give rise to a right of re-entry on the part of the lessor. The dispossessed lessee remains liable under the contract for the obligations. If he stops paying the rent, or performing the covenants contained in the lease and the squatter does not fulfil the obligations then the freeholder may forfeit the lease. Because of this it was argued that it was within the power of the dispossessed leaseholder to surrender the lease, determining the term of the lease and enabling the freeholder to commence an action for possession. Furthermore under the *Fairweather* test the freeholder and the lessee may conspire to

---

48 [1962] UKHL 1, [1963] AC 510

achieve this end. In this way the protection offered to the squatter on leasehold land is much less than in the case of freehold land.

While the decision in *Fairweather* has been accepted in respect of the 'no parliamentary conveyance' rule, its effects have been interpreted differently in Ireland. In the Republic of Ireland the decision was rejected by the Supreme Court in *Perry v Woodfarm Homes Ltd.*[49] The Court in this case held that a lessee with an extinguished title could not assign or surrender that title because if the lessee's title is extinguished then the lessee has nothing but his obligations to the freeholder under the contract contained in the contract/lease. The court stated unequivocally that:

> "a person who has lost all his title to a leasehold estate is not in a position to deal effectively with that estate, … he has nothing to surrender and nothing to assign."[50]

However, this does not mean that the squatter takes the land free from obligations. The freeholder still retains the right to enforce the covenants contained in the lease. In particular the right of re-entry for breach of covenant may be enforced against the squatter, thus dispossessing him. However the Supreme Court is clear that this occurs because of the breach of a covenant contained in the lease and not by surrender by the dispossessed lessee. Given that the law of landlord and tenant in Northern Ireland is also governed by Deasy's Act the decision in *Perry* is likely to be more persuasive in this jurisdiction.[51]

These are the rules that govern adverse possession of leasehold land where the land is unregistered. Where the land is registered the practice of the Land Registry in Northern Ireland has also tended against a strict interpretation of the rule in *Fairweather*. Practice has been to recognise a transfer of title and to enter the squatter as the new owner on the folio of the dispossessed owner.[52] Therefore, while under the construction adopted in either *Fairweather* or *Perry*, the Limitation (NI) Order is entirely negative as far as a squatter of leasehold property is concerned, this rule has been undermined in practice. It is now recognised that the rule in *Fairweather* creates legal difficulties, and the NILC propose to make legislative provision for parliamentary conveyance of title in respect of unregistered land and to formalise the transfer of title system for registered land.[53]

---

49 [1975] IR 104, 118-119 (Walsh J)

50 Ibid 119

51 *cf* Herbert Wallace, *Land Registry Practice in Northern Ireland* (2nd edn) (SLS Legal Publications, 1987) 72

52 NILC *Land Law* (n 1) para 2.68

53 Draft Land Law Reform Bill (Northern Ireland) 201[], section 112. See NILC *Land Law* (n 1) 211

However, following recognition of the inequity caused to many landowners as a result of the operation of the doctrine of adverse possession, there has been a move in English law to tip the scales back in favour of the landowner, making it more difficult for a squatter to achieve title to the land by adverse possession.

CHAPTER 7

Adverse Possession: Challenge and Reform

7.1 Introduction

The last chapter examined the doctrine of adverse possession, and in particular the requirements of that doctrine. This chapter examines the reasons behind the doctrine and the changes that have been made in England and Wales that modify the doctrine and address some of the harsher criticisms that have been made of the way in which adverse possession operates.

It is important to recall that the doctrine of adverse possession has a very long history in land law dating back to Roman times. Over the years it has been amended to address complications as they arose, such as for example the removal by legislation of the requirement being imposed by the Courts that for possession by a squatter to be adverse it must be inconsistent with the future use of the owner.[1] Therefore when considering the reasons that the doctrine exists, it is useful to remember that many of these are rooted in historical circumstances. The evolution of land law over the years has gradually led to the usefulness, and indeed the desirability of the doctrine being called into question. This is particularly the case in respect of registered land. Bear in mind that the doctrine arose specifically to facilitate the investigation of title of unregistered land, it becomes clear how the rationale for the doctrine has altered. With unregistered land a potential purchaser needs to ensure that they will be able to purchase the title to the land free from any prior legal interests in it. Adverse possession facilitates this by ensuring that any claims that have not been asserted for a period of 12 years or more will

---

1 See chapter 6.2

be statute barred, effectively allowing good title to be transferred. It removes the risk for a potential purchaser that someone will appear after the land has been sold and assert title to it. However in the case of registered land, the register is deemed to be conclusive evidence of ownership of land. Therefore if ownership is recorded it is readily apparent to any potential purchaser what, if any, prior interests exist in a piece of land, obviating the need for extensive searches of the title and removing the risk of purchasing bad title.

Bear in mind also at this point that cases of adverse possession where a squatter takes a large portion of land from the true owner are comparatively rare. In most cases where a squatter moves on to the land the landowner is within his/her rights to take legal action to remove them. Provided this is done within the 12 year limitation period then there is no question of the squatter being able to assert title against the owner. Similarly, much more common are cases where a genuine mistake as to boundary is rectified by the operation of the doctrine.[2] This is one of the more justifiable uses of it, as it can save significant legal dispute between neighbours over boundaries. However, high profile cases do still arise, and as a result of this, by the end of the 20th century the continued justification for the doctrine itself was beginning to be called in to question.

The Northern Ireland Law Commission, in their supplementary consultation on land law, considered the law on adverse possession as it stands in Northern Ireland. In the case of unregistered land the doctrine is fundamentally the same as that in England and Wales, so their commentary applies equally to both contexts. They highlight a number of reasons why the doctrine of adverse possession can cause unease among landowners and lawyers.[3] These reasons include:

- It appears to sanction illegality and/or immorality. The effect of the doctrine is to reward those who trespass on the land of others and operates without any requirement of good faith on the part of the squatter. While most people would concede that in the case of innocent boundary mistake a squatter should not be penalised, the situation is different where someone acts in the knowledge that they can benefit from their illegality or immorality. The law commission considered, but ultimately rejected the suggestion that there should be a requirement of good faith interpreted into the existing common law doctrine. This conclusion is based on the judgment in *Pye v United Kingdom*[4] which upholds the validity of adverse possession as a means of controlling the use of

---

2 *Hayes v McGuigan and Others* [2011] NICh 25 [18] [33]
3 Northern Ireland Law Commission, *Land Law* (NI Law Com No 8, 2010) para 12.12
4 *JA Pye (Oxford) Ltd v The United Kingdom* App No 44302/02 (ECtHR, 21 Nov 2005)

land. It is therefore unlikely that any question of morality will be interpreted into the doctrine, and it will therefore continue to operate as before, which leads on to the second criticism of the doctrine.

- The operation of the doctrine imposes severe penalties on innocent landowners. The price that a landowner pays for failing to pay due attention to the use of their land is ultimately forfeiture of that land. It is argued that this imposes a particularly high burden on the owners of large estates where it is more difficult to properly monitor use.

- There is no scope for compensation. Once the right of action is barred the disposed owner does not even have the right of access to court to claim compensation for his/her loss. This is thought by some to constitute a disproportionate penalty on the landowner, particularly given the fact that there is no procedural protection afforded to the landowner under the common law doctrine. The effect of the Limitation Act is to automatically bar the right of access to the court once the 12 year period has expired. There is no mechanism by which the owner can dispute or appeal this (and this was to be one of the key grounds for argument in *Pye*).

- Finally, it is now felt that the original common law rationale for the doctrine does not stand up in the context of registered land. Where title can be easily determined by consulting the register then there is no need for a doctrine of adverse possession to facilitate conveyancing.

These issues came to a head in the case of *Pye v Graham*. Mr Graham had been using land belonging to Pye for grazing and agricultural use without Pye's permission for a period exceeding 12 years. Pye's intention had been to apply for planning permission to develop the land and Graham knew of this intention. Upon expiration of the limitation period, Graham had received a windfall of 25 hectares of land that was suitable for development, and as such of great commercial value. Pye challenged this. In addition to disputing whether or not the requirements of adverse possession had been satisfied, Pye also challenged the outcome on the basis of human rights legislation, namely that the operation of the law on adverse possession constituted a violation of his right to peaceful enjoyment of his possessions as protected by article 1 of Protocol 1 to the European Convention on Human Rights. It is this element of the case that is the focus of this chapter.

From the outset this case had raised questions as to the justice of the situation. Although the High Court, where the case was initially heard, had decided in favour of the Grahams on the question of whether or not adverse possession had been established,[5] the presiding judge commented that the result did not accord with justice and could not be justified by practical considerations.[6] This was based primarily on the fact that the justification for the doctrine – namely the avoidance of uncertainty – did not apply in the case of registered land. In such circumstances, according to the judge, the fact that a registered owner who had sat on his rights for 12 years should be deprived of his property was "illogical and disproportionate", although it should be cautioned that this was probably linked to the size of the windfall in this case, which magnified the perceived injustice to the landowner.

When the case went to the Court of Appeal, the decision of the High Court, recognising adverse possession, was overturned.[7] This was not, however, done on the basis of the injustice of the result. The Court of Appeal considered the question of whether or not the applicant's loss of title constituted a breach of article 1 Protocol 1, and decided that it could not, because what was at issue was the barring of a right to access to the Courts, and not a deprivation of property per se. Thus even though limitation periods limited the right of access to the court, and as a logical consequence deprived a landowner of his property rights, there was nothing in this operation of law that was inherently incompatible with the European Convention. This question was not pursued before the House of Lords, but was raised before the European Court of Human Rights (ECHR) in Strasbourg. At the initial stage the ECHR decided in favour of Pye, suggesting that there had been an unjustified violation of a protected right.[8] However, because of the significance of the question of law being raised, the case went to the Grand Chamber of the European Court of Human Rights, where it was heard by all of the judges from the member states sitting together. It is the 2007 judgment that is the most up-to-date statement of the law.[9]

The challenge that Pye raised in the ECHR was based on the justification for the operation of the doctrine of adverse possession in respect of registered land. Pye claimed that there could be no justification for title to registered land to be lost by adverse possession and that therefore the operation of the Limitation Act constituted a

5   [2000] Ch 676, 693-694
6   Ibid, 709 (Neuberger J)
7   [2001] EWCA Civ 117, [2001] Ch. 804, 813-814
8   *JA Pye (Oxford) Ltd v The United Kingdom* App No 44302/02 (ECtHR, 21 Nov 2005)
9   *JA Pye (Oxford) Ltd and JA Pye (Oxford) Land Ltd v The United Kingdom* [GC], 44302/02, ECHR 2007-III, para [53]

breach of his human rights. The government countered that the doctrine was justified in the public interest; that it could not be considered to be disproportionate; and that it did not impose an excessive burden.

In more detail, Pye attempted to challenge the doctrine from two angles. First of all it was suggested that the doctrine itself could not be justified in the context of registered land. However, if this argument failed, Pye further argued that even if it could be justified, that the absence of any compensation for the loss made the effect of the operation of the doctrine disproportionate to any legitimate aim that it pursued. The scale of the loss incurred, Pye argued, imposed an excessive burden on the applicant companies. Finally it was argued that there was no procedural protection available to the company. What this means is that the companies did not have any opportunity to stop the squatter from asserting title because their own title was extinguished automatically, by operation of law. This phrase 'by operation of law' refers to the fact that under the common law, once a squatter has been in adverse possession of land (meeting the three criteria of having dispossessed the owner; being in possession and the possession being adverse) for the necessary period of 12 years, the Limitation Act works automatically to bar the owner's right of access to the courts. The squatter does not need to take any action beyond remaining in adverse possession for the relevant time, and the owner is given no notification, no opportunity to prevent the operation of the act, and no right of appeal against its operation. This is what is meant by the title being extinguished automatically by operation of law, and why Pye raised the issue of the lack of procedural protection inherent in the doctrine.

The government then responded to these allegations by making three key points:

- There should be no reason to impose a positive obligation on the government to protect the company from their own inattention. This doctrine works by operation of law and is thus a negative operation.

- Going back to the historical context and the public policy issues that accompany land law, the government argued that land is a limited resource, and that therefore it is in the public interest to impose a time limit for recovery. This, argued the government, ensures that land is being used and that it does not become unmarketable because of the risk of title being asserted many years after it is sold. It also more practically prevents land from falling into poor condition from simply being abandoned. If a squatter makes use of land that the owner is not willing to then public policy favours that land remains in use.

- Finally, the government disputed the claim that the operation of the doctrine was disproportionate. They pointed to a number of factors to support this. First the length of the limitation period. 12 years, it was argued, is a perfectly reasonable length of time to expect a landowner to become aware of a squatter on their land. Second, once a landowner does become aware of the presence of a squatter there are legal mechanisms available to allow the owner to recover the land from the squatter within the limitation period. It is therefore ultimately a question of the fault of the applicants in failing to properly manage their land which should not be held to give rise to a positive obligation on the government to prevent them from falling foul of the rules of adverse possession.

Those were the arguments as put forward by the parties. Before moving on to the reasoning of the court, it is worth considering the question of why the government is the respondent in this case.

Human rights law usually operates to regulate the vertical relationship between the citizen and the state. However this case arose as the result of a dispute between two private parties, the property development company, Pye, and the farmer, Graham. While the case went through the UK court system, from the High Court to the Court of Appeal and on to the House of Lords, this remained a private law matter between the two parties. However, when it went to the European Court of Human Rights it became a case against the government. The reason for this is not because the loss of land was the direct result of a legislative or executive act (eg a compulsory purchase order) that would have created a legal relationship between the government and the applicant companies, but rather because the government is ultimately responsible for the legislation that resulted in the loss of the land. This gives rise to state obligations under the European Convention on Human Rights. So because the loss of land occurs by operation of law, effectively as a result of the provisions of the Limitation Act, itself passed by the government of the United Kingdom, the government can be called to account for the effects of that legislation on private parties.

A. What Rights Were Alleged to Have Been Breached?

Article 1 of Protocol 1 to the European Convention on Human Rights provides:

- Every natural or legal person is entitled to the peaceful enjoyment of his possessions. No one shall be deprived of his possessions except in the public interest and subject to the conditions provided for by law and by the general principles of international law.

- The preceding provisions shall not, however, in any way impair the right of a State to enforce such laws as it deems necessary to control the use of property in accordance with the general interest or to secure the payment of taxes or other contributions or penalties.

As with any other right protected under the ECHR, there are limitations that may be put on the right. The Protocol sets out a general statement of the right to be protected – the right to peaceful enjoyment of property – followed by the circumstances in which the right may be limited. To decide this, the Court engages in a two stage examination of the case. First it determines whether the facts of the case fall within the scope of the protected right. If it is decided that an issue does arise under that right, then the Court will decide whether the action taken falls within the scope of one of the permissible limitations to the right. In this regard the arguments made by the government of the United Kingdom are interesting for the way in which they illustrate the doctrine of adverse possession.

Addressing this part of the case, four main arguments were raised by the government in support of the doctrine. Just as Pye tried to allege first of all that the doctrine was unjustified in respect of registered land, but included also lesser challenges to the operation of the doctrine itself, so too the government engaged in this reasoning of first of all refuting that there was any issue to answer under the European Convention, but failing that, addressing the need for a doctrine of adverse possession that would bring it within the scope of a permissible interference. The government therefore argued that:

- The law of adverse possession is a long standing feature of English Land Law. As such the applicant would have been well aware of this limitation on his absolute right to possession of the property when he bought it and then failed to take action to evict the squatter. In this regard adverse possession was no more than the due operation of the pre-existing national legal regime, and as such was clearly prescribed by law.

- The interference with the rights of Pye came from the actions of Graham and the inaction of Pye, and not from the government. As such the operation of the Act was a limitation on the applicant's right of access to the Court and not an interference with property rights.

- That the limitations on property rights inherent in the doctrine of adverse possession pursued a legitimate objective that was clearly in the public interest, namely preventing stale claims from being brought before the Court and ensuring that the reality of unopposed occupation of land and its legal ownership coincided.

- That the measures were proportionate – 12 years was a long limitation period and that Pye could have taken action to evict Graham at any time during this period.

Against this Pye argued that the cumulative effect was a deprivation of the right to possession and that this was more than simply restricting access to Court. They also did not accept that it was their inaction that was responsible for the loss of the land, but that it was the operation of a law, passed by the state and enforced by the national court, which constituted an interference by the state with the applicant's enjoyment of their possessions and that this was a breach of the Protocol.

In the first instance the European Court of Human Rights agreed with the applicant that there had been a breach of their rights and that this breach fell outside the scope of the permissible limitations. This was then reversed by the Grand Chamber – the full court which hears cases which are likely to be of particular legal significance.

The Grand Chamber examined the two parts to the case; whether or not there was an interference with a Convention right; and whether or not that interference could be justified. In considering whether or not there had been a violation of human rights in this case, the Chamber stated that "in order to be compatible with the general rule … an interference with the right to the peaceful enjoyment of possessions must strike a 'fair balance' between the demands of the general interest of the community and the requirements of the protection of the individual's fundamental rights."[10] To achieve this balance there must be a reasonable relationship of proportionality between the means employed and the aim sought to be realised. States would be given a wide margin of appreciation to decide on whether measures taken were proportionate to the aim to be achieved. So in the case in question the issue is whether the effect of adverse possession ie that the owner loses title to his land, is proportionate to the aim to be achieved, ie legal certainty in relation to land.

The Court considered first of all the applicability of the Protocol to the facts of the case. While it agreed with the position of the UK government that ownership of land was subject to the law of the land in relation to issues such as planning permission, compulsory purchase legislation or indeed adverse possession, which could limit enjoyment of ownership rights, it nevertheless did fall within the scope of article 1 Protocol 1. This means that in theory the applicants – Pye – have a right to peaceful enjoyment of their land irrespective of pre-existing legislation.

---

10 Ibid, para [53]

Given that the operation of adverse possession had unquestionably led to an interference with that right, the next question for the court was whether the interference was justified or permissible under the Convention.

On the question of the nature of the interference, the Court held that Pye did not lose their land because of a legislative provision which permitted the state to transfer legal ownership (such as compulsory purchase) but as a result of the operation of generally applicable rules on limitation periods for the recovery of land. This meant that these provisions were not intended to deprive paper owner's of their ownership, but to regulate questions of title in a system in which, historically, 12 years adverse possession was sufficient to extinguish the former owner's right to re-enter to recover possession. This was a generally known provision of land law and the applicant was therefore not affected by a 'deprivation of possessions' but rather by a 'control of land' within the meaning of the second paragraph of article 1.

Having established this was an example of state control of land within the meaning of the article, the Court then had to determine whether the measures taken were proportionate to the aim to be achieved. As part of this the Court considered the existence of a limitation period in light of the reasons given that legal certainty must be ensured, and that defendants must be protected from stale claims. The 12 year limitation period was accepted as pursuing a legitimate aim in the general interest.

When considering whether or not interference with a particular right is justified, the Court will grant to states what is known as a 'margin of appreciation' which recognises that national governments are in a better position than international courts to decide on which laws are necessary within the state. This means that the state has some discretion as to the aims they choose to pursue. The European Court in these circumstances will respect the legislature's judgment as to what is in the public interest so long as it is not manifestly without reasonable foundation. In the context of land law, the Court recognised that the regulation of property is different in different countries, and that this reflects local attitudes to the importance of property. Given the importance of land in the history of law in England and the reasons for the development of adverse possession, the Court accepted that to extinguish title by preventing the former owner from recovering the property could not be said to be 'manifestly without reasonable foundation' and that there existed a general interest in the limitation period and the extinguishment of title at the end of it.

Having decided then that the facts of the case did raise an issue under the Protocol, and that there had been a reasonable aim pursued by the legislation, the final question for the court is whether or not a 'fair balance' had been struck between these competing considerations – namely whether the measures were proportionate to the objective to be achieved. The Court confirmed that in these cases the State enjoys a wide margin of appreciation, meaning that the Court will not exercise too stringent scrutiny of the measures. In this case because of the long history of the doctrine of adverse possession in English land law and the fact that what was at issue was a control of use rather than a deprivation of possession, the Court decided that the doctrine did strike a fair balance. The extinguishment of title was simply a way of regularising the position of the parties upon expiration of the limitation period. The size of the loss in this case was not relevant in determining whether or not the measures were proportionate per se. Indeed the court rejected the idea that compensation should be required in the case of significant loss, stating that this would undermine the logic of limitations per se.

Following Pye the operation of the doctrine of adverse possession is unlikely to be challenged on human rights grounds. This decision has re-affirmed the rationale for the doctrine, and has allowed for its continuation in force as a part of land law.

However, the main issue addressed in Pye – that of the absence of any procedural protection for the landowner, was addressed in England and Wales by the 2002 Land Registration Act, thus creating a clear divergence between the law in Northern Ireland and that in England and Wales in relation to adverse possession of registered land.

Before the 2002 Act the squatter, once he/she had acquired title by adverse possession, could apply to be registered as the owner with the Land Registry.[11]

If time elapsed between his/her gaining title through adverse possession and applying to have his/her title registered, the registered owner would be deemed to hold the land in trust for the squatter (with the legal title remaining vested in the paper owner, but the beneficial ownership vested in the squatter, meaning that if the true owner tried to for example sell the property, the squatter would be entitled to the proceeds of the sale).[12] But apart from that the doctrine operated in exactly the same way as it had for unregistered land – with the title of the owner being extinguished automatically at the end of the limitation period. As we said this is a position that favours the squatter in

---

11 The pre-2002 position in England and Wales is effectively the same as continues to operate in Northern Ireland under the Land Registration (Northern Ireland) Act 1970 and the Limitation (Northern Ireland) Order 1989. See chapter 6.5

12 Land Registration Act 1925 section 75

relative terms, as it does not require any positive action on his/her part to gain title. It is also detrimental to the absent minded landowner who simply loses track of the use of the land and the time elapsing. The position has now effectively been reversed in England and Wales, with the new statutory regime affording much greater protection to the landowner and requiring positive action from a squatter in order to obtain title. The effect of this change and whether or not it was necessary remains a hot topic of debate among the academic community.[13]

7.2 The Land Registration Act 2002

The first significant change introduced by the Act is that establishing adverse possession no longer automatically extinguishes the title of the owner. S96 provides that title to land cannot be extinguished under the Limitation Act 1980. This then precludes the consequence that upon expiration of a limitation period that title will be extinguished. This is intended to protect the proprietor on the basis that the register will be conclusive as to the ownership of the land. This applies to registered estates in land. The key difference to bear in mind is that the effect of the LRA 2002 is to prevent the operation of the Limitation Act in respect of registered land – it no longer applies.

The second change is that rather than adverse possession occurring automatically by operation of law upon the expiration of the 12 year period, under the Act the limitation period will be reduced to 10 years. However, while this initially appears to favour the squatter, the Act also introduces a requirement that the squatter must apply to be registered as the proprietor of the registered estate if he/she has been in possession for the period of 10 years ending on the date of application. At this point the squatter will have to prove that they have been in continuous adverse possession, satisfying all the substantive requirements of the doctrine, for the relevant period. If the period of adverse possession has been interrupted time must start to run again.

There are a number of situations in which a squatter cannot make a valid application to be registered, even if they have been in adverse possession for the requisite time period. These are:

- Where there are possession proceedings against the squatter that are still current.[14] This includes two years after a judgment has been obtained against

---

13 See eg Martin Dixon, 'Adverse Possession and Human Rights' [2005] C & PL 345; Martin Dixon, 'The Reform of Property Law and the Land Registration Act 2002: A Risk Assessment' [2003] C&PL 136

14 LRA 2002 schedule 6 para 1(3)

the squatter. This allows a landowner to take proceedings to remove a squatter without worrying that title could be established while proceedings were still pending, meaning that they had to fend off an application for registration by the squatter at the same time.

- Where the proprietor is an enemy or held in enemy territory. (This essentially ensures that protection provided by a post war statute remains in force. It has little relevance today.)

- Where the proprietor is suffering from mental disability of physical impairment.[15] This means that the proprietor is not disadvantaged through illness which may prevent him/her from addressing his/her affairs adequately.

This leads directly on to the next stage of the process.

If, after 10 years in adverse possession, the squatter applies to be registered as the owner of the land, the true owner and anyone else who has a registered interest in the land will be notified by the registrar of this application. If such a notification is received, the landowner may then serve a counter notice on the registrar requiring him to reject the application (subject to certain exceptions). If this is done then the proprietor has effectively asserted his/her title to the land and the application of the squatter will fail.

If, upon being sent this notification, the landowner does not respond the registrar will enter the squatter as the new proprietor of the estate. Usually the notification is sent to the owner of the estate that the squatter has applied to have registered in his/her own name. In the case of leasehold land, the notification will be sent both to the legal leaseholder and to the freeholder. Although freeholders (landlords) do not have the right to take possession proceedings against the squatter on account of the lease, upon being made aware of the situation they may require that the registered tenant take steps to have the squatter evicted.

So generally if a counter notice is served by the owner the application of the squatter will fail. There are, however, some exceptions to this:

The first is where the owner serves a counter notice, but then fails to take any action to remove the squatter or to regularise his/her position (eg by granting a lease or a licence to occupy the property) within two years.[16] This could also apply if the owner obtained a judgment against the squatter and then failed to enforce it. If the squatter remains in adverse possession for a further period of two years from the original application for registration, then they will be entitled to apply again. Upon this second application the registrar must register him as the owner of the estate.

---

15 Ibid schedule 6 para 8
16 Ibid schedule 6 para 6

The second situation where the squatter may be entitled to be registered despite the objection of the owner is if he/she can establish that they fall within one of the statutory exceptions contained in the Act.[17] These exceptions are:

- Where, under the principles of proprietary estoppel, it would be unconscionable for the registered owner to object to the squatter's application to be registered.
- Where the squatter is otherwise entitled to the land.
- Where the squatter is the owner of adjacent property and has been in adverse possession of the land in question under the mistaken but reasonable belief that he/she was the owner of it.

In these situations it is believed that the balance of fairness plainly lies with the squatter and that he/she should prevail. So what do each of these exceptions mean?

A. Estoppel

Where to allow someone to insist on enforcing their strict legal rights will cause undue harshness to another party, the person can be stopped from enforcing their rights.

To fall within this exception the squatter will have to show two distinct matters; first that it is unconscionable to dispossess him/her and second that the circumstances are such that he/she ought to be registered as the proprietor. This applies the equitable principles of estoppel in statutory form and in the context of land law. To establish this the squatter will have to show that the registered proprietor in some way encouraged or allowed the applicant to believe that he/she owned the land. In this belief the squatter must have acted to his/her detriment, to the knowledge of the proprietor, and that in these circumstances it would be unfair to allow the owner to insist on his/her legal rights in respect of the land. In practice this sort of situation could occur where there is an agreed sale of land but the conveyance is never fully completed, meaning that the land has never legally been transferred.

B. Some Other Rights to the Land

This exception is more straightforward. From time to time there may be cases where the squatter has some other right to the land that would entitle him to possession irrespective of the adverse possession claim, for example where the squatter is entitled

---

17 Ibid schedule 6 para 5

to the land under a will or where he/she had contracted to buy the land and paid the consideration but the legal estate was never transferred.

C. Reasonable Mistake as to Boundary

This applies only where the squatter owns adjacent land and the boundaries have been incorrectly marked on the land, for example the fences dividing properties do not correspond to the title deeds for the land. To be successful in these circumstances the squatter must reasonably believe that the land belonged to him.

If the squatter can demonstrate that they fall within one of these exceptions then they will be entitled to be registered as the owner of the property notwithstanding the objection of the registered owner.

The regime that is in operation in respect of registered land in England now has added considerably to that in force in respect of unregistered land. By removing the automatic extinguishment of title to land upon the expiration of the limitation period, the act now requires that positive action be taken by the squatter to claim title. Although the limitation period has been shortened, the landowner now has the opportunity to prevent a squatter from gaining title. This in effect addresses the concerns raised by *Pye* that there is no procedural protection available to a dispossessed land owner. It has also gone a long way towards protecting the property rights of registered owners. This has arguably been achieved at the expense of the squatter. It has helped to address some of the more cogent criticisms of the doctrine of adverse possession, and has meant that it remains a part of property law into the 21st century.

The reforms are not without controversy however. The practical effect of the veto system is to make it nearly impossible for a squatter to acquire title by adverse possession. It has been argued that these reforms were unnecessary and that they undermine the social function of adverse possession in ensuring that land remains in use and preventing landowners from sleeping on their rights. It has also been argued that the reforms unnecessarily impact on vulnerable populations, and are driven by a portrayal of squatters as immoral or as land thieves.[18] This perception has been strengthened by the recent introduction of legislation that makes squatting a criminal offence in England and Wales.[19]

---

18 See Neil Cobb and Lorna Fox, 'Living Outside the System: the (im)morality of urban squatting after the Land Registration Act 2002' (2007) 27 *Legal Studies* 236
19 Legal Aid, Sentencing and Punishment of Offenders Act 2012 section 144

7.3 Reform in Northern Ireland?

The question of whether or not a veto like the one that now exists in England and Wales should be introduced into the law in Northern Ireland was considered by the Law Commission. In their 2010 report they confirmed that adverse possession plays an ongoing role in dealing with conveyancing problems. The doctrine should therefore apply in the same manner to both registered and unregistered land.[20]

Whereas before *Pye* there may have been a question over the retention of the doctrine per se, this issue has been resolved by the ECHR, and since the *Pye* case there is no question of the abolition of the doctrine nor of radical revision of the core features of the doctrine. However, despite the changes made to the regime in England and Wales, the Northern Ireland Commission had "considerable reservations about introducing a veto scheme into Northern Ireland".[21] This was because they felt that they would be more appropriately introduced in the context of reform of the law of land registration, which was outside the scope of the current consultation. Indeed the reforms brought in as a result of the Land Registration Act 2002 in England and Wales are driven by the requirements of registration and the need to ensure that interests appear on the register. As this system of registration is not as firmly established in Northern Ireland, the Law Commission concluded that until such times as reform is undertaken to the law of registration, there was no need for statutory intervention to amend the doctrine of adverse possession. It therefore looks like the law on adverse possession of registered land in Northern Ireland will remain at odds with that in England and Wales, providing another key point of divergence between the two regimes.

---

20 NILC, *Land Law* (n 3) para 12.2
21 Ibid 12.10

CHAPTER 8

Leases

8.1 Introduction

A lease is an interest in property – it is one of the permissible legal estates that can be created. It is created by contract or deed which grants a proprietary, rather than just a personal, interest in land. This means that the lessee enjoys all the rights associated with property, including the right to possess the property, the right to exclude others, and the right to sell or transfer the property, subject to the terms of the lease. Effectively securing a lease of property has an equivalent effect to owning land in freehold, although these rights last only for the duration of the lease. As a lease is a legal estate it can be registered in the land registry,[1] and as such will bind any subsequent purchasers of land. The proprietary interest created by a lease serves to distinguish it from a licence, which is permission for non-exclusive use of land for a purpose which would otherwise constitute trespass. It is the element of proprietary interest, and the ability to enforce that interest against third parties (including the landlord) that makes it important to be able to distinguish between a lease and a licence. In England and Wales the lease is one of only two remaining legal estates that can be created following the Law of Property Act 1925.[2] The Northern Ireland Law Commission currently proposes that this position should be replicated in Northern Ireland.[3]

In Northern Ireland the statutory definition of the lease is found in the Landlord and Tenant Law Amendment Act (Ireland) 1860, known as Deasy's Act.[4] In England and Wales a statutory definition of the lease, or term of years absolute, is provided in

---

1   See chapter 4
2   section 1(1)
3   Northern Ireland Law Commission, *Land Law* (NI Law Com No 8, 2010) para 3.1
4   Landlord and Tenant Law Amendment Act (Ireland) 1860 (23 & 24 Vict c 154) (Deasy's Act)

Section 205 of the Law of Property Act 1925. In both jurisdictions, however, the law has evolved through common law. While the origins of the law diverge between the two jurisdictions, in practice the way in which the law has been interpreted means that there is very little substantive difference between the two.

8.2 Formalities for the Creation of a Lease

In Northern Ireland certain formalities must be observed to create a lease. This is consistent with the general requirement of land law that any agreement that either creates or transfers an interest in land must be formally executed. The lease must be signed by both parties in accordance with the Statute of Frauds.

Section 4 of Deasy's Act sets these formalities out:[5]

> "Every lease … for any definite period of time not being from year to year or for any lesser period, shall be by deed executed, or note in writing signed by the landlord or his agent thereunto lawfully authorised in writing."

This technically only requires a written agreement, signed by the landlord, but it is good practice to execute a deed.

A tenancy of one year certain or greater requires these formalities to be observed. If they are not then the lease will be void. However, if the tenant takes possession and the landlord accepts rent then a periodic tenancy based on the time between payments will be presumed. Section 4 permits the creation of such short term tenancies without formal documentation. In practice this means that periodic tenancies can be created orally between the landlord and tenant.

In England and Wales a lease will not create a legal estate unless it is made by deed.[6] In addition, following the introduction of the Land Registration Act 2002 any lease over 7 years must also be registered to take effect in law.[7] Leases of between 3 and 7 years must be created by deed but registration, while possible, is not a precondition to taking legal effect. The exception to the rule that a lease must be created by deed is found in Section 54 of the Law of Property Act 1925, which provides that a legal lease may be created where it is for less than 3 years; takes effect in possession; and is at the best rent reasonably obtainable.[8] Thus where the formalities for the creation of a fixed term lease

---

5 Deasy's Act (n 4) section 4
6 Law of Property Act 1925 section 52(1)
7 Land Registration Act 2002 section 27(2)(b)
8 Law of Property Act 1925 section 54(2)

are not met, it is still possible to infer that a lease has been created. This type of lease is known as an implied periodic tenancy. The term of the lease in these circumstances is determined by the interval at which rent is paid. Therefore less formal leases can still be regarded as legal leases where they are not properly executed but fall within the scope of the exception. These informal leases may even be created orally and are exempt from the normal formality requirements of land contracts.[9]

The assignment of an existing lease must also be executed by deed as such a transaction constitutes the transfer of an interest in land.[10] If the land in question is registered then assignment will only be complete upon registration.[11]

8.3 Characteristics of a Lease

The main legislative provision underpinning the creation of a lease in Northern Ireland is Section 3 of Deasy's Act.

This Section provides:

> "The relation of landlord and tenant shall be deemed to be founded on the express or implied contract of the parties, and not upon tenure or service, and a reversion shall not be necessary to such relation, which shall be deemed to subsist in all cases in which there shall be an agreement by one party to hold land from or under another in consideration of any rent."

From this section it can be seen that there are a number of characteristics to a lease. In both Northern Ireland and in England and Wales a lease will have the following characteristics:

- There is Exclusive Possession
- It is granted for a term certain
- There is a reversion to the landlord
- Whether or not there is a rent service
- Irrespective of the intention of the parties as indicated by them

Each of these characteristics will be discussed in turn.

---

9 Law of Property (Miscellaneous Provisions) Act 1989 section 2(5)(a)
10 *Crago v Julian* [1991] EWCA Civ 4, [1992] 1 WLR 372, 376 (Sir Donald Nicholls VC), *Trustees of St John's Hospital v Keevil* [2001] EWCA Civ 1730 (CA) [20]-[21], [39]
11 Land Registration Act 2002 section 27

A. Term Certain

For a term certain to exist the commencement and expiry dates must be certain before commencement of the term. This requirement existed in common law but is also codified in England and Wales in the 1925 Law of Property Act.[12] This requirement was confirmed in the case of *Prudential Assurance Co. Ltd v London Residuary Body* in 1992.[13] In 1930 London County Council purchased a strip of land from a Mr Nathan for the purposes of road widening. The Council then let the strip of land back to Mr Nathan on the following terms:

> "The tenancy shall continue until the land is required by the Council for the purpose of widening the Walworth Road..."

By 1988 Mr Nathan's beneficial interest had passed to Prudential and the Council's interest to the London Residuary Board (LRB). LRB, with no intention of widening the road, gave six months notice to determine the tenancy. Lord Templeman, in the House of Lords, held that there was no leasehold estate for the duration stated in the agreement because there was no term certain – no date of determination. What this demonstrates is that a term certain is an absolute requirement for a lease to exist.

This requirement of a term certain has been questioned in the English courts. In the *Prudential Assurance* case the court stated that there was no clear basis for the rule. The best explanation that has been offered is that it serves to distinguish a lease, which is a determinate interest in property, from the freehold, which is indeterminate. Nevertheless, absence of clear rationale notwithstanding, the requirement that the lease be created for a term certain remains one of the preconditions of a valid lease. Although this issue is not as clear-cut in the case law on Deasy's Act,[14] absent strong evidence to the contrary this should also be presumed to apply in Northern Ireland.

The requirement of a term certain also gives rise to the label 'term of years absolute' which is used to describe the legal estate of leasehold.

A lease can also create a future legal interest in land. This is an agreement to enter into a lease and arises where the terms of the lease stipulate some particular date in the future on which the lease will take effect. To be valid the lease must take effect in possession within 21 years of the date of the grant.[15] If it does not take effect within this time it will not be valid.

---

12 section 205
13 [1991] UKHL 10, [1992] 2 AC 386
14 JCW Wylie, *Irish Land Law*, (4th edn, Bloomsbury Professional, 2010) para [17.13]
15 Law of Property Act 1925 section 205

The definition of the term of years provided in the Law of Property Act expressly excludes certain types of term from its scope. In particular any term of years that is determined by a life (as would have been the case with the legal life estate) is not a valid term of years as it is insufficiently certain.

However leases less than one year duration are expressly included in the definition. From a practical point of view, a lease for 1 year 'from' a particular date begins the next day unless rent is payable on that date. Thus a lease from 1st Jan 2012 begins on 2nd Jan and runs to midnight on 1st Jan 2013.[16]

A term certain can include provision for notice to be given by either side to bring the tenancy to an end – typically a notice to quit or a break clause. This acceptance that the lease may be terminated early does not prevent it from existing for a term certain. So long as an ideal end date is specified the certainty requirement will be met. A term certain also includes periodic terms such as weekly, monthly, quarterly or yearly.

B. There is a Reversion to the Landlord

Under the traditional rules for the creation of estates, a lease is a lesser estate that is carved out of a greater (usually freehold) estate. This means that for the duration of the lease the leaseholder enjoys the rights to the property, but once the lease expires all those rights will pass back to the person who owns the freehold, or his/her successors in title, because the freehold estate will outlast the lease. This applies only in England and Wales. It is related to the requirement that the lease be for a term certain. It must be clear that upon expiration of the lease the property will revert to the freeholder, otherwise again there are problems of distinguishing the nature and extent of the lease.[17]

The position is rather different in Northern Ireland, where Section 3 of Deasy's Act expressly states that a reversion shall not be necessary to the relation of landlord and tenant.[18] This was due to the nature of land holding in Ireland and the moulding of the category of leasehold to accommodate a more arms length relationship between landlord and tenant in Ireland.

---

16 Interpretation Act (NI) 1954 article 39
17 Law of Property Act 1925 section 205 requires that the term of the lease be either certain or "liable to determination by notice, re-entry, operation of law, or by a provision for cesser on redemption...".
18 This difference is due to the way in which land in Ireland was leased on behalf of absentee landlords. Where an agent was acting on behalf of a landlord, the requirement that there be a reversion to the landlord made it difficult for the agent to exercise powers to enforce the lease. See JCW Wylie, *Irish Land Law*, (4th edn, Bloomsbury Professional, 2010) para [17.05]

C. A Rent Service is Not Required

In Northern Ireland, Section 3 of Deasy's Act states that the relationship of landlord and tenant:

> "shall be deemed to subsist in all cases in which there shall be an agreement by one party to hold land from or under another in consideration of any rent."

However this has not been interpreted to mean that rent is a condition of a lease. Although Section 3 of Deasy's Act refers to rent, a lease may still be deemed to exist even where rent is not paid. This means that although the payment of rent may be a useful indicator of the nature of the relationship between parties, the absence of rent will not necessarily preclude the courts from finding that a lease has been created.

It also does not mean that where rent is a condition that a full market rate must be paid. A rent can be simply what is known as a 'peppercorn rent', meaning that it is little more than nominal.

This position is the same in England and Wales. The LPA defines the term of years absolute as "taking effect in possession or in reversion *whether or not at a rent*" (emphasis added).

Initially it had appeared from case law that the courts would consider rent to be a necessary feature of a lease. In the landmark case of *Street v Mountford*,[19] decided in 1985, Lord Templeman stated:

> "…there is no doubt that the traditional distinction between a tenancy and a license of land lay in the grant of land for a term *at a rent* with exclusive possession." (emphasis added)

However the question of the centrality of rent to a lease was clarified a few years later in *Ashburn Anstalt v Arnold*.[20] In this case Fox LJ considered the comments of Lord Templeman in *Street v Mountford* and decided that he did not in fact intend to make rent a condition. He stated:

> "What then is the fundamental right which a tenant has which distinguishes his position from that of a licensee? It is an interest in land as distinct from a personal permission to enter the land and use it for some stipulated purpose or purposes. And how is it to be ascertained whether such an interest in land has been given? By seeing whether the grantee was given a legal right of exclusive possession of the land for a term or from year to year […]. If he was he is a tenant."

---

19 *Street v Mountford* [1985] UKHL 4, [1985] AC 809 (HL), 816 (Lord Templeman)
20 [1988] EWCA Civ 14, [1989] Ch 1, 10 (Fox LJ)

Lord Fox is saying that exclusive possession will be the determining feature of a tenancy. The absence of a rent requirement will not prevent the courts from finding that a lease exists in circumstances where there is clearly exclusive possession.

D. Exclusive Possession

The most significant element that the courts will take into account when determining whether a lease exists is that of exclusive possession. Exclusive possession, meaning that the landlord does not have the right to enter the property without the consent of the tenant for the duration of the lease, is one of the key features of a lease. It therefore falls to the court to determine whether the claimant has in fact been granted exclusive possession of the property in question.

The principle authority in this regard is the decision of the House of Lords in *Street v Mountford*.[21] This case highlights that the court will be more concerned with the features of an occupancy agreement rather than the label that the parties attach to it when considering the nature of the occupancy. As Lord Templeman put it:

> "The manufacture of a five pronged implement for manual digging results in a fork even if the manufacturer, unfamiliar with the English language, insists that he intended to make and has made a spade."

Mrs Mountford was given exclusive possession of a residential flat on a weekly basis at a weekly sum under an express agreement. The agreement was described as a 'personal licence' and the weekly money paid was described as a 'licence fee'. At the time of entering into the agreement Mrs Mountford also made the following declaration:

> "I understand and accept that a license in the form above does not and is not intended to give me a tenancy."

Mrs Mountford subsequently disputed that the occupancy was by licence and sought a declaration that she was in fact entitled to a protected tenancy. The court was therefore asked to determine whether or not Mrs Mountford occupied the property on the basis of a licence only, making her a lodger rather than a tenant, or whether the circumstances of her occupation were such as to give rise to a tenancy.

Lord Templeman stated that there is "no difficulty" in deciding whether there is exclusive possession in the instance of residential accommodation, for the reason that one has to consider whether the person is a lodger or a tenant.

A person will be a lodger:

---

21 *Street* (n 19)

"…if the landlord provides attendance or services which require the landlord or his servants to exercise unrestricted access to and use of the premises."

This could include, for example, where the landlord remains responsible for providing clean linen or for cleaning the room.

A persons will be a tenant where:

"Residential accommodation is granted for a term at a rent with exclusive possession, the landlord providing neither attendance nor services…"

Furthermore:

"Any express reservation to the landlord of limited rights to enter and view the state of the premises and to repair and maintain the premises only serves to emphasise the fact that the grantee is entitled to exclusive possession and is a tenant."

This refers to a clause commonly found in leases that the landlord will have the right to enter the property to inspect it and to carry out any repairs that may be necessary. This is an exception to the principle that the tenant has exclusive possession of the property and is entitled to exclude the landowner from it.

If it is felt necessary to insert such a clause, the court reasons that this is because exclusive possession is being granted, and the occupancy is therefore under a lease rather than a licence, because if it were merely a licence then no such exception would be required.

In *Street v Mountford* the court concluded that because Mrs Mountford had been granted exclusive possession and the landlord did not provide any services that a tenancy had in fact been created.

Lord Templeman admitted that it can be difficult to decide whether there is exclusive possession in some circumstances, but in making its decision the court can take account of:

- the purpose of the grant
- the terms of the grant
- the surrounding circumstances

This will effectively mean looking at the circumstances in which the agreement was made to determine the intention of the parties, both landlord and tenant.

E. Irrespective of the Intention of the Parties

Because it is for the court to decide whether an occupancy agreement is in substance a tenancy, regardless of form, the stated intention of the parties will not be conclusive under the test in *Street v Mountford*. It is possible that in certain situations the courts will find a tenancy to exist in direct contradiction to the expressed intention. And again the court will base its decision on examination of the terms of the agreement, to see which, if any, are indicative of a lease.

The law in Northern Ireland is, on the face of it, a little different. Section 3 of Deasy's Act states that the relation of landlord and tenant shall be deemed to be founded on the express or implied contract of the parties. If taken at face value this provision would have the effect of making a lease a contractual arrangement between parties rather than one which created a legal interest in property.

It would also appear to contradict the rule in *Street v Mountford* by suggesting that it is the intention of the parties that determines whether a lease has been created and not the granting of exclusive possession. Judicial support for this interpretation has been found in the Northern Ireland cases of *NIHE v McCann*[22] and *NIHE v Duffin*.[23]

Both these cases dealt with squatters who paid what was described as 'mesne profits' while in illegal possession of housing executive properties pending eviction. Although in both cases the defendants were in exclusive possession, for a term, in return for consideration, the court held that no tenancy existed because there was no intention to create a tenancy but rather to create a revocable licence until the legal process of eviction took effect. Although it appears that these cases contradict the ruling of the House of Lords in *Street v Mountford*, there are a number of reasons to be cautious. First, the decisions in these cases pre-date *Street v Mountford*.[24] The reasoning of the House of Lords was not therefore taken into account when reaching the decisions. Second, the wording of Deasy's Act need not be read as making the intention of the parties a conclusive feature of a lease. It has therefore been suggested that there is no reason why the rule in *Street v Mountford* should not be applied in Northern Ireland.[25]

Although Deasy's Act appears to suggest that a lease in Northern Ireland is founded on the intention of the parties, in practice the courts have decided cases on an objective rather than a subjective standard, looking at the true intention of both parties.[26] Because Section 3 deems the landlord/tenant relationship to be founded on 'express or implied' contract between the parties then the intention of the parties is an essential element

---

22 [1979] NI 39 (QB), 39 (Murray J)
23 [1985] NI 210 (QB), 210 (Carswell J)
24 Herbert Wallace, 'The Legacy of Street v Mountford' (1990) 41 Northern Ireland Legal Quarterly 143, 148
25 Ibid
26 *NIHE v Duffin* (n 23)

of a tenancy. The fact that the intention may be implied leaves discretion for the court to decide that a tenancy had been created irrespective of the label that the parties have applied. Indeed there has been considerable judicial support in the Republic of Ireland for the view that the question of whether or not a tenancy has been created is essentially a matter of construction in each case.[27] The determining feature will be the way in which the court interprets, or construes, the intention of the parties.[28] Although Section 3 of Deasy's Act was probably intended to introduce a subjective test as to intention (ie the intention as viewed by the parties themselves), in practical terms the courts have searched for objective criteria against which intention can be judged.[29] Therefore the significance of the contractual basis of the lease under Section 3 should not be overstated. There is little evidence of the application of principles of contract law to the landlord/tenant relationship, and there is certainly no case law to this effect. Although a lease is created by contract, once it has been created it is simply regarded as giving effect to the existing common law position that a lease creates an estate or proprietary interest in land. If a strict interpretation were to be insisted upon, the suggestion would be that the relationship between landlord and tenant is contractual only, which would run counter to the whole body of case law on the subject. An example of this can be seen in *Re Courtney*,[30] wherein the court held that the correct words of limitation were needed to transfer a fee farm grant, itself an estate subject to the provisions of Deasy's Act. This was evidence of the fact that a lease is to be treated as an estate in land, not simply a contract. (The crucial difference being the extent to which your rights under the lease can be enforced against third parties).

It is suggested that intention to create a tenancy has always been relevant to the common law and now forms part of the concept of exclusive possession – 'the true intention of the parties', objectively defined, rather than the strict terms of the agreement or the subjective intent of the parties.

These are the key elements that are determinative of a lease. There are, of course, certain recognised exceptions to this general principle.

27 Case law from the Republic of Ireland is not binding on the courts in Northern Ireland, but it may provide useful persuasive authority on how the provisions of Deasy's Act should be interpreted.
28 Wylie (n 14) [17.10]
29 Ibid
30 [1981] NI 58 (Ch), 58

8.4 Exceptions

A. Trespass

Squatters or trespassers will not be deemed to have a tenancy, even if rent is being paid in respect of occupation of a property. This was seen in the Northern Ireland cases of *McCann* and *Duffin*. Whether this exception remains applicable is open to question in light of recent developments in the House of Lords.[31]

B. Sham

In *Street v Mountford* Lord Templeman stated that:

> "The court should be astute to detect and frustrate sham devices and artificial transactions whose only object is to disguise the grant of a tenancy and to evade the Rent Acts."

Effectively this refers to the fact that it is for the court to decide on the question of tenancy, extending also to cover situations where there has been a deliberate attempt to avoid legal obligations. In the case of *Snook v London and West Riding Investments Ltd.*[32] the court defined a sham as:

> "acts done or documents executed by the parties ... which are intended to give third parties or the court the appearance of creating between the parties legal rights and obligations different from the actual legal rights and obligations which the parties intend to create."

If there is bad faith in respect of occupancy the court will not necessarily enforce the legal obligations they believe are the subject of a sham.

C. Purchasers in Possession Prior to Completion

Where a person contracts to purchase (or indeed to rent) land and they go into possession before the transaction has completed, if the sale or lease subsequently falls through, the occupier will be deemed to have a licence rather than a tenancy, even if their possession is exclusive.

---

31 *Bruton v London & Quadrant Housing* [1999] UKHL 26, [2000] 1 AC 406.
32 [1967] 2 QB 786 (HL), 802 (Diplock LJ)

D. Service Occupiers

Where an employee is required to live on site or in a premises provided by the employer as part of the job, this will not be held to create a tenancy.

E. Charity

The scope of this exception is narrowing. Previously it had been the case that where a person was being allowed to live in property on the good will of the owner, even if they were paying rent, the courts would not infer a tenancy. Since *Street v Mountford* this has changed and the courts are more willing to find that where rent is being paid that a contract exists.

F. Statutory Duties

Where a person is granted possession of property pursuant to a statutory duty of a government body this traditionally would not create a tenancy. The most common incidence of this arises under the homelessness legislation.[33] In Northern Ireland the Housing Executive has a statutory obligation to provide temporary accommodation for anyone who is made involuntarily homeless.[34] Any occupancy of property granted under this legislation will not give rise to a tenancy. This may now be subject to article 8 rights to respect for the home.[35]

These are the most common exceptions to the general rule in *Street v Mountford* that where you have exclusive possession it is likely that a tenancy will be held to have been created. What is central to understanding the law on leases, however, is to remember that under the common law a lease has always been treated as creating a proprietary interest – an estate in land. In particular, the emphasis placed by the court on the concept of exclusive possession reflects the idea that a tenant, who has the right to exclude all others, including the landlord, has property rights as traditionally defined.

Recent developments have called into question this clear distinction between contractual and property rights in respect of leases.

---

33 *Westminster CC v Basson* (1991) 23 HLR 225; *Westminster CC v Clarke* [1992] UKHL 11, [1992] 1 All ER 695

34 Housing (Northern Ireland) Order 1988

35 This exception may also be called into question in light of recent developments in the House of Lords and the European Court of Human Rights. See *Kay v United Kingdom* App No 37341/06 (ECtHR, September 21, 2010)

8.5 The Impact of Bruton v London and Quadrant Housing Trust[36]

In this case the London Quadrant Housing Trust held a licence from the local authority of premises that it used to house the homeless. The Trust purported to grant a licence to Mr Bruton but on terms which appeared to give him exclusive possession. The House of Lords, overturning an earlier judgment of the Court of Appeal, held that the plaintiff did in fact have a tenancy, notwithstanding the fact that the Trust did not have an estate in the property, and that this type of occupation was specifically excluded from landlord and tenant provisions. The effect of this was to recognise a form of non-proprietary lease.

The decision provoked much debate with regard to the duality of a lease – as both an estate in land AND a contract between two parties. Orthodox thinking suggests that all leases have this dual nature, but Bruton raises doubts as to whether this is always the case. The Court of Appeal confined their analysis to the contractual relationship between Bruton and the Trust. The fact that Bruton did not have to share the accommodation with anyone else meant that he had exclusive possession. But nevertheless there was no valid tenancy because of the principle *Nemo Dat Quod Non Habet* – you can't give what you don't have. The Trust had only a licence and therefore could not grant a tenancy to Mr Bruton.

However, when the case was appealed to the House of Lords, the court upheld the decision that a tenancy had been created in Mr Bruton's favour. Not only this, but that he could enforce the terms of the tenancy against the Housing Association. This has led to the creation of what has come to be known as a 'Bruton Tenancy'.

Contrary to the conventional understanding of leases, Lord Hoffmann stated that a lease:

> "describes a relationship between two parties who are designated landlord and tenant. It is not concerned with the question of whether the agreement creates an estate or any other proprietary interest which may be binding upon third parties."

The effect of this judgment is to create a new type of contractual, or non-proprietary, tenancy that can be distinguished from a more traditional tenancy in that it does not create or transfer a proprietary interest in the property. In practical terms, this means that the tenancy will be enforceable *only* between the tenant and the person or body

---

36 *Bruton* (n 31)

who created the lease. As there are no property rights created by this type of tenancy, the tenant does not have the right to exclude all others, and specifically not to exclude third parties who may have an immediate claim to possessory title. In *Bruton* the Council who had granted the licence to the housing association revoked the licence. Because the housing association had no estate out of which Mr Bruton's tenancy could be carved, because in effect there was no reversion to the landlord, the effect was to extinguish Bruton's tenancy. A contractual tenancy will be enforceable only against the person who grants it. It cannot create rights or obligations that will bind third parties. Therefore once the person with whom the lease is entered into loses their right to use the land, the tenant will have no enforceable right against the new landlord because they have no recognised legal estate or interest in the property.

This recognition of the new category of 'Bruton tenancy' is a significant development in land law, and represents a blurring of both the rationale behind leasehold as a type of estate, and of the distinction between property and contractual interests.

Subsequent case law suggests that while it has been accepted that exclusive possession may give rise to a contractual lease between the landlord and the tenant, the tenancy remains unenforceable against third parties. Bruton tenancies have not, therefore, been interpreted as creating proprietary rights.[37]

8.6 Types of Tenancy

A lease may be created in law or in equity, creating a distinction between legal and equitable leases.

A. Legal Leases

The most common form of lease is the *term of years absolute*. This type of lease is created by deed in which the dates of commencement and expiration are specified. This does not create any particular difficulties.

Another common form of lease-holding is the *periodic tenancy*.

This type of tenancy still constitutes a legal estate and occurs either where the formalities for the creation of a fixed term lease have not been met but the lease has taken effect in possession, or where a lease for a term of years absolute has expired

---

37 *Kay and Others v London Borough of Lambeth* [2006] UKHL 10, [2006] 2 AC 465 (HL) [143] (Lord Scott), [50] (Lord Nicholls); *Islington LBC v Green, O'Shea* [2005] EWCA Civ 56 [22]-[24] (Blackburne J)

but the tenant remains in possession. It arises by implication where there is exclusive possession and rent is accepted periodically. So for example a group of students agree to rent a house for one year while in their first year at university and pay rent monthly to the landlord. When the lease expires, if they continue to live in the house and to pay the rent each month a periodic tenancy will arise. The term certain in these circumstances will be one month.

The period of the tenancy is determined by the intervals at which rent is calculated or paid – weekly, monthly, quarterly or yearly. Such a tenancy can be ended by either party by notice to quit of the length of the rent period – so one month in this example. The only exception is if the period is yearly, then the notice period is six months.

The third type of tenancy, and one which has now become largely obsolete because of the growth in popularity of the licence, is the *tenancy at will*. This is not a formal lease but effectively just grants permission to use the property. As such, because it does not create a new proprietary interest in the land, it can be terminated at any time. Also because it is less formal than other types of lease it is not subject to the normal requirements of a lease, in particular there does not need to be exclusive possession or a term certain. However this is a largely obsolete type of tenancy, and where such situations arise it is better to apply the law of licences.

Finally there is the tenancy at sufferance. This arises where someone refuses to leave after the expiration of a lease. The landlord in these circumstances neither gives express permission to stay (which would create a tenancy at will) nor asks the tenant to leave (which would negate the 'sufferance' element of the tenancy). Categorisation as a tenancy in these circumstances is important because it will prevent a tenant from claiming land by adverse possession. It can also be converted into a tenancy at will by the landlord giving permission for the tenant to remain. However, if the landlord attempts to evict the tenant, or they remain on the land despite the objection of the landowner, then the tenancy will be deemed to have terminated and possession will become adverse. This again more closely resembles a bare licence and should be characterised under the law of licences rather than as a lease.

B. Equitable Leases

The final categories are ones which arise in equity. First there is an equitable lease that arises where a lease would, legally, be void because of a technicality. This arises when a contract for a lease has been entered into but a deed has never been executed, or when the deed is void because of a technicality. In these circumstances equity will step in to give effect to the terms of the lease. Under the rule in *Walsh v Lonsdale*,[38] if the formalities for the creation of a lease are not complied with then an informal equitable lease will arise. This is possible under the equitable doctrine that "equity regards as done that which ought to be done".[39] A contract for a lease will be as good as a lease. This type of lease is subject to equitable rules and remedies.[40]

Finally, and also in equity, there is also a tenancy by estoppel. This simply means that if there turns out to be some defect in the landlord's title this will not absolve either party from the obligations contained in the lease.

These are the various types of tenancies that can either be expressly created or can be deemed to exist in law or in equity.

While the concept of exclusive possession is relatively easy to define in the context of single occupancy, in circumstances where there is joint occupancy of a property is can be more difficult to establish. There is now a distinct line of authority that deals with the concept of exclusive possession of Housing of Multiple Occupancy (HMOs).

C. Joint Tenancies

Housing of Multiple Occupancy is particularly common among students and young professionals who chose to share accommodation. This is demonstrated in the prevalence of student housing in certain areas of Belfast. However it is not limited to student accommodation. Many of these arrangements are explicitly licence agreements. The difference between the two is relatively easily explained with reference to the obligations undertaken by each party to the agreement.

For example, a landlord advertises rooms to rent in a shared property. The house contains six bedrooms with shared living, kitchen and bathroom facilities. Where the property is let by the room each occupant will agree with the landlord individually to pay their monthly rent. It does not matter how many rooms are occupied or vacant, the monthly rent for that occupant will remain the same, according to the terms of the agreement with the landlord. This is a tenancy in common as each person has a separate interest in the property. It will be the landlord's responsibility to find a sixth person to rent the vacant room. However, if six people go together an ask to rent the whole property, they may wish to enter into a joint tenancy. The key difference is that each of the six people will be jointly and severably liable for the whole rent. If six people

38 *Walsh v Lonsdale* (1882) 21 Ch D 9 (CA), 14 (Jessel MR)
39 See chapter 3
40 In England and Wales the agreement must have been made in writing and signed by the parties to be effective. Law of Property Act (Miscellaneous Provisions) Act 1989 section 2

live in the house then the rent will be divided between the six people. If one person moves out then the remaining five will have to pay extra to ensure that the rent is paid. If the remaining five wish to reduce their rent payments they will be responsible for finding a sixth person to occupy the vacant room, subject to the terms of the lease. This is the practical difference between a tenancy in common and a joint tenancy in shared accommodation. There are advantages to both, and the type of tenancy sought will depend on how the property is to be used. There may, however, be a dispute between the landlord and the tenants as to the nature of the agreement. Two landmark cases decided by the House of Lords have provided guidance on how to determine whether a joint tenancy or a tenancy in common has been created.

In the joint cases of *AG Securities v Vaughan and Others* and *Antoniades v Villiers*,[41] decided by the House of Lords in 1990, Lord Templeman considered that his *obiter* statement in *Street v Mountford* regarding exclusive possession being easy to decide in the case of residential accommodation was not quite so applicable in the case of shared accommodation.

(i) AG Securities v Vaughan and Others

AG Securities owned a flat, which consisted of six rooms in addition to a kitchen and bathroom. The company furnished four bedrooms, a lounge and a sitting room. The company entered into separate agreements with four different applicants. Each agreement was in the same form and was expressed to be made between the company as 'the owner' and the applicant as the 'licensee'. Clause 2 of the agreement provided, *inter alia*, that the licensee agreed with the owner…

- To share the use of the said flat peaceably with and not to impede the use of the said flat by such other persons … to whom the owner has granted or shall from time to time grant licence to use the said flat.

- That if any persons should move out then the others were obliged, upon reasonable notice given by the owner to meet with any prospective new licensee nominated by the owner at the flat to provide an opportunity to agree terms for sharing.

- Not to assign nor permit any other person except any person licensed by the owner to sleep or reside in or share occupation of the said flat or any part of it at any time.

---

41 *AG Securities v Vaughan and Others* [1988] UKHL 8, [1990] 1 AC 417, 462-463 (Lord Templeman)

In practice what happened was that the flat was kept fully occupied. When one agreement was terminated the company invited applications to fill the vacancy. The company took nothing to do with how the occupants shared the flat. It was the practice that whenever a bedroom became vacant upon termination of an agreement, each of the three remaining occupiers, in order of seniority, would decide whether to change bedroom. The applicant for the vacancy was then offered the room least fancied by the others. The applicant, if satisfied, signed his agreement and moved into his bedroom. If he were unable to share the use of the common parts of the flat peaceably he could terminate his agreement, as could any of the others, or alternatively persuade the company to terminate the agreement of the unpopular occupier.

When asked to consider whether the tenants occupied the flat under licence or by joint tenancy, the House of Lords decided that each occupier had only a licence and not a tenancy. The key factor in the decision was that the power to decide who occupied the flat resided with and was exercised by the company. Also the fact that the monthly sum payable by each applicant was not the same was relevant.

In this case the tenants of the flat had sought to establish that they occupied the flat under a joint tenancy. There are, however, a number of features of joint tenancy that made this reasoning untenable in this case.

As discussed above, if the occupiers of property are to satisfy the court that a lease has been created rather than a licence, they must be able to demonstrate that exclusive possession has been granted. Where more than one person is in possession of the property exclusive possession will have been granted on a joint basis. To decide whether or not exclusive possession has been granted in such circumstances, the courts will look to see whether the four unities are present.

These are:

- Unity of possession; all occupants must have an equal right to occupy any part of the premises (subject to agreement between them).
- Unity of Interest; all parties must have the same estate in the premises.
- Unity of time; all parties must have taken their interest in the premises at the same time.
- Unity of title; the parties must have taken their interest in the premises from the same instrument.

In the case of *AG Securities v Vaughan* it was clear that the third and fourth unities were not met, and arguably because of the manner in which the company controlled the property the first two did not exist either.

The circumstances of taking the flat may also be relevant. For example, the court may consider whether the parties intended to live together indefinitely or whether the arrangement was intended to be temporary and flexible when determining whether a licence or a joint tenancy exists. The intention as expressed to the landlord may also be taken into account when looking at the purpose of the grant and at the surrounding circumstances,[42] but this will only be a factor for consideration and will not be conclusive. The courts have, however, demonstrated some flexibility in the application of the four unities. Where the facts of the occupation of a property clearly suggest that exclusive possession has been granted, the courts will not allow the strict formalities of the four unities to prevent a finding in favour of the tenant. This was demonstrated in the case of *Antoniades v Villiers*.[43]

In this case the applicant, Mr Antoniades was the owner of a house. The attic was converted into furnished residential accommodation comprising a bedroom, bed sitting room, kitchen and bathroom. The respondents, Mr Villiers and Miss Bridger were a young unmarried couple. Having spent three months looking for a flat, they viewed the attic flat. The couple required a double bed which Mr Antoniades agreed to provide.

Mr Antoniades and Mr Villiers entered into an agreement, described as a licence, which stated that:

> "the licensor is not willing to grant the licensee exclusive possession of any part of the rooms herein referred to."

It further provided that:

> "the licensee is anxious to secure the use of the rooms notwithstanding that such use may be in common with the licensor and such other licensees or invitees as the licensor may permit from time to time to use the said rooms."

An addendum to the agreement also provided:

> "the flat is for single people sharing and if Mr Villiers marries any occupier of the flat then Mr Villiers will give notice and vacate the flat … No persons will have exclusive possession of the above flat as agreed."

Mr Antoniades and Miss Bridger entered into an identical agreement. Both agreements were signed by both parties and witnessed. Mr Villiers and Miss Bridger moved into the accommodation comprised in the agreement. Mr Antoniades never attempted to use or authorise other persons to use the rooms. After problems keeping up with payments,

---

42 As per the judgment of Lord Templeman in *Street* (n 19) 814-827
43 *Antoniades v Villiers* [1988] EWCA Civ 3, [1988] 2 All ER 309 (CA)

Mr Antoniades gave the couple notice to quit. When they didn't move out he sought an order for possession.

In this case the problem that the respondents faced in establishing that exclusive possession had been granted was that the unity of title was not present. Both had taken their interest in the property from separate agreements. However, notwithstanding the fact that separate agreements had been entered into, the House of Lords concluded that a tenancy did exist. In reaching their decision the court took account of the purpose of the grant, which had been to allow the couple to live together, as well as the surrounding circumstances, particularly the relationship between the occupiers; the course of negotiations; the nature and extent of the accommodation, and the intended and actual mode of occupation. When all of these factors were taken into account it was clear that the two agreements were interdependent, in that both would have been signed or neither, so that they were to be read as one agreement. This interpretation of the agreements in light of the nature of the occupation of the property meant that the problem of the unity of title was overcome.

Furthermore, the court in *Street v Mountford* had highlighted that the court should be astute to detect and frustrate sham devices. In this case the landlord had sought to rely on the clause that he, or whomsoever he may nominate, could move in to the flat with the couple.

The court concluded that the clause permitting sharing with the landlord or his nominee was not genuine, taking into account both the surrounding circumstances of the occupation of the flat and subsequent events, namely that no effort was ever made to move a third party into the flat. Therefore it appears that if it is possible to construe the facts as involving a joint letting to the individuals concerned, by looking at the facts and circumstances of occupation of the property that the court may interpret the terms of the agreements in a way that is favourable to the tenant and which prevents landlords from evading legal responsibilities simply by describing an agreement as a licence rather than a lease.

8.7 Leasehold Covenants

The relationship between landlord and tenant is much more explicitly contractual than that between vendor and purchaser of freehold land. The contractual relationship continues for the duration of the lease. A lease will contain a number of obligations on the part of both the landlord and the tenant. These can include, on the part of the landlord, an undertaking to carry out maintenance and repairs of the property, and to maintain any common areas. On the part of the tenant, the most obvious covenant is to pay the rent. Other obligations might include keeping the property in good order, not to use the premises for specified activities, or not to assign or sublet without permission.[44] All of these provisions will routinely appear in any lease and they constitute express obligations – those that are contained openly in the text of the lease. There can also be what are known as implied obligations that are deemed to flow inherently from the legal relationship created by the lease. Under Deasy's Act two covenants are implied into all leases; first that the landlord has good title to the property and is therefore capable of creating a lease. Second, the tenant will have the right to quiet and peaceable enjoyment of the property during the period of the lease. Conversely, it is implied that tenants that they will give up possession on expiration of the lease and that the premises will be maintained in good repair.[45]

In Northern Ireland Deasy's Act provides that where a lease is assigned, the covenants contained in the lease will be transferred to successors in title.[46] This means that both the benefit (the rights) and the burden (the obligations) of the lease will pass upon assignment. For this to occur two criteria must be met:

- There must be privity of estate between the parties. This means that there was a direct relationship of landlord and tenant between the parties at the time the covenant was breached. Assignees are only liable for breaches that occur while they are responsible for the lease. They will not be liable for any breach that occurs either before the lease was assigned to them or after their interest has been terminated.
- The covenant touches and concerns the land.[47] Assignees will not be liable for covenants that were of a personal nature between the landlord and the tenant. The covenant must relate to the land itself.

If both of these requirements are satisfied then the benefit and the burden of the lease will run with the lease and bind any assignees. This applies to all tenancies.

---

44 This is common practice in Northern Ireland, and possible under Deasy's Act (n 4) section 10 & 18
45 Deasy's Act (n 4) section 42
46 Ibid sections 12 & 13
47 *Spencer's Case* (1583) 5 Co Rep 16a, 77 ER 72; this common law provision was codified in the Conveyancing Act 1881 which referred to covenants as having "reference to the subject matter of the lease" rather than touch and concern.

A. Position in England and Wales

The position in England and Wales is slightly different. Here leases can be divided into two separate categories; those created before 1996 and those created afterwards.

i. Pre-1996 leases

In England and Wales the obligations contained in a lease are enforceable between the landlord and tenant because they are both parties to the lease. Enforcement therefore relied on the doctrine of privity of contract. Prior to 1996 the position was that if the tenant assigned their interest in the lease, the original party would remain liable for any breach of the covenants by the assignee, which would be enforceable against them. If an action was brought against the original tenant and damages were awarded against them, the tenant could bring proceedings against the assignee. This was possible because the law implied covenants into the assignment of a lease. This required the assignee to indemnify the original tenant against liability for breach of covenant.[48] In order for this to happen the two requirements of privity of estate between the landlord and the assignee, and the covenants in question must touch and concern the land must be met.

These rules developed as a pragmatic interpretation of the nature of such obligations and the need to prevent parties from avoiding obligations simply by assigning or subletting their interest in the lease. In practice it would be the assignee who performed the obligations contained in the covenants, but in the event that they failed to do so liability would ultimately rest with the original covenantor. This ensured that the covenants contained in a lease would remain enforceable, even if not technically passing to successors. So in practice then covenants managed to evade the rules on privity of contract by virtue of the interpretation of the courts. But because this situation was being achieved through interpretation, and was somewhat at odds with established legal principle, reform was necessary.

ii. Post-1996 Leases

In 1995 the Landlord and Tenant (Covenants) Act was passed which amended the position. By this time it was felt that given that most leases contained a clause prohibiting assignment without the consent of the landlord, that the landlord should therefore be in

---

48 Law of Property Act 1925 section 77. This continues to be the case for pre-1996 covenants under the Land Registration Act 2002 schedule 12 para 20.

a position to ensure that any assignee was able to meet the obligations of the covenants. This can be achieved by the landlord requiring the tenant to enter into an 'authorised guarantee arrangement' whereby the assignor guarantees the performance of the covenants by the assignee.[49] The 1995 Act therefore abolishes the automatic liability of the original tenant for any breach by an assignee but allows the landlord to seek an express guarantee from the tenant as a condition of giving consent to the assignment of the lease. Any loss that occurs in such circumstances is now borne by the landlord, on the basis that it was his/her responsibility to ensure that appropriate guarantees had been made in respect of the covenants. The only exceptions to this rule are where the assignment of the lease itself has been a breach of covenant, or where it occurs by operation of law because of bankruptcy.

The way in which this is achieved is by annexing the benefit and the burden of the covenants (except personal covenants) to the lease, so that they will pass automatically on assignment. This releases both the landlord[50] and the tenant[51] from their respective covenants.

If it is the landlord who seeks to assign the lease rather than the tenant there are a number of formalities which must be complied with in order to protect the tenant.[52] The landlord must give notice to the tenant which both informs them of the proposed assignment and requests release from the covenants. If the tenant refuses this request then the landlord must apply to the court to be released. The court has the power either to uphold the tenant's objection or to release the landlord notwithstanding the objection of the tenant.

Another modification of the law regulating covenants in leases relates to the status of covenants. Traditionally the position was the only covenants which touched and concerned the land would be enforceable against a successor. This requirement was removed by Section 3 of the 1995 Act.[53] This results in the position that nearly every covenant will pass on assignment. This rule is relatively simple compared to those which pertain to freehold land. For this reason leasehold is an attractive option for landowners. Because both positive and negative obligations will be enforceable where the land is held under a lease, this makes it easier to ensure that covenants are respected.

---

49 Landlord and Tenant (Covenants) Act 1995 section 16
50 Ibid section 6
51 Ibid section 5
52 Ibid section 8
53 Landlord (Covenants) (n 49) section 3

B. Sub Letting

Sub letting a property is different from assignment of a lease. If the lease is assigned all of the terms of the lease are transferred to the assignee, thus creating privity of estate between the landlord and the assignee. Where a property is sublet this transfer does not occur. Rather the original tenant remains responsible for the covenants contained in the lease. This is because there is neither privity of contract nor privity of estate between the lessor and the sub-lessee.[54]

Because of the difficulty in enforcing covenants between a lessor and a sub-lessee, a lease may contain a covenant either prohibiting sub-letting altogether,[55] or restricting the circumstances in which sub-letting may occur.[56] Such restriction will usually require the consent of the lessor before sub-letting can occur.[57] There is no formal process for indemnifying the tenant against breaches of covenants committed by a sub-tenant. At law all covenants will remain enforceable between landlord and tenant, and it is therefore the responsibility of the original tenant to ensure that the subtenant complies with the covenants. This is usually achieved by including all the terms of the original lease in the sub-lease, thus creating covenants between the original tenant and the sub-tenant.

In equity, the rule in *Tulk v Moxhay*[58] provides that covenants contained in the head lease that restrict the use of the property (known as negative covenants) can be enforced in equity by the landlord against the sub-tenant. In England and Wales this equitable rule has been confirmed in Section 3(5) of the 1995 Act.

C. Remedies for Breach of Covenants

Despite the law facilitating the transfer of obligations for leasehold covenants, there will still be circumstances in which it is necessary to seek remedy for breach. This is largely governed by the terms of the contract as agreed by the parties. Common remedies include:

i. Action for damages

A landlord may sue for breach of a covenant contained in a lease and seek to recover damages on the basis of that breach. This also applies to a tenant who may seek damages

---

54 *Northern Ireland Carriers Limited v Larne Harbour Limited* [1981] NI 171 (Ch) (Murray J)
55 Deasy's Act (n 4) section 18
56 Deasy's Act (n 4) section 10
57 See Northern Ireland Carriers (n 55)
58 (1848) 2 Ph 774, 41 ER 1143, 1144. See chapter 10

from a landlord for breach of covenant. In Northern Ireland this action is taken on foot of Section 14 of the Conveyancing Act 1881 which provides for restrictions on and relief against forfeiture of leases.

ii. Termination of the lease

Where one party is in breach of the terms of the lease the other party may seek forfeiture of the lease. This is subject to strict rules.

Waiver

A breach of covenant would usually give the landlord the right to forfeit the lease. However this right may be *waived*. If the tenant breaches a covenant and the landlord waives the breach, he/she will lose the right to sue on the breach, and the right of taking any further action in respect of this breach (such as forfeiture).

In Northern Ireland a waiver must be in writing.[59] The only exception to this is an 'estoppel waiver' where it would be unconscionable to allow the landlord to insist upon a written waiver.[60]

In England and Wales waiver can be either express or implied. It requires both that the landlord knew of a breach of a covenant contained in the lease, but that they led the tenant to believe that the lease would continue notwithstanding the breach. The most common example of this is continuing to accept rent even where a breach of covenant has occurred. Waiver can be used by a tenant as a defence against forfeiture.

8.8 Termination of Leases

A. Expiration of a Fixed Term Lease

As a lease by definition lasts for a finite period of time, upon expiration of the term certain the lease will come to an end. The legal estate then reverts to whoever is entitled to the reversion. This is known as termination by natural effluxion of time.

---

59 Deasy's Act (n 4) section 43. *Craigdarragh Trading Co Ltd v Doherty and Another* [1989] NI 218 (Ch)
60 *Craigdarragh* (n 59), *Belfast West Power Ltd v Belfast Harbour Commissioners* [1998] NI 112 (Ch) 127 (Girvan J)

B. Notice to Quit

If a landlord wishes to retain the power to terminate a fixed term lease before the specified date they must insert a clause in the lease which specifically provides that the lease may be terminated upon a notice to quit. If this term is not included in a fixed term lease then it may not be terminated before the specified date. Where a periodic tenancy exists notice may be given. The notice period will be determined by the nature of the tenancy. For example, a monthly periodic tenancy may be terminated with one month's notice to quit.

If the landlord wishes to serve a notice to quit he/she must follow certain formalities:

- The notice must be in writing.
- It should be clear from the terms of the notice that the tenancy is being terminated. It should also be clear to which property the notice applies.
- The notice should indicate clearly the date of expiry of the lease. Landlords are required to give a minimum of 4 weeks notice to quit a residential property.[61]
- The notice must be addressed to the tenant and delivered to the address contained in the lease. It may be delivered by post, personal service is not required.

Failure by the tenant to comply with a notice to quit will entitle the landlord to bring possession proceedings against him or her. In some circumstances compensation may also be claimed up to the time that the tenant remains in occupation of the premises.[62]

C. Surrender

If it is the tenant who wishes early termination of the lease they may do so by surrender. The landlord must accept the surrender in order to terminate the lease. Surrender can be achieved in law through execution of a deed, or in equity by entering into a contract to surrender the lease. More practical circumstances that will lead to surrender include the landlord accepting possession of the premises; allowing a new tenant to go into occupation of the premises. If these occur then the landlord can be estopped from denying that the surrender has been accepted.

---

61 Rent (NI) Order 1978 article 62
62 This is known as a claim for mesne profits and is based on the rental value of the property.

D. Forfeiture

Where a tenant breaches a covenant contained in the lease the landlord may seek to recover the property by forfeiture.[63] This applies only to breaches other than non-payment of rent.[64] As with a notice to quit, if the landlord wishes to rely on this option express provision must be made in the terms of the lease allowing for forfeiture.

Where a covenant other than payment of rent has been breached, the landlord must serve a Notice under Section 14 of the Conveyancing Act 1881.[65] This Notice must be in writing and addressed to the lessee who is in breach of the covenant. It will outline the nature of the breach, demand that the tenant take action either to remedy the breach or to compensate the landlord for it, and warn the tenant that if action is not taken within a reasonable time, the landlord will exercise his/her right to re-enter the property. If the tenant fails to take action to remedy the breach the landlord may initiate proceedings to gain re-entry. Serving the Notice is a precondition to taking action to re-enter the property.

Where the breach of covenant is non-payment of rent then Section 14 does not apply. Similarly in England and Wales Section 146 does not apply to failure to pay rent. Most leases now include a provision that the landlord may exercise the right of re-entry whether rent is formally demanded or not. This removes the requirement for the landlord to formally demand the rent before taking action. Where rent is in arrears the landlord may apply to the court for a possession order. Where a dispute arises between the parties there is usually provision in the lease to prevent the rent being withheld by the tenant or set off in favour of the landlord.

Relief against forfeiture

Where a landlord seeks to forfeit a lease and re-enter the property the court has an equitable discretion to grant the tenant relief from forfeiture. A starting point for determining whether relief should be granted is found in the Judicature Act (Northern Ireland) 1974. Article 94 of this Act applies to circumstances where the breach complained of is non-payment of rent. This provides that relief should be granted when the rent and arrears are paid, and that the application for relief be made at the earliest opportunity following the enforcement of the order for possession. This almost amounts

---

63 Conveyancing Act 1881 section 14(1)
64 *Shah Din & Sons Ltd v Dargan Properties Management Ltd* [2012] NICh 34 [15] (Burgess J)
65 In England and Wales this procedure is set out in the Law of Property Act 1925 section 146(1)

to a presumption in favour of relief. However in the recent case of *Shah Din & Sons Ltd v Dargan Properties Management Ltd*. Burgess J outlined a number of additional factors that could be taken into account by the court when deciding whether to exercise its discretion.[66] These factors include the conduct of the parties; the wilfulness of the breach by the tenant, the nature of the lease (commercial or residential, for example), the value of the property, and the nature of the relationship between the parties.[67] On the facts of this case relief was not granted. It is not therefore, an automatic entitlement of the tenant but remains at the discretion of the court exercising its equitable jurisdiction.

In both Northern Ireland and England and Wales the courts tend to interpret breaches of covenants as capable of being remedied by the tenant rather than allowing forfeiture of the lease.[68] For example, if forfeiture is sought for non-payment of rent, payment of arrears by the tenant will usually result in relief. However this is at the discretion of the court. If the tenant has a history of non-payment the court may grant forfeiture notwithstanding the payment of arrears.

The tenant may also rely on waiver as a defence to forfeiture. If it can be demonstrated that the landlord knew of the breach of covenant and waived the right to take action then the tenant may gain relief.

---

66 *Shah Din* (n 64) [18]

67 These factors are cited with approval from the Irish case of *Campus & Stadium Ireland Development Ltd v Dublin Waterworld Ltd* [2006] IEHC 200

68 *ETS Vehicles Ltd v Fargate Developments Ltd* [1997] NI 25 (CA) 32-33 (MacDermott LJ); *Glass v Kencakes Ltd and Others* [1966] 1 QB 611, 629-630 (Paul LJ)

CHAPTER 9

Licences and Proprietary Estoppel

9.1 Introduction

A licence is a type of agreement which allows a person to use land but which in principle falls short of creating a proprietary interest in that land. In practice some categories of licence have been interpreted increasingly as creating a limited proprietary interest in land. This chapter will consider the three main types of licences, bare licences, contractual licences and estoppel licences. Some categories of licence create a much greater interest in the land than others. For each of these categories the chapter will consider the main features of the licence and also compare and contrast their features with those of the others. The chapter will examine the manner in which the licence is created, the nature of the interest that it creates, as well as whether or not it is capable of being enforced.

Proprietary interests are interests in land which entail basic property rights such as possession, the right to exclude others, and the right to dispose of or transfer the interest. If you invite someone round to your house for dinner, or to stay for the weekend, there is no question that by opening the door and welcoming them in that you intend to create a proprietary interest in their favour. The effect of your invitation – effectively creating a licence – is simply to prevent their presence on your private property from being trespass.

What this also illustrates is that there are no particular formalities that must be complied with in order to create a licence. There is no requirement that it be executed by deed. An oral agreement, or even an implied agreement can suffice to create a licence.

However, depending on the type of licence, its creation may be governed by other rules, such as rules on the creation of a contract, or rules of equity.

9.2 Categories of Licence

A. Bare Licence

These are the most basic forms of licence. A bare licence is simply permission to enter someone else's land – preventing your presence on that land from being trespass. It is not, therefore, an interest in land, but a right over land. The most common example of this type of licence is where you invite someone to visit your house. They are there with your permission, but this does not mean that you have created any interest in the property for them. The interest is purely personal – not proprietary – in nature.[1] A bare licence is created by the simple act of giving permission.[2] It is not supported by contract or equity and no interest in the property passes with the creation of the licence. However a bare licence will give rise to a basic duty of care towards the licencee.[3]

This category is what is known as a residual category, meaning that it will exist where no other category applies. Such licences need not be confined to short periods of time, but may continue for a number of years without giving rise to a proprietary interest. One of the essential features of the bare licence is that it is revocable at will on the part of the licensor. There is nothing you can do to prevent that licence from being revoked as you yourself have no interest in the land that can be protected. If such a licence is revoked by the licensor the licensee has no remedy.

Also, because a bare licence does not create an interest in the property itself, it is not enforceable against anyone other than the licensor. A bare licence does not create an interest that can be enforced against third parties; it is not even enforceable against successors in title of the licensor. So for example if your neighbour had given you permission to walk across their land to reach the bus stop, creating no interest in your favour but allowing your presence there, but he/she then sells his/her property, the fact that the previous owner had allowed you to walk across his/her land will not bind the new owner – as a personal interest it exists only between the licensee and the licensor.

1 *Thomas v Sorrell* (1672) Vaughan 330, 351: 124 ER 1098, 1109 (Vaughan CJ)
2 *Graham v Northern Ireland Housing Executive* [1986] NI 72
3 Occupiers' Liability Act (NI) 1957 section 2(1)

Similarly, because it is no more than a personal interest, a bare licence cannot be assigned or transferred. This means that you cannot grant another person permission to cross that land on the basis of your licence. If such other person wishes to cross the land they must seek a licence to do so directly from the landowner.

B. Licence Coupled With an Interest

The second type of licence which falls under this basic heading is a licence coupled with an interest. This category has developed to recognise situations where it would not be appropriate to hold that the granting of a licence has created an interest in property, but equally it would not be fair to allow the licence to be revoked at will with no remedy, because of the circumstances which led to the creation of the licence. This arose most commonly where a person did enjoy some interest in the land, such as a profit,[4] and in order to enjoy that interest his/her presence on the land was required. This meant that the purpose of the licence was secondary to the existing interest in the land but did not in and of itself create a new interest in the land. An example of this would be where the interest in question was shooting rights. Obviously the shooting rights cannot be enjoyed if you do not have access to the land. For this reason the existence of a licence will be a necessary implication. But the licence will only last so long as the interest on which it is dependent lasts, as it has no legal status of its own. This reasoning has also more recently been extended to include situations where a person has paid for a service which requires their presence on a particular property. So for example in *Hurst v Picture Theatres* the court held that a person who had purchased a ticket to watch a film in the cinema had a licence coupled with an interest – having paid for the ticket entitling him to permission to be on the property of the cinema owners.[5] However, this differs slightly from earlier cases in that in Hurst the pre-existing right was a contractual right rather than a property right. The fact that interests created by contract can give rise to a licence coupled with an interest was confirmed in the Northern Ireland courts in *Woods v Donnelly* where a licence to draw sand and gravel was also held to have created a licence coupled with an interest.[6] As with the bare licence, no deed is required to create this type of interest.[7] Once the interest has been created the licence cannot be revoked so long as the interest lasts.[8]

---

4   A profit is a form of property right that allows rights over another persons land. See chapter 11
5   *Hurst v Picture Theaters Ltd* [1915] 1 KB 1 (CA) 7 (Buckley LJ)
6   *Woods v Donnelly* [1982] NI 257 (Ch)
7   Ibid; This case considers the English authorities of *Winter Garden Theatre (London) Limited v Millenium Productions Limited* [1948] AC 173 (HL), [1947] 2 All ER 331 and *Hounslow London Borough Council v Twickenham Garden Developments Limited* [1971] Ch 233, [1970] 3 All ER 326
8   Ibid

C. Contractual Licences

The second main category of licences to consider is that of contractual licences. As the title suggests, they are created by contract. This type of licence differs from the bare licence in that it is not granted voluntarily but is founded on valuable consideration,[9] and is commonly categorised as a contractual licence. A contractual licence will create a legal (contractual) interest in the property – but not a proprietary interest. It originates in the terms of a contract, either express or implied.[10] A contractual licence is a sort of a half way house between a personal permission and a proprietary interest. It has been referred to by the Northern Ireland court as 'quasi proprietary' because it creates an interest beyond a mere personal interest but it has not been recognised as creating a proprietary interest. It remains enforceable only against the original licensor under the contract but not against third parties. Similarly contractual licences will bear the other features you would find in a contract. The licensee also enjoys some protection against revocation. In appropriate cases the court will protect the contractual licence by injunction or specific performance.[11] It may also award declaratory relief or damages where appropriate. This was demonstrated in the English case of *Tanner v Tanner*.[12] In this case an unmarried woman had had twins, of whom the plaintiff, a married man, was the father. The plaintiff decided to provide a house for the woman and their children. He bought a house with the help of a mortgage. The woman then left her rent controlled flat and moved into the house. Three years later the plaintiff tried to remove her from the house, because he wanted to move into it with his latest mistress, but she refused on the basis that she was entitled to remain in the house until the children left school. The plaintiff brought possession proceedings against her – purporting to terminate her licence to live in the house. She counter claimed that she was entitled to a beneficial (ie a proprietary) interest in the property. This was rejected by the court, but it did find that she had a contractual licence, which was specifically enforceable and which he could be restrained from breaking. In this case she had already moved out of the property because of the possession order and had been given new accommodation by the local authority. This meant that in effect the remedies of specific performance and injunction would be meaningless. Because the Court of Appeal decided that the possession order should never have been made, she was held to be entitled to damages for the breach.

---

9   *Jones v Jones and Others* [2001] NI 244 (Ch) 255 (Girvan J)
10 Ibid 257. This case also confirms that a contractual licence may attract implied terms where such terms are needed to make the contract workable.
11 Ibid 256
12 *Tanner v Tanner* [1975] EWCA Civ 4, [1975] 3 All ER 776

The contractual nature of these remedies presents no difficulties when dealing with a breach of the relationship between the original contracting parties. However, the situation is more difficult when the original grantor of the licence sells the property. In law, because the interest under a contractual licence is personal only, and not a proprietary interest that would bind third parties, if the original licensor sells the property, the licence would not be enforceable against the purchaser. It is possible that the original grantor would remain liable in damages for the breach, but there would be no possibility for specific performance. This problem has given rise to some rather odd developments in the law.

i. Contractual licences – personal or proprietary?

The case law on contractual licences is limited in Northern Ireland. Beyond confirming the principles outlined, there has been little call for application. Therefore attention should be paid to the case law of the English courts that has developed the concept of the contractual licence.

The development of the contractual licence as a category has by in large been driven by the need to provide some sort of protection to licensees against revocation and to a certain extent this rationale has been reflected in the reasoning of the court, leaving it open to criticism. This is an area of law where it is recognised that bad law has been made, but has now largely been rectified.

The first case where the question of the nature of a contractual licence came to the fore was *Errington v Errington* in 1952.[13] Before this date, it had been firmly established in case law that there was a clear distinction between contractual obligations which gave rise to no interest or estate in land, and proprietary interests, which did. This meant that before *Errington* a licence could be revoked at will, even if there was a contract. The judgment in *Errington* created some confusion in this area of the law.

In this case a father had bought a house for his son and daughter in law. The father had paid the lump sum deposit and the arrangement was that the conveyance remained in his name, but the son and his wife could live in the house so long as they paid the mortgage payments due to the building society. When the last payment was made, the house would be transferred to the son and his wife. So the son and daughter in law moved in to the house and continued to make the payments, as per the agreement. When the father died, however, the son left his wife and went to live with his mother. The daughter

---

13 *Errington v Errington and Woods* [1951] EWCA Civ 2, [1952] 1 All ER 149

in law continued to make the mortgage payments and to live in the house. The mother then brought an action for possession against the daughter in law. The question that was raised for the court was what entitlement, if any, did the daughter in law have to the house. The County Court initially found in favour of the daughter in law, finding that she was a tenant at will and as such any right of action against her was statute barred. The Court of Appeal, in upholding the decision in favour of the daughter in law, looked in more detail at the characteristics of her occupation of the property and at the nature of the permission she had to be there. Lord Denning, delivering the main judgment, decided that the father's promise was a unilateral contract – a promise of the house in return for their act of paying the instalments. It could not be revoked by him once the couple entered on performance of the act (ie making the payments) but it would cease to bind him if they left it incomplete and unperformed. He came to the conclusion that the couple were in fact licensees, having a permissive occupation short of a tenancy, but with a contractual right to remain so long as they paid the instalments. So far this reasoning presents no difficulties. It is how the obligations of this licence are interpreted that diverges from the traditional understanding that a contractual licence was revocable at will. Lord Denning acknowledged that at law, contractual licencees have no legal right to remain, but goes on to suggest that they may have such a right in equity. What he says is that as a result of the intervention of equity, "a licensor will not be permitted to eject a licensee in breach of a contract to allow him to remain." This means that contractual licences now have a force and validity of their own and cannot be revoked in breach of the contract. Lord Denning suggested that in 'appropriate circumstances' a contractual licence can be enforced against a third party. Such appropriate circumstances are deemed to be where the claim of the licencee is supported by an equity – namely where it would be unjust to deny the continued existence of the licence. What Lord Denning did not address, and what led to the criticism of the judgment in *Errington*, was the more fundamental question of whether a contractual licence could be said to constitute an interest that binds third parties in general terms.

Because of this confusion, *Errington v Errington* should not be read as giving proprietary status to contractual licences. While Lord Denning seeks to apply equity to contractual relationships, it is important to remember that this does not create a proprietary interest in the property itself. In this particular case equity prevented the revocation of the licence by a third party. However in general terms, a contractual licence remains enforceable only against the original licensor, and this is on the basis of privity of contract rather than the existence of a proprietary interest. This is because equity will only enforce it on the basis of the promise that was made. It also means that it is not the case that a contractual licence can never be revoked. The conditions for revocation will be contained in the terms of the contract. So for example in the *Errington* case, had the daughter in law failed to keep making the mortgage payments then she would have been in breach of the contract and the licence could have been revoked.

It is important to bear this distinction in mind, because contractual licences should be distinguished from the broader category of estoppel licences. In fact the reasoning of Lord Denning in *Errington* has been criticised on the grounds that the outcome he sought could better have been achieved by using the doctrine of estoppel rather than attributing equitable characteristics to contractual licences. In the later case of *Ashburn Anstalt v Arnold* the court criticised the wide reasoning in *Errington* as being unsupported by authority and unnecessary to reach the decision reached.[14]

The most recent statement on this distinction was made in 2001 in *Lloyd v Dugdale* in which the court re-stated the original principle that a contractual licence is not a proprietary interest that can bind purchasers without notice.[15] This re-statement was necessary because of the considerable confusion that had been created by Lord Denning's creative interpretation of the features of a contractual licence.

ii. Constructive trusts and the status of the licence

While the contractual licence does not have proprietary status, there are limited circumstances in which they may still bind third parties. This happens where a constructive trust is imposed. The leading case in this regard is *Binions v Evans*.[16] In this case the defendant's husband had worked for the same firm for his whole working life. They lived in a house which was owned by the firm. When the husband died the firm granted the wife a licence to remain in the house for the rest of her life. She in turn undertook to maintain the property and pay all the bills and expenses in relation to it. The firm then sold the property, subject to the licence, the purchasers paying a reduced price because of the agreement. Seven months later the plaintiffs tried to remove the defendant from the house. The court held, however, that she had acquired a contractual licence which gave her an equitable interest. This arose by way of constructive trust. The Court held that where a purchaser had agreed to honour an existing licence a constructive trust would arise which would prevent him from later going back on that promise.

---

14 *Ashburn Anstalt v WJ Arnold & Co* [1989] EWCA Civ 14, [1989] Ch 1, 2 (Fox LJ)
15 *Lloyd v Dugdale* [2001] EWCA Civ 1754, [2001] NPC 168, 183
16 *Binions v Evans* [1972] EWCA Civ 6, 1972 Ch 359

A constructive trust is no different from the other types of trust – namely the idea that legal and beneficial interests can be separated in order to protect a party from injustice.[17] The term 'constructive' relates to the fact that in these circumstances the trust is imposed on the parties by the court as a result of the conduct of one of the parties towards the other. That the element of conduct is relevant was confirmed in *Ashburn Anstalt v Arnold*.[18] In situations where a constructive trust is deemed to have arisen the purchaser is deemed to have acted in such a way that it is unconscionable to allow him to revoke an existing contractual licence. This does not imply that the trust is altering the contractual nature of the licence, but rather recognising that an equitable interest may arise. Because of the requirement that the purchaser's conscience must be affected, the trust will bind only that purchaser and not third parties more generally. In *Lloyd v Dugdale* the court set out a six part test for determining whether a constructive trust should be imposed:

- Even where a seller has stipulated that the sale is subject to certain pre-existing rights, there is no general rule that states that a constructive trust will be imposed on the purchaser in respect of the existing licence.

- A constructive trust will not be imposed unless the court is satisfied that the purchaser's conscience is so affected that it would be inequitable to allow him to deny the rights of the claimant.

- This question of establishing the purchaser's conscience will be decided with reference to the obligations undertaken – namely whether they have undertaken some new obligation rather than simply offered to honour pre-existing obligations.

- A contractual licence is not to be regarded as creating a proprietary interest in land.

- Evidence that the purchaser has paid a lower than market price for the land may indicate that he/she has taken on a new obligation, for the purposes of this test.

- It is not desirable that constructive trusts should be imposed on inferences from slender materials.[19]

---

17 See chapter 3
18 *Ashburn* (n 14) 22 (Fox LJ)
19 *Lloyd v Dugdale* (n 15) para 52

This test demonstrates that the use of the constructive trust, although serving to protect some interests under contractual licences, should not be the first option for the courts when faced with such cases. It should not be a default position, and should never be regarded as creating a proprietary interest.

The contractual nature of the interest has been closely safeguarded. A constructive trust cannot be used as a back door to the creation of a property interest by contract. This is partly because the courts want to retain control over the type of property interest that can be created – keeping them limited to those which already exist in law. If you could create property interests simply by contract this would potentially lead to an extremely complicated area of law which would make conveyancing treacherous and would be difficult to adjudicate.

D. Proprietary Estoppel

An estoppel licence, unlike a bare licence or a contractual licence, can in certain circumstances create an interest in land. This is an equitable interest and arises because of the nature of the conduct of the licensor.

Traditionally equity acts as a shield to protect licensees. It is not like contract where a specific cause of action is created, but rather prevents certain actions from succeeding, preventing a licence from being revoked.[20] An estoppel licence, as the name suggests, arises through the operation of the doctrine of estoppel. Estoppel is an equitable doctrine whereby a person can be stopped from insisting on their strict legal rights where to do so will cause injustice to another person. Because of this, estoppel licences can arise as a result of a pre-existing licence, where access to land is already being enjoyed. This can arise, for example, where somebody has been living on or using land for a period of time on the understanding that they will continue to be allowed to do so. For example in the case of *Inwards v Baker*,[21] a landowner had a son who wished to build a house but did not have the money to buy the land he needed. His father allowed him to build on his land, but no title to the property was ever passed to the son. When the father died it emerged that he had, a number of years earlier, drafted a will in which he left the property to another third party. The person who was to inherit the land attempted to remove the son from the property. It was held in this case that the son could not be removed because of the existence of a licence by estoppel.

---

20 *Department of Environment v Leeburn* [1990] NI 135 (QB), 141-142
21 *Inwards v Baker* [1965] EWCA Civ 4, [1965] 1 All ER 446

This is the most basic form of estoppel licence, where, rather than holding that the licensee has any particular proprietary interest in the land, the landowner is simply prevented from revoking the licence. This by itself is not enough to create a proprietary interest in the land, it is simply recognising the existence of the licence and ensuring that it remains in force.

The alternative and more far reaching consequence of establishing a successful claim of estoppel is that the claim will result in the transfer of a proprietary right. The estoppel licence represents an exception to the general rule that any legal estate or interest in land must be created or transferred by deed, duly executed. In cases where an estoppel licence is deemed to have been created, the owner can be held to have conferred an interest in land despite the absence of a deed. In these limited circumstances the promise of an interest in land may give rise to a cause of action.[22] It can be used as an informal mechanism for regulating title to land where there legal formalities have not been met. Proprietary estoppel has featured in a number of cases in the Northern Ireland Chancery Division in recent years.

There are four criteria which must be met in order for this to occur:

- Assurance
- Reliance
- Detriment
- Unconscionability

However, the courts in Northern Ireland, citing the law as it has evolved in England and Wales, have emphasised that these elements should not be read as four discrete elements but rather should be viewed 'in the round'.[23] This means that the court will look at the overall relationship between the parties rather than attributing significance to each individually.

i. Assurance

The element of assurance is relatively straightforward – the landowner must have allowed the claimant to believe that they were permitted or entitled to use the land. This can be done either through refraining from asserting rights in respect of the land, or by

---

22 *McLaughlin v Murphy* [2007] NICh 5 [19] (Deeny J)
23 *McDermott and McDermott v McDermott and Mortgage Trust Ltd* [2008] NICh 5 [36] (Stephens J) citing with approval the decision of the Court of Appeal in *Gillett v Holt and Another* [2000] EWCA Civ 66, [2000] 2 All ER 289

actively encouraging the belief. The belief must, however, be reasonable belief, from an objective standard. Assurance may also extend to leading a person to believe that they are to be given the land. The Court in Northern Ireland has interpreted the element of assurance to require that the behaviour created and encouraged an expectation of a certain interest in land.[24] This may mean, for example, the making of a promise between the parties that land would be passed on by will; that it will be transferred as part of a deal;[25] or may rely on more indirect assurances that a person would be looked after – assurances to which others can testify.[26] The element of assurance may be direct, in that the court will accept that a promise was made and later gone back on. This was the case in *Kinney v McKittrick*[27] and in *Johnston v Johnston and McKee*[28] where promises made were not reflected in the terms of a will. In the absence of evidence of a direct promise the court may infer assurance from the behaviour of the parties, as was demonstrated in *McLaughlin v Murphy*.

ii. Reliance and detriment

The second feature is that of reliance. It is not enough for the landowner to give the assurance, or to create the impression of assurance. The assurance must produce an effect on the claimant. This includes being induced to behave differently, perhaps carrying out work they would not otherwise have had call to undertake. This element of undertaking work or expenditure that would not have otherwise been undertaken is referred to as detriment, which is the third requirement for estoppel. In order to establish a successful claim of proprietary estoppel there must be some causal link between the assurance and the detriment. The element of detriment may take any form, but common examples include spending money or effort to improve land, devoting time or care to the landowner, or passing up other opportunities on foot of the assurance or belief. Case law illustrates some of these points. The ruling of the Northern Ireland Chancery Division in the case of *McLaughlin v Murphy* provides an authoritative statement of the law of proprietary estoppel in Northern Ireland. In that case the daughter of the deceased challenged the provisions of her father's will which left her only a life interest in a property she had renovated and lived in with her family. Considering the facts,

---

24 *McLaughlin* (n 22), *Kinney v McKittrick* [2011] NICh 24
25 *McDermott* (n 23) [16]-[22]
26 *Mulholland v Kane and Kane* [2009] NICh 9 [11]
27 *Kinney* (n 24)
28 *Johnston v Johnston and McKee* [2008] NICh 11

Deeny J highlighted the extent of the detriment that had been suffered. This included on-going expenditure on the house over a number of years to improve the property, as well as work carried out by the plaintiffs themselves on the house. However it was also clear from the case that the detriment relied upon extended beyond financial detriment to include the fact that the plaintiffs had passed up other opportunities to acquire a property of their own. The Court concluded that this would not have been the case had they not had a reasonable expectation that they would acquire an absolute interest in the property.

Similarly in the most recent case of *Kinney v McKittrick* the court found that the plaintiff had acted to his detriment when he relied on an assurance made to him and left secure employment to go and work with his ageing uncle. The loss of other opportunities is a common feature of the case law on proprietary estoppel. In the case of *Mulholland v Kane and Kane*, the court was asked to consider whether a young woman who had maintained a relationship with an older man could be said to have suffered detriment. The plaintiff had spent 30 years working on the farm and caring for the deceased. Witnesses testified that there had been an expectation that she would be left a house and a few acres of land in return. When considering the extent of the detriment suffered, the court accepted that she had worked without proper wages for many years. Yet they also went further to acknowledge that in devoting herself to the deceased, the plaintiff had lost the opportunity to meet other young men, with the result that she had effectively debarred herself from the prospect of marriage. This was held to constitute detriment.

Finally in the case of *McDermott and McDermott v McDermott and Mortgage Trust Ltd.* the court found that a couple who had given up their life in America to come home and live in Northern Ireland had acted to their detriment on foot of a promise from the first named defendant that a house being constructed would be transferred to them. Detriment does not therefore have to be quantified in purely financial terms.

iii. Unconscionability

What these cases also make clear is that claims of proprietary estoppel can arise as a result both of inadvertence, where no will has been made and provision must therefore be sought by other means; and in the case of deliberate deception, where the behaviour of one party gives rise to a claim in equity against them. However it arises, it has been shown in the Northern Ireland courts to be an important way of securing property interests. The courts have confirmed that the element of detriment should be judged at the moment the person who has given the assurance seeks to go back on it.[29] This is the moment at which that person's conduct becomes unconscionable. The element of unconscionability is what frees proprietary estoppel from the formality requirements usually required to create or transfer interests in land. It is also the overarching or holistic category that requires the court to take a broad view of the relationship between the landowner and the claimant when deciding whether or not a claim for proprietary estoppel should be allowed to succeed – effectively the sum of the other three parts. However the over-riding consideration to be taken into account is the extent to which the conduct of the donor has been unconscionable. Without this element the justification for proprietary estoppel does not stand. It is therefore this element that holds the other three together.

E. Effect of Proprietary Estoppel

As outlined, the effect of a successful claim of proprietary estoppel can be to give rise to a proprietary interest. The intervention of equity, however, is limited to the minimum necessary to do equity. The courts in Northern Ireland have confirmed that the intervention of equity in these circumstances will be just enough to redress the detriment and the injustice suffered.[30] This means that the outcome of each case will be determined on its own facts and it is not possible to provide a definitive guide to the nature of the interest that will arise. However, case law provides examples of how the court may decide to discharge the equity.

Where the court decides that the extent of the equity falls short of requiring that a full estate be transferred, the benefit may be quantified in financial terms. This means that the court will try to put a fixed value on the extent of the detriment and that will be the entitlement of the plaintiff. This has been seen recently in cases in both Northern Ireland and England.

In the Northern Ireland case of *Mulholland v Kane and Kane* the court was reminded that the court of equity should do just enough to redress the detriment and injustice suffered by the plaintiff, but should not be extravagant on her behalf. In this case the court decided that the assurance that had been made that the plaintiff would have a house and some land did not require the transfer of the estate of the deceased, but that a sum of money that would allow her to purchase such a property would be appropriate to satisfy the equity. On this basis the plaintiff was awarded £250,000.

---

29 *Johnston* (n 28) [29]
30 *Mulholland* (n 26) [21]

This case demonstrates that an equitable estoppel will not necessarily grant possession to a plaintiff, but will ensure that any equitable interest that may have arisen as a result of a licence will be discharged. Importantly it also does not insist on a continuing licence.

The quantification of detriment was also considered in detail in the English case of *Jennings v Rice* where a childless widow who had died intestate, with an estate worth nearly £1.3 million. From about 1970 the plaintiff, Mr Jennings, had worked for the widow on a part time basis, doing gardening, running errands and taking her shopping. In the late 1980s the widow had stopped paying Mr Jennings for these services, justifying this on the basis that "he would be alright" and that "this will all be yours one day". As the years went on she became increasingly dependent on Jennings, indeed he was providing full time care to her. When the old lady died, Jennings claimed that in looking after her without pay he had acted to his detriment in the expectation that he would benefit on her death. The judge accepted this reasoning, accepting that he had in fact acted to his detriment, but awarded him only the sum of £200,000. Jennings appealed this, claiming that he was entitled to the entire estate, or at least to the full value of the house and contents. But the appeal was dismissed. The court of appeal stated that the value of the equity will depend upon all the circumstances, including the expectation and the detriment. The task of the court was simply to avoid an unconscionable result. Part of this will be to ensure that there is a degree of proportionality between the expectation and the detriment. If the court decides that the claimants expectations were either extravagant or out of proportion to the detriment suffered, then it is open to them to satisfy the equity in another way. In this case the sum of £200,000 was based on the cost of full time nursing care for the plaintiff. It did not go so far as to say that he was entitled to all the property.

This entitlement to a sum from the estate still constitutes an equitable interest in the property.

The second potential consequence of a finding of estoppel is that equity can intervene to grant a licence for someone to remain in possession of a particular property, where the circumstances of the case warrant it. In the case of *Greasley v Cooke*,[31] Miss Cooke had come to live in a house as a maid. A few years later she began to live with one of the owner's sons, as man and wife. From this point on she did not receive any payment for her services, but over the course of 40 years she continued to act as an unpaid housekeeper and also as a nurse to his mentally ill sister. The son, with whom she was

---

31   *Greasley v Cooke* [1980] 3 All ER 710 (CA)

living, eventually inherited the house jointly with his brother. When he died, his brother attempted to have her removed from the house, despite having assured her that she would have a home for life. She counterclaimed on the basis of proprietary estoppel. Initially the court found against the defendant. It was accepted that both brothers had led her to believe that she would be able to remain in the house rent free for the rest of her life, but held that the burden of proving that she had acted to her detriment based on this belief rested on her herself, and that there was insufficient evidence in this regard. On this basis she was not entitled to a remedy based on proprietary estoppel. However, when the case went to appeal it was held that once she had relied on assurances given to her by the brothers, the burden of proving that she had acted to her detriment did not rest on her, but rather it was for the brother seeking to evict her to prove that she had not acted to her detriment on foot of his assurance. If there was no evidence to back up his assertion then the court would draw an inference in her favour that her conduct had been induced by the assurance, and as such, in equity, she would be allowed to remain in the house for as long as she pleased. This effectively created an equitable licence in the property.

Of course the logical conclusion of this line of argument is that there are also circumstances in which the extent of the equity justifies the transfer of the estate. This has occurred in a number of recent decisions in the Northern Ireland court. For example in *Johnston v Johnston and McKee* the court decided that the plaintiff had acted to his detriment on foot of promises that had been made to attract him to come and work the farm and to keep him there. As a result the minimum equity required was to transfer the farm to him, making him absolute owner of the estate. This was the case notwithstanding the fact that it was in direct contradiction to the express terms of the deceased's will. Similarly in *McLaughlin v Murphy* the court decided that the actions of the deceased had given rights to an outright equity in the house.[32]

The fact that an estoppel can create a proprietary interest has been confirmed by the Land Registration Act 2002 in England and Wales.[33] This principle applies equally to registered and unregistered land, and applies also in Northern Ireland.

The final categories of interest to consider are ones that arise uniquely in both jurisdictions of Ireland.

---

32 See also *McDermott* (n 23) and *Kinney* (n 24)
33 s 116

9.3 Conacre and Agistment

Conacre and agistment are informal forms of land holding that allow one person to use the land of another for a specific purpose without creating a proprietary interest. They arise primarily in agricultural contexts. Conacre is a means of using land to grow crops, while agistment refers to the use of land for grazing animals. It is very common for agricultural land in Northern Ireland to be used in this way and in recent years this form of interest has become a feature of larger agricultural business.[34] It is a flexible system of use that does not transfer any interest in the land but allows it to be put to productive use. It arose as a form of interest in land in Ireland because of traditional restrictions on leasehold land, but now performs a similar function to other forms of licence.[35]

9.4 Conclusion

The category of licence in property law has largely developed to replace some of the old categories of tenancies which bore few features of a lease. There is still a great deal of overlap and uncertainty surrounding the categorisation of licences, particularly between the contractual and estoppel varieties. But it is clear that the type of licence created can have a significant impact on the legal relationship created by the parties. And more often than not, as with leases, the true nature of this relationship will be determined by the court, judging on the basis of the characteristics of the occupancy itself and not on the label attached to the agreement by the parties. For this reason it is important to be able to distinguish the features of each category of licence, as well as to be able to explain how licences differ from leases.

---

34 *Maurice E Taylor (Merchants) Ltd v Commissioner of Valuation* [1981] NI 236
35 See JCW Wylie, 'The 'Irishness' of Irish Land Law' (1995) 46 NILQ 332, 342

CHAPTER 10

Freehold Covenants

10.1 Introduction

It is an inevitable fact of life for the majority of people that we will have neighbours. Whether living in the city or in the countryside our lives are potentially affected by property and what other people choose to do with theirs. This can have a significant impact on our enjoyment of our own property, whether through late night noise created by business premises next door, the loss of value of one's own property through failure of neighbours to maintain their own, or inappropriate development of the rural environment. To enable property owners to protect themselves against such difficulties the law provides ways in which the use of property can be restricted.

Property ownership is almost always transferred through a documentary process which includes a contract and deed of transfer. These documents create a contractual relationship between the parties which makes it possible for conditions to be attached to the transfer of the property. These might include conditions such as that the land must be used only for agricultural purposes, or that it may not be used for business purposes, and they are attached where the person transferring the land wants to ensure the ongoing protection of the nature of the land or restrict the use to which it can be put. For example, it is common in modern housing developments to find conditions relating to the maintenance of the property and common areas included in contracts for sale. These conditions do not form part of the estate itself, but may in certain circumstances become an encumbrance on the property. These terms are contractual terms, but are described as 'covenants'. A covenant is a promise made under seal. These can be included within the deed of transfer and are enforceable between the parties to the transaction under the rules of contract law. This means that breaches can be remedied using the traditional remedies in contract. In this regard, where a covenant exists between the two parties to a deed, the position is relatively uncomplicated. So why is this of interest to land law?

The question that arises, and which brings covenants within the scope of land law, is whether the provisions of the covenant become attached to the land in such a way as to affect any subsequent purchasers of that land. Under contract law, the rules of privity of contract mean that any person who was not party to the contract will not be bound by it. In theory this would be the case in relation to covenants. Any subsequent purchaser of the land would not have been a party to the original covenant and would therefore not be bound by it. However, because of the nature of covenants, affecting land as they do, it has gradually been recognised that to insist on a strict contract law interpretation whereby subsequent owners can disregard the provisions of a covenant affecting the land would undermine the rationale for covenants in the first place – namely the protection of the land. Therefore what has been recognised is that a covenant may, in certain circumstances, create a property interest in the land which would then attach to the land in such a way as to affect purchasers.[1] Importantly, these obligations are of the type that would not traditionally attach to land.

There is therefore a move away from contract and towards bringing covenants within the scope of the principles of land law. This is recognised in statute, common law and in equity, all of which regulate covenants. The rules surrounding common law and equitable principles were clarified by statute in 1997 in Northern Ireland.[2] There is therefore clear Northern Ireland law on the creation and enforcement of covenants in this jurisdiction since the 1997 Order. There is also case law and legislation dealing with the modification and extinguishment of covenants in Northern Ireland. However there is little case law in this jurisdiction to illustrate the application of the old rules of common law and equity in the Northern Ireland courts. The discussion of these rules is therefore necessarily developed through established case law of the English courts.

As stated, the 1997 Order does not apply to covenants created before it came into effect.[3] As so many cases still fall to be decided by the common law and equitable regimes in place prior to the 1997 legislation it is important to consider all three sets of rules.

---

1   This is recognised in statute: Property (Northern Ireland) Order 1978 article 3(c)
2   Property (Northern Ireland) Order (1997) Part III
3   Ibid article 34(2)(a)

10.2 The Nature of Covenants

Covenants can be attached to both freehold and leasehold land. The rules will be different depending on the nature of the estate held.[4] The provisions of a covenant will entail either a 'benefit' or 'burden'. The covenantor – that is the person who undertakes the obligations of the covenant – will bear the burden. They will be responsible for fulfilling whatever obligations have been undertaken or for complying with any restrictions placed on the use of the land. The covenantee – that is the person who is attaching the conditions to the land – will enjoy the benefit of the covenant. They can take action to enforce the covenant if any of its conditions are breached. Where the land is sold both vendor and purchaser will want to establish whether either the benefit or the burden of the covenant will continue after the sale.

Broadly speaking there are two types of covenants. There are positive covenants and negative covenants. A positive covenant will require some sort of positive action or expenditure on the part of the covenantor. This could, for example, entail the maintenance of buildings or of roads which cross the land. A negative covenant, also known as a restrictive covenant, will not entail actual expenditure or action, but will limit the manner in which the land can be used. So for example a covenant might prevent the covenantor from building on a piece of land, restrict the type of building;[5] or restrict the type of business that can be carried out from the property.[6] As such they are used to protect the character of a particular area, whether rural or urban eg housing developments.

For example:

- Mark owns 1 acre of land but he decides to sell half of it to Peter. In the sale Mark retains a right of way across the half acre he is selling to Peter and Peter covenants (promises) to ensure the upkeep of this right of way. This is a positive covenant as it requires the landowner to carry out certain acts for benefit of another persons' land.

- Helen is selling her home in Hillsborough to Kate. She wants to ensure that the house will be used as a family home so in the deed Kate covenants not to use the house as a bed and breakfast. This is a negative covenant as it requires landowner to refrain from doing certain things.

---

4   This chapter will deal exclusively with freehold covenants. For rules on leasehold covenants see chapter 8.
5   *Danesfort Developments Ltd v Mr and Mrs M Morrow and Richard Palmer* [2002] 4/55, R/45/1999 [33]
6   *McNicholl v Thomas Mullan & Anthony Mullan* [2001], R/49/1999 [20]-[24], [37]-[44]

However, as stated, the difficulty arises when either party to a covenant sells or otherwise transfers their interest in the land to a third party. It is then that it is important to be able to identify whether either the benefit or the burden of the covenant will pass with the land.

10.3 Property (NI) Order 1997

The Property (NI) Order of 1997 codified the position in relation to covenants on land in Northern Ireland. The Order replaces the rules of common law and equity relating to the enforceability between owners of estates in fee simple of covenants burdening and benefiting those estates.[7] The legislation applies to covenants made in Northern Ireland after 10 January 2000. This means that it is a relatively recent development, and as such is still of limited application because disputes surrounding covenants that were created before this date must still be decided with reference to the old rules of common law and equity as discussed in this section. The Order attempts to simplify the rules regulating covenants by providing a statutory basis for their enforcement.

The key provisions of the Order are found in article 34 which lists the types of freehold covenants that will be enforceable, whether restrictive or not. As such the legislation alters the position that had previously pertained whereby the covenants would be enforceable only where they were restrictive in nature. Article 34(4) lists the types of covenants that will be enforceable:

   a. Covenants in respect of the maintenance, repair or renewal of party walls or fences or the preservation of boundaries.

   b. Covenants to do, or to pay for or to contribute to the cost of, works on, or to permit works to be done on, or for access to be had to, or for any activity to be pursued on, the land of the covenantor for the benefit of land of the covenantee or other land.

   c. Covenants to do, or to pay for or contribute to the cost of, works on land of the covenantee or other land where the works benefit the land of the covenantor.

   d. Covenants to reinstate in the event of damage or destruction.

   e. Covenants for the protection of amenities or services or for compliance with a statutory provision (or a requirement under it), including:

---

7   Art 34(1)

   i. Covenants (however expressed) not to use the land of the covenantor for specified purposes or otherwise than for the purposes of private dwelling.

   ii. Covenants against causing nuisance, annoyance, damage or inconvenience.

   iii. Covenants against interfering with facilities.

   iv. Covenants prohibiting, regulating or restricting building works or the erection of any structure, or the planting, cutting or removal of vegetation (including grass, trees and shrubs) or requiring the tending of such vegetation.

   f. Covenants in relation to a body corporate formed for the management of land.

Thus, the new legislation covers a wide variety of covenants, both positive and restrictive in substance. Under the Order these covenants will run with land and this will no longer need to be scrutinised under the rules of common law or equity. The legislation is also clear that this is a conclusive list of the types of covenants that will be enforceable.[8] This removes ambiguity as to whether other types of covenant may also be argued to be enforceable under the previous common law or equitable rules. Because the Order replaces the old rules, covenants falling outside its scope will not be enforceable. The Order also addresses the question of who is entitled to enforce an existing covenant. It clearly remains the case that the original parties to the covenant remain bound by its terms.[9] However the policy of article 34 is that any relevant covenants can be enforced by the owner *for the time being* of the benefited land against the owner of the burdened land.[10] The covenant therefore attaches permanently to the whole and every part of the land and will run with that land. In this way the statutory regime consolidates many of the principles that already exist in equity.[11]

There are, however, some exceptions to the type of covenants covered by the Order. It will not apply to:

   a. Covenants contained in a deed made before 10 January 2000.

   b. Covenants contained in a deed made in pursuance of an obligation assumed before this date.

   c. Any covenant for title. This is essentially a guarantee that the former vendor had good right to convey or lease the whole of the property and the

---

8   Ibid article 34(4), which states that the listed covenants, *and only covenants of those kind*, are enforceable. (emphasis added)

9   Ibid article 34(3)

10 Ibid article 34(4)

11 See section 10.5

interest he/she had agreed to sell. Alternatively it can refer to covenants for quiet enjoyment – where the owner's enjoyment of the property will not be disturbed. This relates to the implied covenant in all leases that the tenant will be entitled to quiet enjoyment of the property for the duration of the lease. This falls outside the scope of the Order.

d. Covenants that bind only the covenantor. This may occur in circumstances where a person is granted an estate in property on the condition for example that they continue to live there with their elderly mother. This is clearly not a covenant that touches or concerns the land, nor could it effectively be passed to a different person as it is essentially based on the conduct of the individual in the context of a family relationship. This type of obligation will not be deemed to have run under the Order.

e. Any covenants to which article 25 applies (ie covenants affecting land after the redemption of ground rents).

Therefore from 2000 the position is much clearer for vendors and purchasers as to whether covenants will be enforceable. This is a significant improvement on the previous position whereby the enforceability of the covenant had to be scrutinised under the laws of both common law and equity. However as stated, the Order does not apply to covenants that were created before it came into effect. It is therefore necessary to know the old common law and equitable rules that will determine the enforceability of these historical covenants.

10.4 The Common Law Position

To be able to enforce a covenant in common law you must be able to establish that both the benefit and the burden have passed. This is a two part test. It must be demonstrated first, that the benefit of the covenant itself is capable of being passed and has done so, and second that there is a person against whom the burden can be enforced. Therefore for each of these regimes, we must consider separately the running of the benefit and the burden. The applicable rules differ depending on which is at issue but it must be established that both have run.

A. The Running of the Benefit

The benefit of a covenant will run in common law under the rules stated in *Smith and Snipes Hall Farm v River Douglas Catchment Board.*[12] In this case the covenantor was the River Authority, who had entered into an agreement with the owner of land surrounding the river to make good the banks of the Eller River, which was liable to flooding, and to improve drainage in the surrounding land. This work was intended to make a permanent improvement to the flooding and also included an undertaking that they would maintain the banks so as to prevent future flooding. In consideration of the agreement the landowners contributed to the cost of the repairs. In 1946, six years after the repairs had been carried out, the river burst its banks and destroyed a significant quantity of crops. In the intervening period the original covenantee – that is the owner of the farm for whose benefit the covenant had been entered into – had sold the land. The question at issue was whether the successor in title to the farm could enforce the covenant against the river authority – essentially whether the benefit of the covenant had passed with the land or whether it had been extinguished upon sale of the land. The court set out the test for deciding whether or not the benefit attached to the land or was simply a contractual agreement. There were 5 criteria:

- The Covenant must touch and concern the land (ie it must benefit the land by altering the mode of occupation or value of the land rather than the individual). Because in this case the effect of the covenant was to transform the land from bog meadows into useable agricultural land, this part of the test was met.

- It must be intended when the covenants are made that the benefit should run with the land so as to be available to subsequent owners.

- The original covenantee must have had a legal estate.

- The new owner of the land must have the same legal estate as the original covenantee.

- The deed in which the covenant was created must have made clear what land was to benefit from the covenant.

Thus, if all these criteria are present then the covenant will be held to run with the land, making it an interest in property rather than simply a contractual obligation. In this case the Court of Appeal was satisfied that all the necessary criteria had been met and the Covenant was deemed to have run with the land and was enforceable against the river authority as the original covenantor. This is known as being directly enforceable.

---

12   [1949] 2 KB 500, [1949] 2 All ER 179 (CA), 506-508 (Tucker LJ), 514-517 (Denning LJ)

This test reflects the provisions of the Conveyancing Act which states that covenants are deemed to have been made with 'the covenantee, his heirs and assigns',[13] thus presuming that this intention is present in all circumstances.[14] However this is just one part of the equation and the other requirements will still have to be fulfilled.

Therefore the right to enforce a freehold covenant will only pass to successors of the covenantee if they own the land that is to be benefited by the covenant. This is because both parties must own the same estate. The benefit of a freehold covenant will not pass where a lease is demised rather than freehold. Conversely, it is irrelevant whether a covenantor, such as the River Authority, owns any land or not – the covenant can still be enforced. It is also irrelevant in these circumstances whether the covenant is positive or restrictive in nature. In this case the covenant was positive, requiring expenditure on the part of the Board. This did not stop it from being enforced. This is because the River Authority had been a party to the original agreement – they themselves had made the promise. There was therefore no reason why it should not be enforced against them.

It is therefore interesting to note that it is possible for the benefit to be held to have run because it is not imposing obligations on a party other than the original covenantor who undertook them in the first place. Rather it is the beneficiary who has changed.

The position and the rationale are a little different where you want to establish that the burden of a covenant has passed with the land. In such circumstances you are acting contrary to the principles of privity of contract and holding the successor in title liable for obligations undertaken by his/her predecessor and enforcing against him/her an agreement to which he/she was never a party. This has meant that the courts have been more reluctant to hold that the burden of a covenant can pass with the land.[15] At best it has been achieved indirectly.

B. The Running of the Burden

There are a number of possible situations where the burden will be indirectly held to have run:

---

13 Conveyancing Act 1881 section 58(1). In *Roake and Others v Chadha* [1983] 3 All ER 503 (Ch), [1984] 1 WLR 40, 46-47 (Paul Baker QC) it was held that the presumption of intention resulting from section 58 could be rebutted by express words indicating a shared intention that the benefit of the covenant not be annexed to the land.

14 In England, section 58 has been replaced by the Law of Property Act 1925 section 78, which uses the words "successors in title or the persons deriving title under him or them", which has been interpreted by case law as meaning that it annexes the covenant to the land without the need to prove the other conditions.

15 *Austerberry v Corporation of Oldham* (1885) 29 Ch D 750, 773-774 (Cotton LJ)

i. Where the estate in question is determinable/conditional

Land can be transferred subject to certain conditions. In the case of determinable conditions, if they occur then the transfer of the property will be void. Effectively if land is sold subject to a covenant in the form of a condition subsequent (or a determining event) and the condition is broken then the vendor can reclaim the land. In this way the landowner can ensure that any burden on the land can be enforced. (So for example a house is sold on the condition that the owner agrees not to paint it yellow. This condition represents the burden of the covenant. If the owner then paints the house yellow the condition has been broken and the sale is void.) This is a rather extreme means of ensuring that a burden runs.

ii. Where a rentcharge is placed on the land

A rentcharge is a perpetual obligation by which the owner of land is bound to pay an annual payment charged upon the land. Positive conditions can be attached to the rentcharge which, if not performed, will entitle the owner of the rentcharge to re-enter the land and perform the acts in question at the expense of the land owner. Rentcharges are rare in Northern Ireland and as of January 2000 can no longer be created by virtue of article 29 of the Property (NI) Order 1997.[16] This means that they are of limited use in ensuring that the burden of a covenant can run.

iii. Rule in *Halsall v Brizell*[17]

This rule states that a person claiming any substantial right conferred by a deed must submit to any corresponding burden in the deed. The facts of this case were that land was subdivided and conveyed to a number of purchasers. In the deed of conveyance the purchasers were granted a right of way in return for which they covenanted to contribute to the cost of its maintenance. When the successor in title of one of the original purchasers questioned his obligation to contribute, the court found that if he wished to continue to use the right of way he would only be allowed to do so if he submitted to the burden of contributing to its upkeep. This rule effectively enforces reciprocity where both benefit and burden exist.

---

16 Similarly in England and Wales the Rentcharges Act 1977 prohibited the creation of any new rentcharges.
17 *Halsall and Others v Brizell* [1957] Ch 169, 182 (Upjohn J)

iv. Indemnity agreements

These arise where an agreement is inserted into a deed by which the owner of land will require a purchaser to indemnify against any future breach of the covenant, regardless of ownership of the land at the time of the breach. So for example, if X sells some land to Y and Y covenants to maintain a boundary wall, because there is privity of contract between X and Y, X can insert a provision into the contract whereby Y will have to indemnify (ie compensate) X if the covenant is ever breached. If Y later wants to sell the land to Z, Y will remain liable to compensate X if Z breaches the covenant. As a result, Y will insist that Z enter into a similar indemnity agreement meaning that if X sues Y for breach of the covenant, Y can then sue Z. In this way compensation for breach of the covenant occurs by virtue of a chain effect.

These methods of indirect enforcement at common law at least provide some possibility of remedy against the current holder of the relevant land, but if the object is to have the burden directly enforceable then they are not exactly efficient. Consequently, equity has intervened to make direct enforcement of burdens possible in certain circumstances.

10.5 The Equitable Rules

A. The Running of the Burden in Equity

Because of the difficulties that arose in common law in trying to make the burden of a covenant directly enforceable, equity has developed specific rules to achieve this. This was first provided for in the case of *Tulk v Moxhay (1848)*.[18] This case was the first case in which the burden of a restrictive covenant was allowed to be enforced by successors in title.

The general principle established in this case was that the burden of a restrictive covenant will run with the land to which it relates to so as to bind all successors in title of the original covenantor, except a bona fide purchaser for value without notice of the covenant. This addresses the difficulty in common law that an assignee cannot be held to be directly liable for a covenant, even where they knew of its existence. Traditionally, equity will step in to mitigate the effects of the common law and where a successor in title knows of the existence of a covenant on a piece of land that they buy, the burden

---

18 *Tulk v Moxhay (1848)* 2 Ph 774, 41 ER 1143

of that covenant will be binding on them, irrespective of the fact that they were not an original party to the covenant.

There are four requirements which must be met before the burden of a covenant will pass in equity; the covenant must be restrictive; it must be for the benefit of the land; it must be intended to pass with the land; and it will be enforceable in equity only.

i. Covenant must be restrictive

First, the covenant must be restrictive.[19] The burden of a positive covenant will not run automatically. Where there is ambiguity or doubt it will be for the Court to decide whether or not a covenant is restrictive in nature.[20] So for example in *Tulk v Moxhay* itself the covenant stated that the owner would keep and maintain the land in a open state uncovered with buildings. Although the wording of keep and maintain sound as if they are imposing a positive requirement on the landowner, the court determined that the covenant was in fact restrictive as it simply prevented building on the land (and indeed there had been no positive action taken in respect of the land, which had fallen into disuse). Conversely in the case of *Rhone v Stephens*[21] it was argued that a covenant to maintain a roof was restrictive so as to run with the land, but this was found not to be the case. So even where the parties have used a particular wording with the intention of either enforcing or avoiding obligations, the court can disregard the form of the covenant and instead look to the substance.

ii. Covenant must benefit the land

The second criteria is that the covenant must exist for the benefit of the land owned by the covenantee, ie it must touch and concern the land and not merely benefit the covenantee in his/her personal capacity. The person seeking enforcement must generally be the current owner in possession of the land to be benefited. In *London County Council v Allen* the defendant's predecessor in title had covenanted with the council not to build on a part of the land which had been purchased from them.[22] Allen then built on the land but by this time the Council no longer owned any land nearby

---

19 *Haywood v The Brunswick Permanent Benefit Building Society* (1881) 8 QBD 403 (CA), 408-409 (Cotton LJ)
20 See for example *In the Matter of a Reference by George Conville & Marie Conville* [2002] 2/70, R/64/2000, 4
21 [1994] UKHL 3, [1994] 2 AC 310, 317-319 (Lord Templeman)
22 [1914] 3 KB 642 (CA)

which would be affected by the breach. It was held that the covenant must be made for the benefit of certain land, some of which must remain with the covenantee or his successors. As the council no longer had any land near that of Allen, the breach did not touch or concern their land and as such the burden did not run.

iv. Burden must be intended to pass

The third criteria is that the burden of the covenant must be intended to pass with the land, meaning that there must be an intention that subsequent owners will be bound by it. In Northern Ireland, by virtue of Section 58 of the Conveyancing Act 1881, unless a contrary intention is expressed a covenant will be deemed to have been made on behalf of the covenantor, his heirs and assigns.

v. Covenant will be enforceable in equity only

Finally, since the burden is only enforceable in equity, the interest under the covenant is equitable only – it does not create a legal interest. What this means is that the legal rights of the owner remain the same under common law, but equity will prevent them from being enforced. It does not vest a legal right in the covenantee. An equitable interest will not bind a bona fide purchaser for value without notice of the covenant. It will, however, be difficult for a purchaser to claim that they bought land without notice of the covenant because of the Registration of Deed and Registration of Title systems under which the purchaser will be deemed to have notice of the covenant (ie any purchaser could reasonably be expected to have made inquiries as to any interests that might exist in relation to it.)[23] If the land is registered, however, the covenant must also be registered against it in order to bind the purchaser.[24] This is because of the fact that the register is deemed to be conclusive as to the ownership of land and any charges and interests in it. If the covenant is not registered then the purchaser will not be deemed to have notice of it.

B. The Running of the Benefit in Equity

Equity has also developed its own rules for when the benefit of a covenant will pass. In such cases the plaintiff must establish that:

---

23 See chapter 3
24 Land Registration Act 1970

- they are the holder of the land to which the benefit relates
- the benefit has passed to them

Proof that the benefit has passed can be established in four ways:

i. Express assignment

This means that the benefit of the covenant is passed as part of the transaction when a new owner acquires the land. This was the case in *Re Union of London & Smiths Bank's Conveyance, Miles v Easter*.[25] This case sets out the conditions in which the benefit of a covenant can be expressly assigned to a purchaser, thereby binding the covenantor. The Court stated:

> "in order that an express assignee of a covenant restricting the user of land may be able to enforce that covenant against the owner of the land burdened with the covenant, he must be able to satisfy the Court of two things. The first is that it was a covenant entered into for the benefit or protection of land owned by the covenantee at the date of the covenant … Secondly, the assignee must be able to satisfy the Court that the deed containing the covenant defines or contains something to define the property for the benefit of which the covenant was entered into…"

This means that the court must be able to establish exactly what piece of land the covenant is to benefit. If this cannot be done then assignment will fail as a means of passing the benefit, as happened in this case.

ii. Transfer on death

If the new owner acquires the land and the benefit of the covenants under will/intestacy of the former owner. In *Newton Abbot Co-op Society Ltd v Williams & Treavold Ltd*[26] an ironmonger sold land that was subject to a covenant that it would not be used for ironmongery. Years later the property was used for that very purpose and it was held that the benefit of the covenant had passed by operation of law (ie under the will) to her heir even though the covenant was not specifically mentioned. This means that where the land is obtained under a will it will not matter that the beneficiary was not party to the covenant as they take the land as it is – subject to the covenant.

---

25 [1933] Ch 611 (CA), 625 (Bennett J)
26 [1952] Ch 286 (Upjohn J)

iii. Express annexation

Express annexation means that the covenant is expressly included in the deed of conveyance. Where land is added to another piece of land (ie the plot of land is increased in size) that is already subject to a covenant, if there is express annexation of the covenant then this means that the new land will also be subject to its terms. This also operates where land that is subject to a covenant is broken up by sale. The effect of express annexation in these circumstances would be to ensure that both the remaining land and the piece that has been sold remain subject to the covenant. It effectively means that a purchaser of any part of the land will still benefit from the provisions of the covenant and it cannot be argued that the covenant did not apply to the particular area of land that was sold. This will be indicated by the wording of the deed or covenant. It must precisely specify the land to be benefited and not merely refer to the covenantee, his heirs or assigns. This ensures that the extent of the affected land can be accurately determined. In *Rogers v Hosegood*[27] a covenant was created in respect of a property 'and every part thereof' to the benefit of the vendor, his heirs and assigns and others claiming under them. Because the covenant was expressly annexed to the benefited land a purchaser of part of the benefited land was able to enforce the covenant even though he was originally unaware of its existence. If the benefit is not annexed to 'every part thereof' then annexation may be ineffective if the covenant is not capable of benefiting the whole land. Similarly if the benefited land is sold in parts rather than as a whole annexation may not succeed.

In respect of covenants made in England and Wales after 1952, Section 78 of the Law of Property Act 1925 has the effect, in the absence of contrary intention, of annexing the benefit of a covenant even if express words of annexation are not used. In *Federated Homes v Mill Lodge properties Ltd*[28] it was held that because, under Section 78 a covenant made with a covenantee is also deemed to have been made with his/her successors in title the effect is to annex the benefit. This implies that where a restrictive covenant exists that touches and concerns the land, annexation is to the whole of the land and any parts thereof.

The position is a little different in Northern Ireland. In contrast to the inference in the absence of contrary intention contained in Section 78, in Northern Ireland, the Conveyancing Act of 1881 continues to apply to pre-2000 covenants in Northern Ireland. The wording of Section 58 does not refer to the covenantee's successors in title

---

27 [1900] 2 Ch 388 (CA), 397-398 (Farwell J)
28 [1979] EWCA Civ 3, [1980] 1 WLR 594 (CA), 601-602 (Brightman LJ)

or persons deriving title under him or them, or the owner or occupiers for the time being of the land that the covenantee intended to be benefited. The section was confined to the covenantee, his heirs and assigns, words which suggest a more limited scope of operation than is found in Section 78. This is confirmed by the *Sainsburys v Enfield* case.[29]

10.6 Housing Developments

The term Housing Development is of relatively recent origin. However the practice of building large numbers of similar houses in close proximity to each other is not a new one. These types of developments were previously described as 'estate schemes'. Despite the change in terminology over the years, the underlying legal principles remain applicable.[30]

An estate scheme occurs when a developer builds a number of houses for sale but wishes the character of the area to remain constant after all the houses have been sold. The rules on estate schemes continue to be of relevance of modern day housing developments where developers wish to maintain the character of a development. To achieve this, the developer will sell each house subject to a covenant that operates between the purchaser, the developer and all other owners in the development. In practice this means that any of the owners can enforce the terms of the covenant if there is a breach. This is, however, subject to certain rules. These were set out in the 1908 case of *Elliston v Reacher*.[31]

A. Title must derive from a common owner

The first rule is that the plaintiff and the defendant must derive title from a common owner. This simply means that the houses were originally bought from the same developer. As these rules relate to the running of a benefit, it should be assumed that this means original title. If someone who has originally bought their house from the developer subsequently sells the property, the new purchaser will still be deemed to have derived title from the same common owner. Title passes as if in a chain, which remains traceable back to the same common owner.

---

29 *J Sainsbury Plc v Enfield London Borough Council* [1989] 1 WLR 590 (Ch),
30 *Conville* (n 19)
31 *Elliston v Reacher* [1908] 2 Ch 665 (CA)

B. Estate must be subject to common restrictions

The second is that the common vendor must have laid out the estate in plots that were subject to common restrictions. This means that all the plots in the development must be subject to the same restrictions. Variation of the terms of the covenants may undermine this principle.

C. Restrictions must be intended to benefit all plots

Thirdly, the common vendor must have intended the restrictions to benefit all of the plots sold. It will not be enough if the covenant only operates in respect of some properties but not all.

D. Reciprocity

Fourthly, the plaintiff and the defendant must have purchased their plots on the basis that the restrictions would benefit the other plots. This again reinforces the idea of reciprocity when considering the running of benefit. It would be inequitable to allow one landowner to enforce a covenant against another if they themselves were in breach of the same obligations. Therefore, it goes back to the idea that if you want to enjoy the benefit you must also shoulder the burden.

E. Scope of covenant must be clearly defined

Finally, for a benefit to be enforced under an estate scheme, the area covered by the scheme must be clearly defined.[32] This simply recognises the principle that the courts must be able to identify the land to be benefited.

These have traditionally been the rules which govern estate schemes. They are relatively common in modern housing developments, and can prove extremely useful in dealing with problem neighbours. The rules have also been relaxed somewhat in recent years. *Re Dolphin's Conveyance* in 1970 provided that so long as the area to be covered is clearly defined and there is clear intent to establish a scheme of reciprocal obligation then the courts will not insist that the other rules are satisfied.[33]

---

32 *Reid v Bickerstaff* (1909) 2 Ch 305
33 *Re Dolphin's Conveyance* [1970] Ch 654, 659-662 (Stamp J)

This issue was addressed by the Lands Tribunal for Northern Ireland *In the Matter of a Reference by George Conville and Marie Conville*.[34] In this reference the Tribunal was asked to decide whether a restrictive covenant applied as between all leaseholders within a housing development or existed only between the original lessor and the lessee. The Tribunal relied on the idea of a 'community of interest' as providing the necessary foundation for potentially holding that other leaseholders would be entitled to enforce the terms of the covenant. In this case it was decided that no such community existed. This was because although all tenants took their title from a common vendor, the covenants contained in each lease were not the same. A scheme of reciprocal obligation was therefore not established.

These are the rules that have developed in common law and in equity to determine when a covenant can be enforced either by or against a successor in title of an original party to the covenant. But what happens if the successors in title do not want to remain bound by a covenant? Are there any means by which they can have it removed?

10.7 Discharge and Modification of Restrictive Covenants

Under the Property (Northern Ireland) Order 1978 in certain circumstances one may apply to the Lands Tribunal for the removal or modification of covenants. The order applies to various impediments to the enjoyment of land held either in freehold or leasehold so long as at least 21 years of the lease have already run.[35] These impediments are defined in article 3 of the Order. It is important to note that the definition only provides for one type of positive covenant to be modified or removed – those to pay for or execute works for the benefit of other lands.

Article 4 of the Order grants the Lands Tribunal the power to determine the scope of the covenant. Under article 4(1) the Tribunal may determine the existence of an impediment burdening the land, the nature and extent of the impediment, and address if the impediment is enforceable, and if so by whom. Where such cases raise a significant issue of law, the Tribunal may refer the case to the Court of Appeal for a decision.[36]

---

34 *Conville* (n 20)
35 Property 1978 (n 1) article 5(2)
36 Ibid article 4(2)

Under article 5(2) of the 1978 Order the Lands Tribunal has a discretionary power to modify or extinguish a relevant covenant where proceedings are brought to establish or enforce the existence of an obligation arising under such a covenant. An application to the Lands Tribunal for modification or extinguishment of a relevant impediment (burden) under this order may be made by any person interested in the lands which includes someone contemplating purchasing the lands.[37]

In order to have the covenant modified or extinguished the applicant must show that the impediment "unreasonably impedes the enjoyment of the land or if not modified or extinguished would do so."[38] The test is whether or not the burden placed by the covenant is presently unreasonable. This is different from determining whether a covenant is void *ab initio* on the grounds of public policy. The test of 'presently unreasonable' recognises that the covenant may at one time have played a useful function in relation to the land but the circumstances that gave rise to the covenant have changed and its purpose has now gone.

In considering an application, article 5(5) of the Order requires the Tribunal to consider a number of specified matters. The matters to be taken into account will be:

a. The period at, the circumstances in, and the purposes for which the impediment was created or imposed.

b. Any change in the character of the land or neighbourhood.

c. Any public interest in the land.[39]

d. Any trend shown by planning permissions (within the meaning of that Planning Order) granted for land in the vicinity of the land, or by refusals of applications for such planning permissions, which are brought to the notice of the Tribunal.

e. Whether the impediment secures any practical benefit to any person and, if it does so, the nature and extent of that benefit.

f. Where the impediment consists of an obligation to execute any works or to do any thing, or to pay or contribute towards the cost of executing any works

---

37 See generally Norma Dawson, 'Modification and Extinguishment of Land Obligations Under the Property (NI) Order' (1978) 29 NILQ 223

38 Property 1978 (n 1) article 5(1). In England and Wales this is governed by the Law of Property Act 1925 section 84

39 The legislation provides that such public interest includes matters as exemplified by the regional development strategy formulated under article 3 of the Strategic Planning (Northern Ireland) Order 1999 or any development plan adopted under Part III of the Planning (Northern Ireland) Order 1991 for the area in which the land is situated, as that plan is for the time being in force.

or doing anything, whether the obligation has become unduly onerous in comparison with the benefit to be derived from the works or the doing of that thing.

g. Whether the person entitled to the benefit of the impediment has agreed either expressly or by implication, by his acts or omissions, to the impediment being modified or extinguished.

h. Any other material circumstances.

In Northern Ireland article 5(5) has been interpreted as giving the Tribunal discretion as to the weight it attaches to each of these criteria.[40]

What is clear from this list of criteria is that the Tribunal can approach the question of the enforceability of covenants in light of the circumstances pertaining at the time the application is made. Rather than enforcing covenants that may no longer serve any practical use, due to the changing nature of an area, for example, the Tribunal has the power to balance any ongoing benefit enjoyed as a result of the covenant against the changing context in which it applies. This allows the Tribunal to recognise the evolution of land use and provides flexibility to extinguish or modify covenants that continue to restrict the use of property but provide little demonstrable utility.

The order is not clear as to who may object but presumably this includes those entitled to the benefit of the impediment. The impediment may be extinguished or modified; new impediments may be added or substituted in the light of the extinguishment or modification of the old one.[41] New impediments should only be substituted with the agreement of the person applying for modification. However if agreement is not forthcoming the Tribunal has the power to refuse the application.[42]

There must be clear and justifiable reasons for requesting that a covenant be modified or extinguished. The fact that an applicant simply wishes for greater flexibility in the use of the land will not be sufficient grounds for modification or extinguishment. The policy of the Lands Tribunal is not to give applicants a 'blank cheque'. Rather the applicant must make a specific proposal that allows both the person entitled to the benefit of the covenant and the Tribunal to assess the merits of the application.[43]

---

40 The decision of the Lands Tribunal in *Danesfort* (n 5) suggests that the discretion available under the legislation is wider than that granted under the equivalent provisions in England and Wales.
41 Property 1978 (n 1) article 6(2)(a)
42 Ibid article 7
43 *McNicholl* (n 6) [39]

Compensation may be awarded on modification or extinguishment as calculated under article 5(6). The Order recognises two situations in which compensation may be appropriate. Firstly, the loss of the benefit of the covenant may produce loss or disadvantage to the owner of the property. While the Order does not give guidance on what loss or disadvantage means in this context, it may include, for example, a possible loss of value of the property where the nature of the surrounding area is changed. Extinguishing a covenant preventing building on agricultural land in the countryside, for example, may well be detrimental to other land owners in the area where the nature of the area changes from rural to sub-urban.

The second situation is where the owner of a property that has been burdened by a covenant has suffered direct financial loss because the price obtainable for the property was reduced because of the burden of the covenant. In these circumstances the Tribunal may direct the applicant to pay an appropriate sum to the property owner to compensate for this loss.

Finally where the loss likely to be incurred in either of these circumstances will impact on the value of a property to such an extent that it will negatively affect the security provided for a mortgage, the Tribunal may order that such compensation be paid to the mortgagee to prevent loss.[44]

For these reasons it can be quite difficult to have a covenant lifted. There must be good reasons to demonstrate why the covenant will no longer benefit the land. As consideration of the enforceability of covenants has tended to focus on the benefit to the land itself (seen in the requirements that a covenant must touch and concern the land and not merely benefit the individual landowner) mere inconvenience or commercial limitation to the landowner will not be sufficient reason to have a covenant lifted.

While the Lands Tribunal has the power to extinguish or modify covenants, they may also be discharged or modified in the following situations:

A. Common ownership

If the benefited and burdened land falls into the same ownership then any covenants will become extinguished. This is straightforward, there is no longer any need for the covenant as it is no longer a matter of agreement between two parties. There is no longer an outside party against whom the landowner wishes to protect his/her interest.

---

44 Property 1978 (n 1) article 5(6)(b)

B. Agreement between parties

By release or modification by agreement of the parties. This can also be deemed to have happened in equity where there has been acquiescence in a serious breach of the terms of the covenant.

C. No ongoing benefit

If the covenant is obsolete, in that it is no longer benefiting the land, it may be set aside in equity.

10.8 Remedies for Breach of Covenant

Remedies include the standard equitable injunction or damages in lieu of an injunction. However it is important to note that as always these remedies are subject to discretion and are exercised in accordance with settled principles of equity.

10.9 Apartment Living and the Problem of Collective Responsibility

Although leasehold covenants are considered in more detail in chapter 8, the operation of leasehold covenants in situations such as apartment living is worth mentioning in this context. Although leasehold covenants are often understood to refer to obligations between and landlord and tenant in a short-term residential tenancy, the majority of urban property in Northern Ireland is owned under a long lease. Whilst these can no longer be created, they nevertheless remain common.[45] This means that the landlord/tenant relationship continues to apply and the rules on leasehold covenants will dictate whether a covenant will be enforceable between successors in title.

The question of leasehold covenants intersects with that of freehold covenants when it comes to the question of apartment living. The past 20 years have seen a significant increase in the number of apartments being built and sold in Northern Ireland. These apartments are transferred to private ownership, but remain reliant on common structures such as entrances and stairways. While a freehold covenant could

---

45 Property Order 1997 (n 2) article 30

be entered into between the developer and the initial purchaser, the rules on freehold covenants outlined in Section 10.4 demonstrate the practical difficulties entailed in ensuring that the covenants will remain enforceable between successors in title when apartments are sold on. Given the nature of apartment living, and the reliance of all owners on the maintenance of common areas, covenants play an extremely important role. Recognising the growing difficulties caused by the increase in apartment living in Northern Ireland, the Law Commission have embarked on a consultation on Apartment Living that seeks to explore the legal issues raised and recommend specific legislative reform in this area.[46] The spectacular decline in the property market in Northern Ireland has led to well-publicised problems for owners of apartments. The inability of home owners who have found themselves in the unfortunate position of living in an incomplete development highlights the importance of having clear laws on the responsibility of developers in these situations. It is necessary that the means by which obligations can be enforced be clear for vendors and purchasers alike. On a less drastic level, complaints about the difficulties of ensuring the proper management of common areas in apartment blocks have led to calls for law reform in the area.[47]

The most common and most convenient way of dealing with these types of developments has been to sell a leasehold rather than a freehold estate to such properties. This means that in law the landlord/tenant relationship is maintained, but in practice a lease of several hundred years will be demised, granting the equivalent in practice of freehold tenure. The popularity of the lease for this type of property is reflected in the fact that it is one of the exceptions to the rule that new long leases may no longer be created in Northern Ireland.[48]

The rules on the passing of leasehold covenants are simple compared to those which pertain in the case of freehold land, and for this reason leasehold has been an attractive option for landowners in situations where covenants need to be enforced between neighbours. The fact that the law regulating freehold covenants will not facilitate the enforcement of positive obligations against successors in title is irrelevant if flats are held under long lease. The lease has therefore long been accepted as a suitable framework for creating rights and obligations between parties.[49] As both positive and restrictive obligations will be enforceable where the land is held under a lease, this makes it easier

---

46 Northern Ireland Law Commission, *Apartments* (NI Law Com CP No 15, 2012)
47 Ibid 11.25-11.26
48 Property Order 1997 (n 2) article 30(5)(e)
49 NILC *Apartments* (n 46) 6.4

to ensure that covenants are respected. In addition selling property as a leasehold estate rather than a freehold is a convenient way of imposing identical obligations on owners and thereby controlling land through the imposition of covenants that can be enforced between parties.[50]

The key question for the Law Commission's consultation is how to balance the rights of individual ownership of an apartment with the collective responsibilities entailed in shared spaces.[51]

10.10 Proposals for Reform?

In England and Wales this anomaly in relation to people buying property on long leases has been addressed with the introduction of the concept of commonhold to try and bridge the gap between freehold and leasehold land.[52] The Commonhold and Leasehold Reform Act 2002 provides for a specific type of freehold that exists where a number of residential units share a common area and share facilities.

Using the example of an apartment block, with commonhold each flat can be sold as a freehold property rather than under a long lease, with the developer remaining as the land owner. This does not apply to short leases, but only where the purchaser is paying the full market value of the property. In addition to buying the freehold in their own individual apartment, the purchaser will also become a member of what is known as the commonhold association – a company limited by guarantee whose members are the owners of each individual apartment. The common areas of the building, for example staircases and lifts, will then be vested in this company. It will be for the Commonhold Association to determine the rights and responsibilities of each freeholder in the building. These will be contained in what is known as a Commonhold Community Statement (CCS) which freeholders will sign up to and which will then make the covenants contained in it enforceable against them. These obligations will also bind purchasers. In the case of positive covenants this runs directly counter to the established rules relating to freehold land and so it is expressly provided for by Section 16 of the Act. The CCS will typically address obligations such as insurance, repairs and maintenance – ones which are of central importance to the concept of commonhold, and are provided for by the Act itself.

---

50 Ibid Ch 6
51 Ibid 11.1
52 Commonhold and Leasehold Reform Act 2002

Details of the operation of commonhold are not of specific relevance to the law in Northern Ireland. The 2002 Act provides detailed guidance on how a commonhold will come into being, including the requirement that all units within the development be held on common hold and that reciprocal obligations are undertaken by each apartment owner.

While it had been thought that commonhold should be introduced in Northern Ireland,[53] the most recent statement from the Law Commission suggests that this is no longer likely. Indeed the extent of the embeddedness of leasehold tenure in the law in Northern Ireland, and the ability of conveyancers to work with this system to ensure the enforceability of obligations means that there is little to be gained by introducing a new form of title for apartments. This is particularly the case when the leasehold rules are working effectively. Where problems arise it is with the ongoing management of the common areas. The proposal is therefore to address this through reforming company law to provide an appropriate mechanism for the enforcement of the obligations of companies responsible for the management of apartment buildings.

In this regard we see an appropriately contextualised approach from the Law Commission that recognises that land law in Northern Ireland responds to its social context.

---

53 NILC *Apartments* (n 46) 11.7

CHAPTER 11

Incorporeal Hereditaments

11.1 Introduction

It is a feature of land law that at any one time there may be a number of different interests in that land. These might include interests in land that fall short of ownership of the land but nevertheless give the person with the interest a right over that land. These interests are known as 'incorporeal hereditaments' and fall within the scope of the law of real property. 'Incorporeal' refers to the fact that there is no physical form to these interests, they simply exist as abstract rights. Where such rights exist they are proprietary in nature. This means that they will attach to the land and will be enforceable against third parties. One of the most common examples of an incorporeal hereditament is the right of way. Its effect is to allow the beneficiary of the right to cross a piece of land that belongs to another person. It does not matter who owns the land in question. If it can be established that a right of way exists then it will continue to bind whoever owns the land.

There are four main categories of incorporeal hereditaments:

- Easements
- Profits à prendre
- Periodic rents and annuities
- Rent charges

This chapter will concentrate on the first two of these categories.

11.2 The Definition of an Easement

Easements do not amount to ownership of the land, they do not grant exclusive control or possession of the land, but rather the holder of an easement has ownership of the right to do the prescribed action over the land of another for the benefit of his/her own land. Broadly speaking, an easement can be either positive, in that it allows a third party act on the land of another for the benefit of their own land, or negative, in that it restricts a landowner from acting on his/her own property in a certain manner so as to protect another property. The question of what constitutes an easement has traditionally been decided by the courts, and there is flexibility of approach to recognise changing contexts.[1] However the courts have shown themselves to be reluctant to recognise new types of easements. This is because an easement is a proprietary right that will burden the land. They should not therefore be created too easily where a contractual right or a permission would suffice.[2] A number of different types of easements are recognised by the law, but some are more common than others. For example, rights of way that allow access to one property across another is a commonly recognised form of easement. Similarly easements allowing drainage or water supply across a neighbouring property are also common. An easement also exists in relation to the support provided by one terraced or semi-detached house to another. The owners of both houses will enjoy a legally recognised and enforceable easement in respect of that support meaning that one neighbour cannot remove a supporting wall between the properties.

Easements should also be distinguished from other types of rights that are often mistaken for easements. These include licences, which may allow use of one person's land by another but do not create a legal interest in that land;[3] freehold covenants, that impose restrictions on the use of property, but are created in a different manner than easements;[4] and public rights of way that are exercisable by the public in general rather than between private parties.[5] These rights may appear similar to easements in their operation, but they are fundamentally different interests and care should be taken to distinguish them.

The question of the nature and creation of easements is not one that has featured heavily in Northern Ireland case law. Therefore the key principles relied upon in

---

1 Northern Ireland Law Commission, *Land Law* (NI Law Com No 8, 2010) para 4.39
2 See M Haley & L McMurty, 'Identifying an Easement: Exclusive Use, *De Facto* Control and Judicial Constraints' (2007) 58 NILQ 490
3 See chapter 9
4 See chapter 10
5 These rights of way are governed by the Access to the Countryside (Northern Ireland) Order 1983

Northern Ireland law remain those that have evolved in the English courts. There are, of course, examples of where these principles have been applied in Northern Ireland, and these are highlighted where appropriate.

The test for the existence of an easement was laid down by the Court of Appeal in *Re Ellenborough Park*.[6] The Court in this case outlined four essential characteristics of an easement. These are that there must be two separate pieces of land, known as the dominant and servient tenements; an easement must accommodate or benefit the dominant tenement; the dominant and servient owners must be different persons; and the right claimed must be capable of forming the subject-matter of a grant. Taking each of these conditions in turn, if an easement is to exist:

A. There must be both a dominant and a servient tenement

An easement is a property right attached to land. Therefore the person acquiring an easement does not acquire it personally but acquires it for the benefit of the land. For this reason incorporeal hereditaments are known as 'appurtenant' rights, in that they appertain to the land. The easement must benefit one piece of land, known as the dominant tenement, and act as a burden on another piece of land, known as the servient tenement. The dominant tenement need not be adjacent or attached to the servient tenement. Both tenements simply need to be sufficiently near each other to allow the exercise of a right over one that accommodates the other.[7]

The effect of this rule is that an easement cannot exist independently of the land. It is "an essential element of any easement that it is annexed to land and that no person can possess an easement otherwise than in respect of and in amplification of his enjoyment of some estate or interest in a piece of land".[8]

This requirement of a dominant and a servient tenement also highlights the fact that an easement cannot exist 'in gross' – that is to say that it cannot exist simply for the benefit of an individual. This is because the easement will constitute a burden on the servient land that will bind subsequent purchasers. There must therefore be a very clear rationale for the existence of the right. The existence of the land benefited by the easement underpins and justifies the conferral of property status.

---

6   *Re Ellenborough Park* [1955] EWCA Civ 4, [1956] Ch 131 (CA) 140 (Evershed MR)
7   *Pugh v Savage* [1970] EWCA Civ 9, [1970] 2 QB 373 (CA), 381 (Cross LJ)
8   *Alfred F Beckett Ltd v Lyons* [1967] Ch 449 (CA), 483 (Winn LJ)

B. Accommodation of the dominant tenement

The benefit of an easement must 'accommodate and serve' the dominant land. This requirement ensures that there is some nexus between the land and the right attached to it. However this requirement relates more accurately to the enjoyment of the land and as such the easement must be reasonably necessary for the better enjoyment of the dominant land. This was seen in *Re Ellenborough Park*[9] where the Court held that the right to enjoyment of the park was similar to the right to use a garden for normal domestic purposes. Although the use of the park did not have any *necessary* connection to the enjoyment of the properties it did enhance their enjoyment and could therefore be considered an easement. What is important is the extent to which the right enhances the property and benefits the owner in his/her capacity as owner of the property rather than simply as an individual.

The requirement that the benefit to the dominant land be clearly identifiable is demonstrated in the approach taken by the courts to interpreting the extent of the right created by an easement.

In the case of *Peacock and Another v Custins and Another*,[10] the defendants acquired title to a house and a strip of land (the servient tenement). The land was subject to a right of way to land which benefited property adjoining the rear of the premises which had been acquired by the claimants in 1976 (the dominant tenement). The benefit of the right of way existed "for all purposes in connection with the use and enjoyment of the property hereby conveyed". The dominant land was clearly marked on the plan annexed to the conveyance. However the claimants sought to establish that the right could be exercised to benefit a separate but adjoining piece of land also owned by them. The defendants replied that use of the right of way to access land other than the dominant property constituted trespass.

The court was asked to consider the following point of law: where the owner of a dominant tenement possesses a right of way for 'all purposes' over a servient tenement, may he make use of that right of way to access and cultivate (in conjunction with the dominant tenement) other property which lies adjacent to the dominant tenement? The court held that the scope of a right of way is determined by the terms of the grant specifying the dominant tenement, for the purposes of which the right is created. Use that falls outside the terms of the grant will constitute trespass. In such cases the court has the power to determine the scope of the grant. In this case the grantor had not

---

9   *Re Ellenborough* (n 6)
10   *Peacock and Another v Custins and Another* [2002] 1 WLR 1815 (CA), [2001] 2 All ER 827

authorised the use of the right of way for the purpose of cultivating the adjacent land, nor could it be said that cultivation of this land was merely ancillary or incidental to the use of the dominant land. Therefore use of the right of way to cultivate land other than that specified in the grant was not permitted and constituted trespass. What is clear from this case is that the easement exists to accommodate a specific piece of land. It is not simply a broad and generally exercisable right of the landowner.

The purpose for which the easement was granted will also be relevant. The existence of an easement does not guarantee that it can be used for purposes other than that intended at the time of the grant. This was demonstrated in the recent Northern Ireland case of *Hearty v Finnegan and Finnegan*.[11] In this case the plaintiff enjoyed a right of way, acquired by prescription,[12] for agricultural purposes. He applied to the court for a declaration that this should be recognised as a right to way for 'all purposes' to allow him to develop the site. The court considered the question of whether the proposed change of use of the land would constitute a 'radical change' to the use of the easement, or would simply represent an intensification of its existing use. In circumstances where radical change of the use is such that it would not have been in the contemplation of the parties at the time the easement arose, then it will not be recognised. However, if the new use simply represents an intensification of the use of the easement that has been created then this will be permitted. In this case what was proposed was changing the use of land from agricultural use, including grazing, to development of residential property. The court was asked to determine whether the extent of the increase and alteration of the use of the land would impose a significant additional burden on the servient land. The court held that it would, and therefore rejected the application for the easement to be recognised as existing for 'all purposes'.

This highlights the importance that the burden of the easement be clearly defined.[13] Accommodation of the dominant land is not a licence to claim rights additional to those intended at the time of creation of the easement. Accommodation of the dominant land may also include business interests. For example, in the case of *Moody v Steggles* it was held that the erection of an advertising sign on a neighbouring property could constitute an easement.[14] However it will need to be demonstrated that the right claimed benefits the business carried on from the property and not simply the individual. For

---

11 [2009] NIQB 21
12 See section 11.3.D
13 See also *Karl Armstrong and Margaret Elaine Armstrong v Phelim Bernard Shields and Rosaleen Shields* [2010] NICh 10
14 *Moody v Steggles* [1874-80] All ER Rep Ext 1512 (Ch) 1512 (Fry J)

example, in *Hill v Tupper*[15] the plaintiff was granted the sole and exclusive right to put pleasure boats on a canal. When someone else tried to run pleasure boats, the plaintiff, a leaseholder beside the canal claimed an easement and sought to remove the newcomer. The court held that this was just a personal right not related to use of land and therefore did not accommodate the dominant tenement. Whether the right claimed is reasonably necessary for the better enjoyment of the dominant tenement or whether the right claimed is too tenuous to amount to an easement can be subject to dispute.

C. Ownership or occupation of the dominant and servient tenements must be by different persons

This requirement prevents a person having an easement over his/her own land. It is logical that the owner of the dominant and servient tenement must be different people – you don't need rights in the nature of easements over land that you already own. What is important is that the estate in possession belongs to different people. It is therefore possible for a tenant to establish an easement in respect of land that belongs to a landlord but is subject to a lease. This is particularly true in Northern Ireland where leasehold was a common form of landholding. To exclude leasehold relationships from this criterion would have had an extremely restrictive effect on the application of the law of easements in this jurisdiction.[16]

D. Any right claimed must be capable of forming the subject matter of a grant

The fourth of the *Ellenborough Park* requirements is that the right must be capable of forming the subject matter of a grant. That is, it must be capable of being created by deed. The general rule is that all easements lie in grant. The legal presumption is that all easements have at some point been created by a deed, even if it is not possible to prove this.[17] For this reason any easement must comply with the rules of grants:

    i.   There must be a capable grantor and grantee. In the first instance this means that the person purporting to make the grant has a legal estate in possession from which they can create the grant. As a general rule an easement cannot

15 *Hill v Tupper* (1863) 2 H&C 121, 159 ER 51
16 See JCW Wylie, 'The 'Irishness' of Irish Land Law' (1995) 46 NILQ 332
17 See section 11.3.C

exceed the existing property right.[18] For example, if the grantor owns only an equitable estate then the easement will also be equitable.

ii. It must belong to a category of property rights that are regarded as capable of grant.

In order to determine whether a right falls within a category of rights capable of forming the subject of a grant, the court has established criteria by which the validity of grants can be assessed. These are:

i. Is the right conferred too wide or too vague?

ii. Is the right conferred inconsistent with the proprietorship or possession of the alleged servient owners?

iii. Is it a mere recreational right with no utility or benefit?

i. Is the right conferred too wide or too vague?

A right cannot be recognised as an easement if it is excessively wide or vague. The right must therefore be expressed (or be capable of being expressed) in a definite manner. In basic terms, it should be specific. The easement must be able to be clearly defined. This is usually interpreted as requiring that not only the benefit but also the means by which it is to be received must be identifiable. For example, a right of drainage would fall within the scope of this definition, but a right to a TV signal would not.[19]

The categories are not closed and within these categories there is room for variation. Generally however the courts will be sceptical of novel rights and will insist that they are specific and definable. Problems therefore arise with matters of taste, for example in *William Aldred's Case*[20] the right to a 'fair prospect' (good view) was too vague to be recorded in a deed with any degree of certainty. This therefore cannot be an easement. In *Webb v Bird* it was held that there can be no easement to the general flow of air over land in order to turn a windmill for the same reason.[21]

It is also unlikely that the courts will recognise rights that require expenditure on the part of the owner of the servient tenement. Easements will generally be negative in operation in that they will simply require an act of sufferance from the landowner. They

---

18 *Wall v Collins* [2007] EWCA Civ 444 [34]-[38] (Carnwath LJ)
19 *Hunter and Others v Canary Wharf Ltd* [1997] AC 665 (CA), 701-709 (Lord Hoffmann)
20 *William Aldred's Case* [1610] 9 Co Rep 57b, [1558-1774] All ER Rep 622, 623-624
21 *Webb v Bird* (1863) 13 CB (NS) 841, 843; 143 ER 332, 333 (Wightman J)

cannot be held to impose positive obligations on the owner of the servient tenement.[22] For example, in respect of an easement of support for a house the owner of the servient tenement is under no duty to keep the supporting building in good repair but merely to refrain from actually removing or damaging it.[23]

It is also unlikely that an easement will exist where the interest prevents the owner of the servient tenement from doing something on his/her own land. The main exceptions are rights of support, which prevent the servient owner from removing a supporting wall, and a right to light insofar as it will prevent building.

ii. Is the right conferred inconsistent with the proprietorship or possession of the alleged servient owners?

As a general proposition, a right is not an easement if it conflicts with the proprietorship or possession of the servient tenement or if it results in the exclusion of the servient owner or occupier. While the owner of the dominant tenement enjoys a right over the servient tenement this right cannot amount to an excessive infringement on the proprietary rights of the servient owner. In particular it is important to note that no right will be recognised as an easement where the effect of such a right would be to give joint or exclusive use of the land.[24] The principal test that the alleged easement cannot overly infringe on the servient owner's property rights is set out in *Copeland v Greenhalf.*[25] In this case it was claimed that a right of way included the right to leave vehicles parked in the land. When the plaintiff sought to prevent this activity the defendant claimed he had an easement that permitted him to use the lane in this way. The court held the right claimed was too extensive to be defined as an easement. This was outside the normal idea of an easement as it involved the exclusive use and enjoyment (possession) of the strip of land and was therefore not capable of constituting an easement.

Upjohn J held:

> "It is virtually a claim to possession of the servient tenement, if necessary to the exclusion of the owner, or at any rate, to a joint user, and no authority has been cited to me which would justify that a right of this wide and undefined nature can be the proper subject-matter of an easement."[26]

---

22 *Liverpool City Council v Irwin and Another* [1977] AC 239 (HL) 256 (Lord Wilberforce)
23 *Phipps v Pears* [1964] EWCA Civ 3, [1965] 1 QB 76 (CA) 81-84 (Lord Denning MR)
24 For detailed discussion of this requirement see Haley & McMurty (n 2)
25 *Copeland v Greenhalf* [1952] Ch 488, 498 (Upjohn J)
26 Ibid 498

However exclusive possession is a matter of degree. In *Wright v Macadam* the right to store coal in a shed was considered to be an easement.[27] Similarly, depending on the extent of the claim, the right to park cars on the land of a neighbour may or may not be classified as an easement.[28] In the more recent case of *Moncreiff v Jamieson* the House of Lords held that the right to park can, in some circumstances, constitute an easement.[29] However, this will depend on the particular context of the land. In *Batchelor v Marlow*[30] it was ruled that the exclusive right to park six cars on a strip of land between the hours of 8.30am to 6.30pm from Monday to Friday was too extensive. Conversely, in *Hair v Gillman* the right to park a car on a forecourt that could accommodate four cars was capable of being an easement provided that it did not relate to any one specific space.[31]

Therefore it can be seen that there is ambiguity as to what may or may not constitute an easement. The court will exercise its discretion when deciding on the fourth of the *Re Ellenborough* criteria.

iii. Is it a mere recreational right with no utility or benefit?

An easement must be a right of benefit and utility and not one of recreation and amusement. As outlined, it must enhance the enjoyment of the property and not simply provide a benefit to the owner. This mirrors the requirement that the easement must accommodate the dominant land.

Having established the types of rights that may be recognised as forming an easement, it is now necessary to turn to the manner in which easements are created.

11.3 The Creation of Easements

If an easement is being claimed over someone else's property, it is not enough to show that the right asserted satisfies the characteristics of an easement. It must also be shown that the claimant acquired this right in some recognised way. An easement may be created in five ways:

---

27 *Wright v Macadam* [1949] 2 KB 744 (CA) 752; [1949] 2 All ER 565, 561 (Jenkins LJ)
28 *Moncreiff v Jamieson* [2007] UKHL 42 [26]
29 Ibid
30 *Batchelor v Marlow* [2001] EWCA Civ 1051
31 *Hair v Gillman* (2000) 80 P & CR 108 (CA) 116 (Chadwick LJ)

A. By statute

Rights are created by statute, for example, to enable companies and public authorities to run pylons or pipes through land, as easements. Statutes concerning the provision of gas, water, electricity and other services will typically allow for the creation of easements over land in favour of the service provider. The procedure for acquisition is set out in the statute.[32]

It is a basic principle that apart from easements created by statute, easements may be created only by way of a grant. Such a grant may be express, implied, or presumed.

B. By Deed

i. Express grant

An express grant will be made by the owner of the servient tenement. It can be granted either to the existing owner of a neighbouring property, provided that this grant is executed by deed, or granted to a purchaser on sale of the land. The grant will operate for the benefit of the land sold. In the case of grant as part of a sale the easement will be created by the execution of the deed of conveyance.

It is advisable to identify the dominant tenement expressly at the time of transfer, although in the absence of express identification the court will examine all the relevant circumstances to identify the dominant tenement.[33]

ii. Express reservation

Alternatively, an owner who is selling only part of his/her land may wish to retain, for the benefit of the part he/she keeps, an easement over the part he/she sells. This will be an express reservation. Any reservation must be clearly and unequivocally expressed in the terms of the deed. This includes specifying the extent of the easement and specifying the dominant tenement within the deed.[34] If the easement is not clearly defined it will be more difficult to assert rights under an easement by reservation.

Where a legal easement is created by deed the appropriate words of limitation must be used to specify the extent of the easement. In Northern Ireland this means that legal

---

32 See eg The Electricity (Northern Ireland) Order (1992)
33 *Johnstone v Holdway* [1963] 1 QB 601 (CA) 611-612 (Upjohn LJ)
34 *Armstrong* (n 13)

easements can be created in fee simple or for life, or on a long lease, as all of these estates remain part of the law. In England and Wales a legal easement can only be created in fee simple or for a term of years and not, for example, for life.[35]

In Northern Ireland a grant that does not meet the relevant criteria can still be regarded as an equitable easement if it was given for value and evidenced in writing or supported by part performance, thus constituting a specifically enforceable agreement. Equity will then treat the informal arrangement as a specifically enforceable agreement, and the other party will be estopped from denying the grant of the easement.[36]

Where an easement is created either by express grant or by express reservation the interest should be registered to ensure it will continue to burden the land. If the land is registered then the easement should be registered against the title to the property.[37] If the land is unregistered then the easement should be registered as a burden in the Registry of Deeds.[38] This will ensure that any subsequent purchaser of the property will have notice of the easement and will be bound by it.

C. By Implication

In some situations the courts can imply the creation of an easement notwithstanding the absence of any express grant by the parties. Where it is allowed, the law will imply that an easement has been granted to the alleged dominant owner. This is known as an implied grant. In these cases implication is based on what is perceived to be the intention of the parties. They are not granted expressly but are implied by the courts in situations where an individual sells or leases part of his/her land. Therefore if evidence can be shown that the parties didn't intend for any easement to arise from their conduct or the circumstances of the case, this will usually rebut an inference on the part of the courts. However where easements are created by implication they will be legal easements. This is because the court implies that a grant must have been made.

As with implied grants, the court, in certain circumstances, has the power to imply that an easement has been reserved over the servient tenement. This is known as an implied reservation. The principles are the same as for implied grant, but the test will be stricter for an implied reservation. This is because in the case of implied reservation the seller is not undertaking to burden his/her own land, but rather is seeking to impose the

---

35 Land Registration Act 2002 ss 27(2)(d). In the register of title of the servient land and (only if also registered land) the register relating to the dominant land (schedule 2, para 7).
36 *McManus v Cooke* (1887) 35 Ch D 681, 697 (Kay J)
37 Land Registration Act (NI) 1970 section 39(1), schedule 6 Part 1
38 Registration of Deeds Act (NI) 1970

burden on the purchaser who may not have agreed to it. This also reflects the principle that a seller cannot derogate from his/her grant. This means that a seller will not be allowed to grant land and then subsequently go back on his/her word by claiming rights for him/herself in the land. If an easement is to be reserved it should be done expressly at the time of the sale of the property and with the consent of both parties.

There are four main ways in which easements may arise by implication. They are:

- Easements of Necessity
- Easements by common intention
- The rule in *Wheeldon v Burrows*[39]
- Section 6, Conveyancing Act 1881

i. Necessity

Where land is conveyed in circumstances that render it impossible for the land to be enjoyed without an easement, an easement may be implied into the grant of transfer as an easement of necessity. This usually arises where a right of way is necessary to gain access to a property. What is important is that the easement is absolutely necessary for the use of the property. It will not be enough to argue that the easement sought simply provides a more convenient route of access to the property. It must be the only route of access.[40] In these circumstances the courts will infer that because the easement is necessary for the enjoyment of the property that the parties must have intended to create such an easement. No easement of necessity will arise if the parties expressly exclude the implication of such an easement in terms of the deed.

A clear distinction should be drawn between implied grants and implied reservations. If the owner of a dominant tenement seeks to establish the existence of an implied reservation, it must be clear that the retained land would be unusable without the easement. The courts will interpret these criteria more strictly in the case of implied reservation than in the case of implied grant. This is because if an easement is necessary for the use of retained land then it should be expressly created by deed. The court will therefore lean against the seller in these circumstances.

ii. Common intention

Necessity may simply be considered to be part of the wider concept of common intention.

39 (1879) 12 Ch D 31 (CA) 49 (Thesiger LJ)
40 *Manjang v Drammeh* (1990) 61 P & CR 194

Where the parties can demonstrate shared intention as to the use of the land, then an easement may be implied. For example, in *Stafford v Lee*[41] an area of woodland was sold. The only access to this woodland was via a private road but no express right of way was granted. Thirty-four years later Stafford wished to build a house in the woodland. To do so he needed access for construction vehicles. Lee claimed that there was no right of way and denied him access. The court outlined two criteria that needed to be established. The first was that it must be possible to demonstrate a common intention between the parties as to the intended use of the land. Second, the easement must be necessary to give effect to this common intention. In the case in question the deed itself and a plan of the land that was included in the conveyance, together with surrounding facts, allowed the court to decide that the land had been sold for the purposes of housing development. Therefore a right of way for relevant machinery was both intended and necessary.

Similarly in the case of *Wong v Beaumont Property Trust Ltd* Mr Wong took a lease of cellars for the purposes of opening a Chinese restaurant.[42] As a condition of the lease he undertook to eliminate smell and to comply with all relevant health regulations. There was however no ventilation in the property. To install the necessary ventilation an easement was required over the property of the landlord. Lord Denning held that an easement of ventilation could be implied because the purpose for which the property was leased was sufficiently definite. If an easement were denied Mr Wong would be denied proper enjoyment of the property under the lease. Therefore an easement by common intention could be implied. This was despite the fact that neither party knew that the easement would be necessary at the time the lease was granted.

These cases demonstrate that the doctrine of 'implied common intention' is broader than that of necessity. However this option is possible, but not always permissible.

iii. The Rule in Wheeldon v Burrows[43]

The rule in *Wheeldon v Burrows* arises where a landowner sub-divides land, selling one portion and retaining another. In these circumstances, if the landowner has been accustomed to crossing one part of the land to reach the other, this may give rise to what is known as a quasi-easement. Quasi-easements are rights that satisfy some of the requirements of easements in that they benefit the quasi-dominant land and are capable of being the subject matter of a grant, but they are not full easements as the

---

41 *Stafford v Lee* [1992] EWCA Civ 17, (1993) 65 P & CR 172
42 *Wong v Beaumont Property Trust Ltd* [1964] EWCA Civ 4, [1965] 1 QB 173
43 *Wheeldon v Burrows* (1878) 12 Ch D 31

dominant and servient tenements are owned and occupied by the same person. Where the landowner disposes of the land that has benefited from the quasi-easement the right will be elevated to the status of easement and will become a burden on the servient land. The servient land in these cases is the land that has been retained.[44]

For example, John owns two adjoining pieces of land, Green Farm and Yellow Meadow. His house is located on Green Farm. He regularly walks from his house across Yellow Meadow, which is the quickest way to access the road. John's right to walk across Yellow Meadow is not an easement as he owns and occupies both pieces of land. But, John's right of way is a quasi-easement in that it is a right which benefits him in his use of Green Farm as a residence, and a right of way is well established as a right which is capable of being the subject matter of a grant. If John sold Green Farm to Simon and retained Yellow Meadow for himself, Simon may be able to use the rule in *Wheeldon v Burrows* to claim a right of way leading from his house, over Yellow Meadow, to the road.

There are three elements that must be satisfied for the rule in *Wheeldon v Burrows* to operate:

- The right claimed must be continuous and apparent
- It must be reasonably necessary for the enjoyment of the land granted
- It must have been used at the time of the grant for the benefit of the land granted

It is important to note the rule applies only to implied grants of easements, and not to reservations. *Wheeldon v Burrows* itself concerned an implied reservation of light. *Burrows* therefore did not succeed. This rule will also apply where both the dominant and the servient land are transferred to different owners.[45] The words continuous and apparent indicate the need for some feature on the servient tenement which can be seen on inspection and which is neither transitory nor intermittent eg drains or paths.[46] The absence of such a feature resulted in failure to establish an easement on this ground.

It has now been proposed that the rule in *Wheeldon v Burrows* should be replaced in Northern Ireland with a statutory scheme that regulates the rights and obligations that accrue when land is divided. Section 17 of the draft Land Law Reform Bill provides a clear statutory footing for the operation of this rule. This makes slight amendment to the criteria in *Weeldon v Burrows* in that it requires the continuation of:

> "all facilities which were previously available to the disposing title holder … and were actually enjoyed … immediately before the agreement to dispose or disposal

---

44   *Close v Cairns* (NICh, 23 April 1997)
45   Ibid
46   *Ward v Kirkland* [1967] Ch 194, 225 (Ungoed-Thomas J)

… as regularly as their nature permitted and which in all the circumstances it is reasonable should continue to be available…"

iv. Due to the operation of Section 6 of the Conveyancing Act 1881[47]

Section 6 removes the need to expressly transfer pre-existing easements over property when that property itself is being transferred. Where there is a pre-existing easement over the land at the time that it is conveyed then the easement will be conveyed with the land by the power of the statute and without the need for any express words to that effect. The benefit of an existing easement will pass automatically on the conveyance of the dominant tenement without any need to mention it expressly in the deed of conveyance.

Section 6(1) of the Conveyancing Act 1881 provides:

> "A conveyance of land shall be deemed to include and shall by virtue of this Act operate to convey, with the land, all … liberties, privileges, *easements*, rights and advantages whatsoever, appertaining or reputed to appertain to the land, or any part thereof, or at the time of the conveyance demised, occupied or enjoyed with, or reputed or known as part or parcel of or appurtenant to the land or any part thereof".

The effect of Section 6 of the Conveyancing Act 1881 can be excluded by evidence of contrary intention,[48] and indeed it is good conveyancing practice to expressly exclude its operation in any deed of transfer. Section 6 applies only where there the dominant and servient tenements are in different ownership or occupation before the conveyance in question unlike the rule in *Wheeldon v Burrows* which applies where both tenements were in common ownership prior to transfer.

The effect of Section 6 may also be to create new easements. To operate in this way there must have been diversity of ownership or occupation before the conveyance. In other words, the land in issue must be in the freehold or leasehold ownership of different owners. The grantor must have had power to create the easement, and the right must be, in its nature, capable of existing as an easement. A permissive right that an occupier is enjoying by licence pending completion can thus be elevated to an easement.

The objective of this provision was to imply these words into all conveyances thereby removing the need for conveyancers to draft long detailed clauses, for example listing all of the specific easements that are being transferred with a piece of land. However, in certain circumstances Section 6 has the effect of creating new easements. This is the

---

47 Equivalent to the Law of Property Act 1925 section 62 in England and Wales
48 section 6(4)

case where rights that fell short of being easements are elevated on conveyance of the property. For example, if a licence is granted to allow someone to use land and the land is subsequently sold, the effect of Section 6 can be to upgrade that licence into an easement, notwithstanding the intention of the grantor of the licence or the purchaser of the property.

The operation of Section 6 can therefore be regarded as controversial in so far as it has the potential to create legal rights contrary to the intentions of the parties. The Northern Ireland Law Commission has therefore recommended that Section 6 be replaced with a provision that ensures that only existing rights will pass on conveyance and that new rights should not be created by operation of this statute. Section 95(3) of the draft Land Law Reform Bill clarifies that only existing rights will pass with a conveyance.

D. By Prescription

Where there is a long enjoyment of a right that is capable of forming an easement, then an irrebuttable presumption arises as to its legality. The method of acquiring an easement by long use is known as prescription and arises where the law presumes that an easement was granted because of the continuous long use by the prescriptive user. The principle is that long use of land may eventually mature into an easement. However the use of the land must be 'as of right'. This means that the person seeking to establish that an easement has arisen by way of prescription must be able to demonstrate that they used the land as if they were entitled to do so. It will be for the person asserting the right to prove, on the balance of probabilities, that it has been established.[49] The effect of this will be that the court will indulge the legal fiction that long use indicates that a grant was actually made. Easements arising by prescription will be *legal* easements.

As outlined, a key principle on the creation of easements is that they must arise in a grant. In the case of prescription, there is no grant – its existence is implied by law. The rules are judge-made, but have been modified by statute.

There are four general requirements of prescription. The use of the land must be:

- open and notorious (discoverable upon inspection)
- adverse (without the owner of the servient land's permission)
- continuous and uninterrupted[50]
- for the statutory period

---

49 *Seamus McFerran and Dermot McFerran v Patrick McFerran and the Trustee of the Property of Patrick McFerran (a bankrupt)* [2005] NICty 2 (Smyth J)
50 Prescription Act 1832 (2 & 3 Will 4 c 71) section 2

Enjoyment or use of an easement as of right therefore requires that the use should have been *nec vi, nec clam* and *nec precario* –without force, without secrecy and without permission. There has been significant emphasis placed on the requirement that the use of the land be 'as of right' – meaning without permission.[51]

In drawing the distinction between permission and acquiescence the court has given useful guidance on all three requirements for use 'as of right'.

The case of *Dalton v Angus* has been interpreted as providing 5 key indicators that use of land was 'as of right – namely that it was without express permission. Where there is doubt the court will seek to establish (i) is there a use of the servient owner's land? If so (ii) is there an absence of a strict right to carry on that use? If so (iii) does the servient owner have knowledge (actual or constructive) of the use? If so (iv) Does the servient owner have the ability to stop the use (practically or legally)? If so (v) has the servient owner abstained from stopping the use for the period required for a successful prescriptive claim?[52]

This interpretation of the judgment in Dalton provides a useful framework for thinking about the meaning of permission in the context of prescription.

Where these criteria are met then it will be established that the use of the land was as 'of right'. For a claim of prescription to be successful the claimant must be able to demonstrate 20 years continuous use. If the use of the land over the period preceding the claim has been intermittent, or falling short of what would ordinarily be understood as 'continuous' then it will not give rise to an easement.[53]

However, if it can be demonstrated that there has been 20 years continuous use 'as of right' then an easement may be held to arise by prescription. There are currently three ways in which this will be achieved.[54]

i. Prescription at common law

If it can be demonstrated that the right claimed has been exercised since time immemorial then the courts will presume that an easement exists. The beginning of time was arbitrarily fixed by the Statute of Westminster at 1189.[55] However, it is not necessary

---

51 *McFerran* (n 49)
52 See Martin Dixon, *Modern Land Law* (7th edn) Routledge, 2010, 301, citing *Charles Dalton v Henry Angus & Co* (1881) 6 App Cas 740 (HL)
53 *McLean v McAuley* (NICC, 2 January 2006) [24] (Smyth J)
54 For a detailed discussion see Law Commission, *Easements, Covenants and Profits Á Prendre* (Law Com CP No 186, 2008)
55 Statute of Westminster 1275 (3 Edw 1 c 5)

to actually prove that the easement has been in existence since 1189, the courts will be prepared to presume this to be true if 20 years of use can be demonstrated. However, if it can be proved that the easement has not been in existence since 1189, an easy matter for example in the case of a building that was only constructed in the last 100 years, then such a claim will fail.

ii. Doctrine of lost modern grant

In order to get around this the courts have been prepared to indulge in a fiction that where user as of right has been demonstrated for 20 years an easement must have been granted but the deed has been lost. Since this is a fiction, evidence that no such grant was ever made is irrelevant. Such a claim can only be thwarted if it can be shown that such a grant was impossible. In this respect the courts are not prepared to presume that a landlord would grant an easement to a tenant and they insist that there must have been a capable grantor and grantee, thus if a company owned the land but did not have the capacity to grant easements no easement could be granted.

iii. Statute – Prescription Act 1832

The 1832 Act created two different time periods, a shorter period of 20 years and a longer period of 40 years. The difference between the two is not exactly clear. However, 20 years' continuous use will only give rise to a rebuttable presumption that an easement exists. As with the other forms of prescription, user must be as of right so – the existence of oral permission will defeat the claim. However, the longer period once complete is absolute and indefeasible unless written permission has been given.

Shorter period

In relation to the shorter period, the Act provides that an easement enjoyed as of right and without interruption for a period of 20 years prior to the date an action is brought will raise the presumption that an easement was granted. Establishing use as of right for the shorter period of 20 years defeats only claims that the right could/did not exist prior to the commencement of the period. Such a claim can, however, be defeated by:

- showing some 'interruption'
- showing that the right claimed as an easement would not qualify under the 'Re Ellenborough' test

- showing that it was objected to by the owner of the land claimed to be the servient tenement, or that it was a secret

or

- that it was only exercised by mere permission/licence of the said owner consent, written or oral, is fatal since it means that the user is permissive

It should be noted that it is *not* possible to acquire an easement by prescription for the benefit of an interest for a term of years (or lesser interest). Although the use of the right may be *on behalf* of the owner of the fee simple, for example by its tenant, if established, it is for the benefit of the dominant fee simple against a servient fee simple.

Longer period

In relation to the longer period, the same user without interruption for a period of 40 years before an action is brought makes the title to an easement or a profit 'absolute and indefeasible' unless it has been enjoyed by *written* consent. With the 40 year period it appears that use itself is determinative and that the existence of the easement cannot be rebutted if 40 years use can be established.

iv. Easement of light

Because the right to light was the hardest right to establish at common law, the 1832 Act made special provision for rights of light. Under Section 3 a period of 20 years use without interruption is absolute and indefeasible unless enjoyed by consent in writing.

Thus under the 1832 Act it is easier to acquire an easement of light than any other easement as it requires only 20 years enjoyment as opposed to 40 years for all other easements. Also an easement of light acquired in this way does not need to be acquired as of right (without force secrecy or permission) of these, only written consent will defeat a claim. Deductions are not made in relation to the prescription period for light unlike other easements.[56]

Perhaps unsurprisingly, the law on prescription is regarded as being long overdue for change. The Law Commission has proposed that the law should be significantly simplified in this area. A new statutory scheme to replace the existing provisions of the 1832 Act has been proposed. While retaining the statutory prescription period of

---

56 An interesting example of the importance attached to easements of light was the Rights of Light Act (NI) 1961 which guaranteed easements of light to owners of bomb damaged property to register burdens that would prevent light being blocked.

20 years, the Commission propose criteria for prescription that largely simplify the existing law, including clarifying the requirement that the right claimed should be capable of forming an easement and the requirement that it be enjoyed openly and peaceably. The position on continuous use is clarified in that an interruption of use for a 12 month period will terminate the running of the prescriptive period; and the extent of the easement is clarified a being 'commensurate' with the right enjoyed during the prescriptive period.[57]

Under the Commission's proposals the effect of a 20 year prescription period running against the owner of the servient land owner will be to automatically vest the right in the dominant land owner. In particular there will be no requirement that the owner of the dominant land apply to the court to have the right recognised, nor will registration be a precondition to the easement taking legal effect.[58]

11.4 Easements Arising in Equity

As with most other interests in property, easements are capable of existing in law and in equity. Easements that are *only* capable of being equitable rights arise principally:

• under a contract to grant a legal easement, which is never completed

• by proprietary estoppel

Estoppel is a doctrine that prevents someone from going back on a representation or induced belief that they will not strictly enforce their legal rights. Where this representation has led another to act to his/her detriment, an easement might be recognised in equity as a remedy.[59]

It is important to be able to distinguish between legal and equitable easements for a number of reasons. These include the effect that the easement will have on potential purchasers of land and being able to identify whether the benefit or the burden of an easement will run with the land. An easement can add significant value to land, and conversely the failure to create an easement that is necessary for the enjoyment of the land can have significant adverse implications for the owners. Likewise an easement may constitute a burden on land that a potential buyer is not willing to undertake. It is

---

57 Draft Land Law Reform Bill (Northern Ireland) 201[], section 9. See Northern Ireland Law Commission, *Land Law* (NI Law Com No 8, 2010), 150
58 Ibid 150
59 *Crabb v Arun District Council* [1975] EWCA Civ 7, [1976] Ch 179 (CA) 197-198 (Scarman LJ)

therefore important to be able to distinguish the different types of easements and the extent to which they will bind a purchaser of the property.

11.5 Discharge and Modification of Easements

A. Statute

A statute may extinguish an easement expressly or by implication.

B. Release

The way in which an easement is discharged by private act is by release. Release may be either express or implied. To take effect in law an express release must be made by deed. However, a specifically enforceable agreement to release an easement will, on general equitable principles, operate as a release in equity.

C. Abandonment

An implied release will occur where the dominant owner abandons the easement or profit: that is, he/she ceases to enjoy the right with the intention of giving up the right permanently. Non-use is not sufficient to abandon a public right of way; there must also be an intention to abandon.[60]

D. Unity of possession and title

An easement is automatically extinguished where the dominant and servient tenements are in common ownership and occupation, as one of the essential requirements of an easement is thereby lost. There will not, however, be any extinguishment if, although there is a union of the fee simple estates, there is no unity of possession because one of the tenements has been let. Nor will there be any extinguishment if there is unity of possession without unity of fee simple title. The easement will simply be suspended during the concurrent possession.

---

60 *McLean* (n 53) [4] (Smyth J)

11.6 Profits à Prendre

A profit is a right to take something from someone else's land. Generally this must be part of the land, such as turf, minerals or wild creatures living naturally on the land such as fish and game. The key aspect of a profit is that it can exist in gross and can be conferred on a person rather than for the benefit of land. This is what distinguishes a profit from an easement.

CHAPTER 12

Co-ownership

12.1 Introduction

A central feature of land law is that more than one person can have an interest in land at any one time. While this may refer to different types of interests or to estates that vest at different times, it can also refer to the situation where two or more people purchase or inherit land together. In these situations they are referred to as co-owners because they both hold the same estate in the same land concurrently. The law of co-ownership differs in Northern Ireland from that which applies in England and Wales. In Northern Ireland there are two forms of legal co-ownership; the joint tenancy and the tenancy in common.[1] The way in which land is owned will determine the rights of each party in respect of the property. The rules apply equally to freehold and leasehold estates. It is therefore possible to hold freehold land under either a joint tenancy or a tenancy in common.

This area of land law has been of increasing significance in recent years due to the boom and subsequent crash of the property market in Northern Ireland. With house buyers now facing negative equity and banks seeking to enforce commercial loans against property, being able to distinguish between a joint tenancy and a tenancy in common is important. The nature of the interest held in a property will determine the ability of a lender to enforce security against that property, or may determine the extent of the legal protection available for a family home. These issues will be discussed in light of the legal rules on co-ownership.

---

1   In England and Wales only the joint tenancy is a legal estate. The tenancy in common exists only in equity. Section 36 LRA 1925

12.2 Forms of Co-ownership

As outlined, the two main ways in which people co-own property in Northern Ireland are by joint tenancy or tenancy in common. There are two other types of co-ownership which will not be dealt with in detail in this chapter as they are primarily historic forms. These are:

- *Coparcenary*

  Traditionally the eldest male in the family took any property on intestacy. If there were no males within a family, the females inherited as coparceners.[2] This meant that they inherited jointly, all with equal shares. The only way in which coparcenary can arise nowadays is if a tenant in tail dies without barring the entail, leaving the fee tail to pass to female descendants.

- *Tenancy by Entireties*

  As husband and wife were considered to be one entity in the eyes of the law, when property was transferred to a husband and wife, they did not take the property as joint tenants. They took a tenancy by entireties – the law looked at them as one owner, the husband would exercise any powers of management. Under the Married Women's Property Act 1882, tenancy by entireties was abolished and the wife takes her share as a joint tenant and has the power to exercise her rights over this share.

12.3 Joint Tenancy and Tenancy In Common

A joint tenancy is defined by two key features – the right of survivorship and the four unities. If these two features are not present then all that has been created is a tenancy in common.

A. Features of Joint Tenancy

i. The right of survivorship

If two or more persons have joint tenancy of an estate in the land each is entitled to a single interest in the whole land. Together they are legally regarded as being a single

---

2   This rule was abolished by the Administration of Estates Act (Northern Ireland) 1955

owner, individually they are regarded as owning nothing and it is impossible for any joint tenant to claim to have a specific share of the property. This is the form of co-ownership that (usually) exists where real property is held by a husband and wife or by trustees. The reason for this is the right of survivorship that exists between joint tenants. Where property is held under a joint tenancy, on the death of one of the tenants the property will automatically pass to the other tenants by operation of law. This is because on the death of one joint tenant, his/her interest in the land also dies.[3] This reflects the central concept of the joint tenancy that each tenant owns the whole of the property, not simply a divided share in it. Instead, the right of survivorship comes into play and the property is said to be freed from the concurrent interest of the deceased. Importantly this is so even if the deceased joint tenant has tried to pass their property within their will. In this case the right of survivorship will trump the terms of the will and his/her heirs will not succeed to it.

As time passes, the right of survivorship will eventually result in the property being owned by one person. The number of joint tenants decreases with time until one joint tenant remains alive who is entitled to sole ownership of the property.

ii. The problem of commorientes

Commorientes arises where two or more people die in circumstances where the order of their deaths is not clear. In a joint tenancy where the tenants die simultaneously, for example in a car crash, there are no joint tenants left to exercise the right of survivorship. If it can be demonstrated that one tenant survived the other, even by seconds, then the right of survivorship will operate and the property will be inherited by the heirs of the party who survived longest. However if it cannot be demonstrated who survived, in Northern Ireland the common law treats the tenants as dying at precisely the same time. In these circumstances the share of each joint tenant will pass under their will or by the rules of intestacy to their heirs. These heirs will then take as joint tenants. This is clearly unsatisfactory in the modern day where there can be any number of heirs. The right of survivorship might operate between parties who have no discernible relationship and who have not contracted into a co-ownership arrangement of this sort. This problem was addressed in England and Wales by Section 184 of the Law of Property Act 1925 which introduced the presumption that the youngest of the commorientes was the last to die and therefore his/her estate is entitled to the property.

---

3   Ibid section 44(d)

A different approach is proposed for Northern Ireland. In order to address the difficulties created by the simultaneous death of joint tenants, the Northern Ireland Law Commission has proposed that commorientes be treated as an event which severs the joint tenancy. This means that in the event of both tenants dying together they will be treated as having held the land in common at the time of their deaths.[4] This would mean that the property could pass by will to the heirs of each party, who would inherit it as tenants in common rather than joint tenants. This approach is reflected in the draft Land Law Reform Bill,[5] but is does not currently form part of the law of the jurisdiction.

iii. Corporations

A limited company is a legal not a natural person, therefore where a company is a joint tenant it will (theoretically) survive any natural joint tenants (people).[6]

iv. The four unities

In addition to the right of survivorship there are four essential elements to a joint tenancy. If one (or more) of these 'four unities' is absent then a joint tenancy will not exist (and a tenancy in common will arise instead).

The four unities are:

- *Unity of possession*

    This unity must be present for a joint tenancy to exist. Under this principle each co-owner is entitled to possession of the whole land.[7]

- *Unity of interest*

    The co-owners must all possess the same interest in the land. The co-owners must have the same estate with the same rights and obligations. If one owner has a greater interest than another then a joint tenancy does not exist.

- *Unity of title*

    Joint tenants must all derive their title from the same document (eg will or conveyance), or act (such as the taking of adverse possession).

---

4   Northern Ireland Law Commission, *Land Law* (NI Law Com No 8, 2010) para 7.15-7.16
5   Draft Land Law Reform Bill (Northern Ireland) 201[], section 58. See NILC (n 4) 176
6   For this reason, until the Bodies Corporate (Joint Tenancy) Act 1899, corporations were not permitted to hold property as joint tenants.
7   That ownership is equal is recognised in the Administration of Justice (Ireland) Act 1707.

- *Unity of time*

  Finally, for a joint tenancy to exist the interest of each tenant must vest at the same time.

These four unities are necessary conditions for the existence of a joint tenancy, but they are not sufficient, since even where all four are present, there may be a tenancy in common. It is only where the four unities and the right of survivorship exist in concert, that there will be a joint tenancy.

B. Tenancy in Common

Whereas for a joint tenancy to exist all four unities must be present, in situations where property is co-owned but these requirements are not met, the relationship that arises is a tenancy in common. With a tenancy in common only the unity of possession will be present. This is because possession is an inherent characteristic of property rights. It means that all parties will be equally entitled to possession of the property, even if they do not in fact exercise that right.

Under a tenancy in common each tenant has a distinct and separate interest in the property. This means that their legal interests in the property are distinct, not that possession of the property itself is divided. This would be the case for example where a group of friends agreed to buy property together because they could not afford to buy individually. The intention here is not to create a joint legal interest but rather that each person would have an entitlement to the property equal to what they had contributed to the purchase.

The tenancy in common is also quite different from the joint tenancy in that there is no right of survivorship. Where a tenancy in common exists a tenant may pass his/her ownership rights to another by sale or mortgage, in his/her will or via intestacy. If one co-owner dies then their interest in the property will pass to their successors in title, not to the other co-owners. In order to ensure that a tenancy in common is created the intention of the parties should be expressly stated in the deed of conveyance.

A tenancy in common may also arise where a joint tenancy is severed (see section 12.5).

C. Comparative Advantages and Disadvantages

Each form of co-ownership has a key advantage and disadvantage by which they can be distinguished. Traditionally the courts of equity regarded the doctrine of survivorship in respect of a joint tenancy as unfair – who ultimately gains outright title to the land is essentially a matter of chance and may not reflect the actual wishes/intentions of the parties. Conversely, because of the absence of a right of survivorship in respect of a tenancy in common the title can, particularly over a number of generations, become fragmented. For example, if Andrew, James and Ryan purchase the fee simple of 'the Brooke' as joint tenants and they later agree to sell the property to Philip, Philip's solicitor will simply investigate the single deed of conveyance by which ownership was transferred. However, if they purchased as tenants in common, Philip's solicitor will have to consider them as three separate entities. This can cause problems. If, for example, before the property was sold, Andrew died, devising his (undivided) share to his sons, Max, Kieran and Dylan, as tenants in common (of that share) and James also died, leaving his (undivided) share to Emma and Amy as tenants in common (of that share), Philip's solicitor would then have to investigate the title of Max, Kieran, Dylan, Amy, Emma and Ryan, all of whom would have *legal* interests in the property.

If we bear in mind that legal interests will bind subsequent purchasers of the land, and will make it more difficult to establish good title, it can be seen that whilst a tenancy in common may be fairer, a joint tenancy is much more convenient from a conveyancing perspective.

In England and Wales the solution to this problem caused by the legal tenancy in common was to convert it into an equitable arrangement. Under the Law of Property Act 1925 where two or more people owned land concurrently the title to that land was deemed to be held as a legal joint tenancy. Each co-owner held the land on trust for the benefit of themselves and the others. Therefore each person owned both a legal and equitable interest in the property. This meant that the tenancy in common ceased to exist as a legal interest. Where one joint tenant died their legal interest in the land could not be passed under will or intestacy but the surviving joint tenants would continue to hold the land on trust for the benefit of the heirs of the deceased tenant.

Earlier proposals for reform in Northern Ireland had suggested introducing the same mechanism.[8] However the most recent proposals indicate a change of direction and favour the retention of the legal tenancy in common.[9]

---

8   Committee on the Registration of Title to Land, Registration of Title to Land in Northern Ireland (1967) ('The Lowry Report'). Working Party of the Faculty of Law, QUB, Survey of the Land Law of Northern Ireland (1971). Office of Law Reform, Department of Finance & Personnel, Belfast, Final Report of the land Law Working Group (1990).

9   NILC *Land Law* (n 4) 7.4. The Commission justifies this recommendation on the basis that parties should remain free to devise their own methods of holding land. In the Northern Ireland context the specific examples of undivided grazing agreements and the increase in apartment living were cited as

D. Uncertainty: In Common, or Joint Tenancy?

The common law courts and the courts of equity take differing views on a joint tenancy and a tenancy in common which has made the creation and operation of co-ownership complicated. When looking at co-ownership, it is always necessary to consider the form of co-ownership which has been created at common law and in equity, noting that they might not always be the same.

Generally the terms of the deed or will under which two or more persons acquire their interest will make clear whether they hold the land as joint tenants or tenants in common. However, this is not always the case and, if no express declaration that the co-ownership is to take one form or the other is apparent, the courts must decide which was intended.

Despite the existence of the legal tenancy in common, for reasons outlined, the law tends to favour the joint tenancy. There will therefore be a strong presumption that where two or more people own property together that it is held as a joint tenancy and that the legal and beneficial interests are divided equally between the parties.[10] If the intention is to create a joint tenancy, such as a husband and wife purchasing a family home, then there is no need for the presumption to be rebutted. However there are a number of good reasons why people may not want to enter into a joint tenancy. These may include where property is purchased as an investment, or where a couple cohabit but do not intend that survivorship would operate in respect of the property. In these circumstances, even where no contrary intention is expressed, equity may infer the existence of a tenancy in common. Therefore if co-owners want to ensure that the equity in the property is also held as a joint tenancy it is advisable for them to expressly state that that is the case.

It is common, therefore, for individuals to be joint tenants of the property at common law but to hold the estates on trust for themselves in equity as tenants in common. So if one joint tenant dies, the remaining tenants will take the property through the right of survivorship. However, the surviving joint tenants must hold that interest on trust for the deceased joint tenant's estate or successors.

The common law presumes that if two or more people are entitled to possession, they will hold as joint tenants. This presumption can be rebutted by reference to the terms of

key reasons to exercise caution in this area.

10 The *Law Society of Northern Ireland v B* [2011] NICh 21 [21]-[27]

the disposition or by the absence of one of the four unities. If one of the four unities is absent, then there can be no joint tenancy. If unity of possession exists, then a tenancy in common will have been created.

It is also possible to expressly create a tenancy in common rather than a joint tenancy by including words of severance in the terms of the disposition. The effect of these words is to indicate that the co-owners intend to take distinct shares. Such words can include: 'to be divided between'; 'share and share alike'; 'in equal shares'.[11]

Despite the starting point that parties intend the beneficial ownership of the property to follow the legal title to it, in certain cases equity will intervene to alter this division of beneficial ownership. These cases arise either where the parties argue that their intention was not to create a joint beneficial title, or where fairness requires that the presumption of joint beneficial interest be overridden. In these circumstances the tenancy in common will operate in equity. The co-owners will therefore continue to hold a joint legal tenancy, but the beneficial interest will be held on trust. This creates a situation where you have a legal joint tenancy but an equitable tenancy in common. The equitable rules will dictate each party's entitlement to beneficial ownership of the property.

This is an area of law where there has been considerable development in recent years. There is currently a 'live debate' on the question of whether the court can impute or attribute an intention that beneficial ownership should differ from the legal ownership.[12] This has arisen primarily in the context of family homes, but has raised significant questions about the nature of co-ownership. Two recent cases in the Northern Ireland courts have addressed this issue, and in doing so have engaged with key developments in the House of Lords in respect of family property.[13]

However there are also a number of more straightforward situations in which equitable intervention is common.

i. Multiple title

Where two or more people hold the legal title to the property and they have provided the money for this property in equal shares the parties will generally hold the title as joint tenants. This reflects the presumption that where property is conveyed into joint

---

11 JCW Wylie, *Irish Land Law*, (3rd edn, Tottel Publishing, 1997) para [7.15]

12 *Bank of Scotland Plc v Brogan and Another* [2012] NICh 21 [29] (Deeny J)

13 *Stack v Dowden* [2007] UKHL 17, [2007] 2 AC 432, *Jones v Kernott* [2011] UKSC 53, [2012] 1 AC 776

names without any declaration of trust that both the legal and beneficial interests in the property are joint and equal.[14]

The second situation which falls under this heading is where the purchase money is contributed in unequal proportions. If two people are purchasing property and contribute unequally to the purchase price of the property, they may describe themselves as joint tenants however equity will presume that they hold the property on trust for themselves as tenants in common in equity in shares proportionate to their contributions. This presumption may be rebutted by the circumstances of the acquisition or the terms of the conveyance showing a contrary intention. Increasingly it is also challenged in the context of family property.

ii. Non-recognition on the title

It may sometimes be the case that more than one person contributes to the purchase price of property, but only one person is recognised on the title as the owner. In such a circumstance equity will once again presume that there was no intention on the part of the party not mentioned to give away his/her interest, and therefore the recognised owner will be deemed to hold the property on trust for him/herself and the unrecognised owner as tenants in common in shares proportionate to the shares of purchase monies paid.[15]

iii. Mortgages

Where two or more people (or companies/banks/institutions) loan money on the mortgage of a property, whether they have advanced the money in equal or unequal shares, they will be presumed to take the property as tenants in common in equity. The right of survivorship is inconsistent with the commercial nature of the transaction.

iv. Presumption of advancement

This is a presumption that arises due to the relationship between two parties. Where certain relationships exist it will be presumed that one party intended to make a gift to the other and that the intention was not therefore that the beneficial ownership

---

14 *Law Society* (n 10) [21]-[27]
15 *Bull v Bull* [1955] 1 QB 234 (CA), 236-237, 239 (Denning LJ)

should reflect the relative contributions of the parties. This will apply primarily in family relationships, most notably between parent and child. For example, in a market where property prices are high it is not uncommon for parents to help their children to purchase their first property. If a parent and their child purchase a house together, they both contribute to the purchase price and the house is put into the child's name, the normal rule will not apply. Under the traditional rule both the parent and child would be entitled to the property as tenants in common in equity. However the presumption of advancement will apply so that the child will take the property in both law and equity, giving the child the entire beneficial ownership notwithstanding the contribution made by the parent. This presumption also traditionally applied between husband and wife, but was recently abolished by article 16(1) of the Law Reform (Miscellaneous Provision) (Northern Ireland) Order 2005.

However, the best way to rebut any of the above presumptions is to include an express statement in the conveyance/will stating that a joint tenancy rather than a tenancy in common is intended.

All of these examples emphasise the relative financial contribution that the parties have made to the purchase price of a property. The presumption is therefore that beneficial interest can be calculated using the straightforward and certain criteria of who contributed what. However there are exceptions to this rule, and cases where the court has discretion to quantify beneficial interest based on either direct or indirect contributions. This is possible under Section 17 of the Married Women's Property Act, which gives the court the power to determine the relative rights of spouses in property in the event of a dispute between them, and the Matrimonial Causes (Northern Ireland) Order 1978 which gives the court the power to direct a transfer of property between spouses in certain circumstances. This arises primarily where one spouse, traditionally the wife, seeks a declaration of a beneficial interest in the property. This may be necessary either because she is not named at all on the deeds, or because she is seeking to establish that her beneficial interest exceeds a 50/50 division of the property. It is unfortunately the case that most such cases arise as a result of marriage breakdown where there is dispute over the division of property.[16] The rules in this area have evolved significantly in recent years, and probably now accord much more with justice than in the past.

---

16 For detailed discussion of this see Heather Conway, *Co-Ownership of Land: Partition Actions and Remedies* (2nd ed, Bloomsbury 2012) Ch 9

12.4 Who owns the Family Home?

Where legal title is jointly owned both parties will enjoy protection from the law. However it is also common for title to family property to be registered in only one name even though a spouse or partner may be in actual occupation of the property and making financial or other contributions to it. Where the contributions being made are financial it is easier to quantify the extent of the beneficial interest generated as it will generally be commensurate with the contributions. However it has also long been recognised that there are circumstances in which non-financial contributions should also give rise to a beneficial interest.

In Northern Ireland it is established law that a spouse who does not hold legal title to a shared property may nevertheless be deemed to have a beneficial interest in that property. However this was never an automatic entitlement by virtue of marriage. In the 1972 case of *McFarlane v McFarlane*[17] the court considered the factors to be taken into account when determining if a wife could be said to have established a beneficial interest in property. The first, and most straightforward, consideration was whether she had made direct financial contributions to the purchase of the home. The concept of direct contribution was interpreted narrowly to include only direct financial contribution to the purchase price of the property or towards mortgage repayments. Where this could be established then the wife would acquire, by way of a resulting trust,[18] a share in the property proportionate to her contributions. Under these rules the position of a wife in relation to the family home is no different from that of any joint tenant who purchase property together. However the court then goes on to consider the extent to which indirect contributions may also give rise to an interest in the property. Indirect contributions are defined as those which have added to the resources out of which the property has been acquired. This may include work done or services rendered that have relieved the spouse of some of the financial obligations entailed in property ownership. However, the existence of such indirect contributions alone would not be sufficient to give rise to a beneficial interest in the property. They must be accompanied by an agreement between the parties that demonstrated a mutual intention that the wife would be entitled to an interest in the property. Such intention could not be imputed by the court. Finally, any indirect contributions that were unrelated to the acquisition of the property could not found an equitable interest in it. This sets a very high threshold for a

---

17 [1972] NI 59 (CA)
18 The resulting trust arises 'as a result' of her contribution and gives her an equitable share in the property. See chapter 3

wife to establish that she has made a sufficiently clear contribution to the purchase of the property, and arguably blurs the distinction between direct and indirect contributions by requiring a demonstrable link between the contribution and the purchase of the property. By way of example, in the case of *Northern Bank v Beattie*,[19] the court considered the fact that the wife had used her earnings to pay the bills as evidence of her having made an indirect contribution to the mortgage repayments through relieving her husband of responsibility for such outgoings and allowing him to use his earnings to make the mortgage payments. However, when it came to determining the extent of her interest in the property, the court relied heavily on the financial contribution. In a rather harsh line of reasoning, the judge calculated her entitlement based on her net financial contribution, noting that it would have been less on weeks where she had a day off. Further when ill health as a result of pregnancy prevented the wife from returning to work, this resulted in a significant reduction in her perceived 'contribution'. The judge noted that this resulted in a greater reduction to her overall contribution, which should mathematically give rise to a much smaller share. However, recognising the unfairness this would cause, he awarded a one quarter share in the property. What this reasoning demonstrates is the link between direct contribution and an interest in the property.

These cases make it clear that the equitable division of property has traditionally followed a rigid formulation that has been primarily concerned with certainty in property transactions. These cases arise in the context of what Murray J described as 'the eternal triangle', referring to a husband, the mortgage lender and the estranged wife.[20] It is a fact of life that when marriages are going well and mortgage repayments are up-to-date there is little need to address the question of who owns what in respect of family property. It is only when marriages or mortgages hit difficult times that the question of whether and to what extent a wife owns a beneficial interest in the property become significant. Being able to establish a beneficial interest in the property, particularly one that enjoys priority over the interest of a mortgage lender, can be the difference between keeping or losing the family home.[21] However the fact that questions of co-ownership are often integrally linked to the ability of mortgage lenders to enforce security has resulted in a restrictive approach to questions of division of property. Recent developments in the law suggest a more flexible approach to the division of family property and an increased willingness by the courts to use their discretion to achieve a just outcome.[22]

---

19 [1982] 18 NIJB (Ch)
20 Ibid
21 For further discussion of this see chapter 13
22 See Andrew Hayward, 'Finding a Home for 'Family Property': Stack v Dowden & Jones v Kernott' in

A. Recent Developments – Quantifying Beneficial Ownership

As the earlier cases in this area demonstrate, the approach taken by the courts to the division of beneficial ownership has been to presume that equity follows the law, save where it can be demonstrated that there was a clear intention otherwise. It is however possible for the parties to rebut this presumption. Where it is contended that equity should not follow the law, then the burden of proof rests on the party seeking to rebut that presumption. To do this they will have to satisfy the court that there was a common intention that the beneficial interest should differ from the legal interest.

In the UK Supreme Court case of *Jones v Kernott*,[23] cited with approval in Northern Ireland in *Bank of Scotland v Brogan*,[24] the court suggested that the presumption can be displaced by showing either that a different common intention existed at the time the home was acquired, or that the course of dealings between the parties was sufficient to demonstrate that their common intention as to ownership changed over time. Such intention must be objectively established from the conduct of the parties.[25] However it was also emphasised that the presumption should not be displaced readily, and that to justify such equitable intervention the facts of the case would need to be very unusual. Where the presumption is rebutted the court can then quantify the beneficial interest of each party in light of the course of dealings between them.

The focus of the recent cases has been purportedly less on the details of direct and indirect contributions, but rather on how the intentions of the parties can be discerned from a range of factors that extends beyond financial contributions.[26] In the two recent cases of *Law Society of Northern Ireland v B*; and *Bank of Scotland v Brogan*, the court has recognised the claim of a wife to a share in family property. Importantly the share recognised has not been determined solely on the basis of financial contributions made, but has been quantified in light of an entire course of dealings between the parties. Protection of the equitable interest in these cases has been achieved by the imposition of a constructive trust,[27] giving effect to the common intentions of the parties.

N Gravells (ed) *Landmark Cases in Land Law* (Oxford, Hart 2013)

23 *Jones* (n 13) [51] (Lord Walker of Gestingthorpe, Baroness Hale of Richmond)

24 *Brogan* (n 12)

25 *Jones* (n 13) [51]

26 *Law Society* (n 10) [20] (McCloskey J)

27 A constructive trust arises by operation of law, by identifying the common intention of the parties and dividing beneficial ownership accordingly. See chapter 3

The cases differ in that in *Law Society* the wife did hold joint legal title to the property with her husband. A course of dealings which had involved heavy borrowing against the property led to a claim on the part of the wife that there had been an agreement between herself and her husband that he would relinquish his beneficial entitlement to the property and that she would be entitled to full beneficial ownership. In *Brogan* the situation was different in that the wife was not named on the title to the property and was seeking to establish the existence rather than the extent of her beneficial interest therein. In both cases the court examined the entire course of dealings between the parties in an attempt to establish the existence of a common intention that would rebut the presumption that equity follows the law in terms of property ownership.

However, it is interesting to note that in both cases the question of 'contribution' still remains closely linked to financial considerations. In *Brogan* it was suggested that the rearing of children, which Deeny J characterised as "an intrinsic part of the role of wife and mother ... particularly in rural Northern Ireland", was in and of itself unlikely to point to ownership of the property. Rather much greater emphasis was placed on work carried out running the farm to allow the husband to seek work in Dublin, and on a direct financial contribution that had been made to the purchase of the property. Similarly in *Law Society* the fact that the wife who was seeking to protect her beneficial interest in the property had obtained paid employment and ensured that mortgage payments were kept up-to-date by arranging them through her own personal bank account were taken as evidence of an agreement between the parties that the wife would enjoy the whole beneficial interest in the property.

However what is evident is the shift from relying solely on contributions to the purchase or maintenance of the property that would give rise to a resulting trust towards recognition of a course of dealings that requires the imposition of a constructive trust to reflect the true intentions of the parties in terms of ownership.

These decisions are also significant in that they introduce an element of uncertainty into the property transaction. In both cases wives in possession of family property were seeking to establish that they had beneficial interests in the property that would enjoy priority over a mortgage. In both cases this argument was successful. In *Brogan* the outcome was that the existence of the beneficial interest prevented an action for partition of the property, meaning that the mortgage could not be enforced against the undivided share of the wife.[28] In *Law Society* the result was even more extreme. As

---

28 See chapter 13 for further discussion of mortgages

the court accepted the argument that the intention of the parties was that the husband should relinquish his entire beneficial ownership of the property the lender was left with no interest against which their security could be enforced.

From the decision in *Law Society*, which draws heavily on precedents set in the House of Lords, it seems that the courts are now more willing to exercise discretion when it comes to quantifying the extent of beneficial interest in family property.[29] This is, however, subject to restrictive interpretation. It has been re-affirmed in *Brogan* that this should only happen in exceptional cases. It is unlikely, therefore, to become the norm that the court interferes in the presumed division of ownership. Further there must be very clear evidence of the intention between the parties, and this will not be inferred lightly. And finally, to introduce a Northern Irish angle to the debate, it seems that such intentions are only likely to be inferred in cases where the couple is married. In *Brogan* it was suggested that marriage indicates a much higher degree of commitment between the parties than a decision to live together, and therefore it is more likely that a common intention in terms of shared ownership can be inferred in such circumstances. While it had been suggested in England and Wales that the rules should apply equally to cohabiting couples, dicta in *Brogan* suggests a perhaps more conservative approach will be taken in Northern Ireland. Deeny J suggested that he did not accept that the social conditions were necessarily the same as in England and that therefore "we should not slavishly follow a view that might seem appropriate in some parts of that jurisdiction."[30]

12.5 Severance

The common law recognised that where there is a joint tenancy, events could occur which would 'sever' the joint tenancy and render the co-ownership a tenancy in common.

Severance of a joint tenancy will not end co-ownership; it will merely convert the joint tenancy into a tenancy in common. Severance is the means by which a joint tenancy is divided into shares, disallowing the operation of the right of survivorship.

There are two different ways in which severance can occur. Where the joint tenancy is severed at law, the legal ownership of the property is converted from a joint tenancy into a legal tenancy in common. Where the joint tenancy is not formally severed the

---

29 This is possible under the Property (Northern Ireland) Order 1997 which gives the court the power to quantify a sale or division of the family home or to quantify the extent of the strict legal rights of the parties.
30 *Brogan* (n 12) [34]

severance will have no effect on the legal ownership, which will remain as a legal joint tenancy, but the equitable ownership will be severed. This will result in an equitable tenancy in common.

The most commonly cited explanation of the ways in which severance may occur was set out in the Irish case of *Williams v Hensman*:[31]

> "A joint tenancy may be severed in three ways: in the first place, an act by any one of the persons interested operating upon his own share may create a severance as to that share … Secondly, a joint tenancy may be severed by mutual agreement. And, in third place, there may be a severance by any course of dealing sufficient to intimate that the interests of all were mutually treated as constituting a tenancy in common."

The best way to establish severance is to demonstrate mutual agreement between the parties. This may occur, for example, when a couple decide to separate and agree to sell the family home. However it will not always be possible to prove mutual agreement. In these cases the court may look at the course of dealings between the parties to establish where there was an intention to sever the joint tenancy.[32]

Such determination will focus on whether the acts and dealings of the parties indicated an intention to treat the property as held in common rather than jointly. If this is the case then the court may infer an agreement to sever the joint tenancy.[33]

These principles continue to form the basis of the law on severance in Northern Ireland.[34] For the purposes of satisfying this test there are a number of examples of what may constitute an act or course of dealings.

A. Severance at Common Law

i. Acquisition of another interest

If one of the joint tenants is given an additional interest at the time of the creation of the joint tenancy, this will not affect its creation. However, if one of the joint tenants

---

31 *Williams v Hensman* (1861) 1 J&H 546, 547; 70 ER 862, 867
32 See *Law Society* (n 10)
33 *Wilson v Bell* (1843) 5 Ir Eq R 501; See Heather Conway, 'Joint Tenancies, negotiations and consensual severance' [2009] C & PL 67
34 For more detail on severance in Northern Ireland see *Conway* (n 16)

subsequently acquires an additional interest this will sever the joint tenancy.[35] This happens because the unity of interest is no longer present. The tenant who has acquired the additional interest will in these circumstances become a tenant in common in relation to the other co-owners. The remaining tenants continue to stand as joint tenants in relation to one another.

ii. Alienation

If a joint tenant sells or otherwise transfers his/her interest in the property to another person this will invoke a severance. The severance occurs in these circumstances because the unity of time and unity of title are both destroyed. The acting joint tenant (vendor) severs his/her ownership from the remaining joint tenants and the purchaser becomes a tenant in common in relation to the remaining joint tenants. Where a contract is signed by the joint tenant to alienate his/her interest (with consent), this will effect a severance in equity until such time as the actual conveyance of the interest occurs.[36] A severance will generally also occur where a lesser interest in the property is sold for example, the creation of a lease.

This is a significant aspect of the law on severance because its effect is to allow a joint tenant to unilaterally sever the joint tenancy without the knowledge or consent of the other joint tenants. As the law currently stands this must be done by way of another *inter vivos* disposition of land.[37] Common ways of achieving this outcome would be to create a mortgage or charge against the joint tenant's share of the property,[38] to create a lease in favour of a third party, or to simply transfer their share to a third party to be held on trust for their own benefit.[39] Each of these methods falls short of the tenant actually disposing of his/her entire estate, but falls within the definition of alienation to allow him or her to sever the joint tenancy. The Northern Ireland Law Commission has proposed that statutory provision be made for severance by way of serving a notice.[40] This would reflect the freedom of a joint tenant to unilaterally sever a tenancy because

---

35 *Wiscot's case* (1599) 2 Co Rep 60b
36 This occurs under the Rule in *Walsh v Lonsdale* (1882) 21 Ch D 9 (CA)
37 Severance cannot be achieved by testamentary disposition. See Martin Dixon, *Modern Land Law* (7th ed, London, Routledge, 2010) 178
38 Under article 50 Property (Northern Ireland) Order 1997 the effect of a mortgage or charge is to sever the joint tenancy.
39 Where this is done the use is executed under the Statute of Uses 1634, re-uniting the legal and beneficial ownership of the property but severing the joint tenancy.
40 NILC *Land Law* (n 4). This mechanism is already available in England and Wales under the Law of Property Act 1925 section 36(2)

of a change in circumstances and would also address the current state of affairs whereby unilateral severance can only be achieved by way of another disposition. However, under these proposals the severance would not take effect in law unless and until the notice of severance is registered either in the Land Registry or the Registry of Deeds, as appropriate.[41]

iii. Act of a Third Party

Unlike in the previous cases, the severance of a joint tenancy as a result of the act of a third party exercising statutory powers is involuntary, ie it is done by parties other than the joint tenants themselves. Some statutory provisions vest power in parties to transfer proprietary interests in property that belongs to another person. If the owner is a joint tenant, the exercise of this statutory power will lead to a severance of the joint tenancy. A common example of this occurs on bankruptcy, whereby a person's property is transferred to the Official Assignee to sell or dispose of to pay off creditors. Such transfer to the Official Assignee will sever a joint tenancy automatically and regardless of the consent or lack thereof of other joint tenants. Similarly the effect of a third party registering a charge against the property will be to sever the joint tenancy and transfer the tenant into tenants in common with equal and divided shares.[42]

iv. Surrender

It is possible for a joint tenant to surrender his/her interest to the other joint tenants. In this case there is no severance but instead the other joint tenants are entitled as if the tenant surrendering was dead.

B. Severance in Equity

A severance in equity will occur where the recognised intention of the parties is for the joint tenancy to be severed, even in the absence of formalities that may be required in order for a severance to be affected in law. When a severance occurs in equity the joint tenancy still exists with regard to the legal title but the beneficial interest will be held as a tenancy in common.

---

41 NILC *Land Law* (n 4) 34
42 See decision *Law Society* (n 10)

i. Mutual agreement

A mutual agreement among joint tenants that they will hold as a tenancy in common will amount to a severance in equity. It may affect a severance in equity even where the parties have not taken any steps to enact their intentions – or where they have done so through, for example, the creation of a contract.

It must be an intention that all co-owners share and have expressed, as opposed to a secretly declared intention of some co-owners. However it is often the case that this intention has not been expressly stated and the courts must look to the behaviour of the parties to decide if it is impossible to imply or infer such intention.

ii. Course of dealings

By 'course of dealing', we mean not only negotiations that fall short of actual agreement but also the way in which the property itself has been dealt with by the parties involved. So even if there is no agreement, a severance in equity will occur provided it can be shown that relations between the co-owners have been altered to the extent that they no longer consider themselves as joint tenants but rather as tenants in common. If a course of dealing is sufficient to show that the interests of all were mutually treated as constituting a tenancy in common this will affect a severance in equity even though the course of negotiations may fall short of a formal agreement. The important point is that the co-owners perceive themselves as tenants in common. According to *Williams v Hensman*, when a severance depends on an inference of this kind without any express act of severance, it will not suffice to rely on an intention, declared only behind the backs of the other persons interested.[43]

C. Effect of Severance

In Northern Ireland the effect of severance is to convert a joint tenancy into a tenancy in common. This can occur both in law and in equity.

In England and Wales the effect of severance is the conversion of the beneficial entitlement to a joint tenancy into an equitable tenancy in common. This technical distinction is necessary because in England and Wales tenancies in common have been abolished at law and are now recognised only in equity behind a trust in land. Consequently, Section 36(2) of the Law of Property Act 1925 provides that no severance

---

43 *Hensman* (n 31) 558, 867

of a joint tenancy of a legal estate is possible but severance of a beneficial joint tenancy (behind the trust) remains possible.[44] In Northern Ireland, because tenancies in common are still possible at law and because trusts of land are not imposed to give effect to co-ownership, this rule is not necessary.

Where a joint tenancy is severed the party effecting severance will be entitled to a divided share directly proportionate to the number of joint tenants at that time.[45]

12.6 Determination of Joint Tenancies and Tenancies in Common

Where all rights in the land become vested in one person co-ownership will come to an end. Alternatively the parties may agree by deed that the land be physically divided and the former co-owners will have exclusive rights over their divided share. In Northern Ireland, where the parties cannot agree to the nature of such a division the Partition Acts 1868 and 1871 enable any co-owner to apply to the court to have the property partitioned or sold and the land or proceeds divided according to the shares of the parties.[46] There are three ways in which co-ownership may be brought to an end altogether.

A. Sale

If all the co-owners consent to a sale, the property may be sold, and the purchaser will then take it free from the rights of the joint tenants or tenants in common, whose interests will shift to the proceeds of the sale. Each will then have a right to the proceeds proportionate to the extent of their interest in the property.

B. Partition

Partition results in the land being physically divided, with one part going to each co-owner. There are two circumstances in which this may arise. The first is where one party seeks to release their interest in the property. In these circumstances partition can be achieved voluntarily by agreement between the co-owners, executed by deed. For a

---

44 This does not prevent a joint tenant of the legal title releasing his/her interest to the other joint tenant(s) and dropping out of legal ownership of the land.

45 Unless they actually agree upon some other arrangement. *Barton* v *Morris* [1985] 1 WLR 1257, 1260; [1985] 2 All ER 1032, 1036

46 In England and Wales reference to the court should be made under section 14(1) of the Trusts of Land and Appointment of Trustees Act 1996

voluntary partition to occur the land itself must be capable of being divided. There may therefore be practical limitations to the benefit of partition.[47] In order to combat this practical difficulty, the Partition Acts of 1868 and 1871 gave the courts the discretion to order the sale of the property where partition was not a reasonable prospect. This power can be invoked where one party owns more than half of the property and seeks to force a sale. This happens, for example, in respect of matrimonial property where partition of a dwelling house is not feasible but the parties seek to release their respective interests in the property. It can also happen where a mortgage is secured on the interest of one party and that party defaults on their repayments.[48] In these situations the courts may make an order that the property be sold, unless it sees good reason to the contrary.[49]

Partition can also be forced upon the parties where circumstances require. This arises where a mortgagee seeks to enforce security against a property that is co-owned. In these circumstances partition of the property is a necessary prerequisite to enforcing that security against the debtor's share of the property. Article 48 of the Property (NI) Order 1997 gives creditors the power to request an order for partition under the Partition Acts. This is necessary because security cannot be enforced against the owner of an undivided share whose interest is not subject to the mortgage.[50] Where partition is ordered the proceeds of the sale will be distributed between the parties in accordance with their interest in the property.[51]

C. Union in a Sole Tenant

Co-ownership will end where all the property becomes vested in only one of the co-owners. With a joint tenancy this will eventually happen through the operation of survivorship, unless severance has taken place. With a tenancy in common or a severed joint tenancy, union in a single co-owner will occur only where one tenant acquires the shares of the others by grant, will, or operation of law.

---

47 See for example *Brogan* (n 12) where a dwelling house and its immediate curtilage were deemed unsuitable for partition. See also *Beattie* (n 19); *Ulster Bank Ltd v Shanks* [1982] NI 143
48 *Law Society* (n 10)
49 Partition Act 1868 (31 & 32 Vict c 40, amended 39 & 40 Vict c 17) section 4; for further discussion of this power see chapter 13.
50 section 63(1) Conveyancing Act 1881; *Tubman v Johnston* [1981] NI 53
51 For discussion of the application of article 48 see Heather Conway, 'Nearly, But Not Quite: Partition Actions in the Wake of Article 48 of the Property (NI) Order 1997' (1999) 50 NILQ 116

CHAPTER 13

Mortgages

13.1 Introduction

In recent years mortgages have become a common topic of discussion. During the property boom mortgages were freely available on good terms even to those who had previously thought property ownership to be beyond their reach. However as the property market slowed down the topic of conversation shifted from the ready availability of mortgages to the unwillingness of banks to make funds available for mortgage lending. For a number of years is has been acknowledged that a significant number of homebuyers in Northern Ireland now have mortgages that exceed the value of their properties, and that others are simply unable to keep up the repayments on a mortgage secured on an overpriced property they cannot afford to sell. Therefore while the law of mortgages is a technical area of land law, it has very real application to everyday life. This chapter will explain the key concepts of mortgages as they pertain to land law. It will explain the ways in which a mortgage can be created, the various rights and responsibilities of the borrower and the lender, and it will also consider the legal assistance available to those who fall into difficulties with mortgage repayments.

13.2 What is a Mortgage?

A mortgage is a mechanism by which borrowing can be secured against property. Given the relative value of real property, it is a fact of life that most people will need a mortgage to be able to purchase property. It is therefore also inevitable that banks will want some means of ensuring that a loan advanced to purchase such property will be repaid. The law of mortgages seeks to strike a balance between these competing interests. On one hand it is important that purchasers are able to access finance, but on the other if the bank cannot be assured that the debt can be enforced they will be reluctant to lend. Striking a balance that ensures adequate protection for both parties to the mortgage transaction is therefore essential.

A mortgage contains elements of both contract and property law. The creation of a mortgage consists of two steps. These are the agreement to create a mortgage, which stipulates the terms of the agreement; and the execution of the mortgage itself. The contract is a specifically enforceable agreement to create a mortgage. The form the mortgage takes will depend on whether the land is registered or unregistered, discussed further in section 13.5. Once created a mortgage generates a proprietary interest in the land. The mortgagee will acquire a legal interest in the property of the mortgagor. This interest will only last so long as the debt remains outstanding. Once the debt is repaid, along with interest and charges, the mortgage will be released or discharged, thus bringing the mortgagee's interest to an end.

However, if the borrower becomes unable to repay the loan, the lender may claim against the property. When a mortgage is created both the borrower and the lender have certain rights that are protected by law.[1]

13.3 Terminology

It is common to speak of the bank 'giving' you a mortgage. The public perception of the mortgage transaction is that a mortgage is something that is granted by the bank to the customer. This is not, however, an accurate representation of the mortgage.

The terminology can therefore be a little confusing.

The *mortgagor* is the person who borrows the money. The money is used to buy the property and in return, a legal charge is created by the borrower in favour of the lender. This is of course a basic example. In practice the mortgagor may be a third party who agrees to guarantee a loan for someone else. For example, a parent may agree to create a mortgage on their own property to raise the deposit for a child to purchase their first home. It does not matter on which property the loan is secured. Further, while it is often

---

1   See section 13.6

the case that the money borrowed on foot of a mortgage is used to buy property, it is not necessarily restricted to this purpose. It is possible to create a mortgage to secure borrowing for other purposes such as home improvements. The key principle is that the mortgage secures the loan against property by creating an interest in that property for the lender.

The *mortgagee* is the person or company who lends the money. They are the person in whose favour the charge is created.

Therefore the bank does not 'give' you a mortgage, but rather you create a mortgage in favour of the bank.

13.4 Types of Mortgage Facility

There are two main ways in which a mortgage can be structured. These are as a repayment loan or as an interest only loan.

A. Repayment Loan

With a repayment loan all the capital and the interest are paid off in instalments made over a fixed period of time. If a borrower has a repayment loan, they will often take out a life insurance policy to ensure that the loan can be repaid should they die during the term of the mortgage.

This type of mortgage is the most common form of mortgage where people intend to acquire ownership of the property. If the repayments are met over the course of the mortgage term then at the end of the term the debt will be repaid and the mortgage will be discharged.

B. Interest Only Loan

With an interest only loan, over the fixed period the borrower repays interest to the lender but does not repay capital. However, once the loan period expires, the borrower will still have to repay the original capital amount to the lender. The borrower must therefore have some other means of raising the capital at the end of the period of the loan.

These types of mortgage were popular when house prices were rising and property was purchased as a first step on to the property ladder. If the value of the property rises then it can be sold and the mortgage repaid from the proceeds of sale, leaving a profit for the purchaser. However, the purchaser takes a risk that the value of the property falls and they are left with a mortgage that cannot be repaid from the proceeds of sale. In 2013 it was estimated that about 40% of mortgages in Northern Ireland were interest only. It is anticipated that a significant number of these mortgagors will be unable to repay the loan when the term of the mortgage ends.[2]

13.5 The Creation of Mortgages in Northern Ireland

Mortgages can be legal or equitable. The nature of the mortgage will determine how it is created and how it is protected. As with other classes of interest, whether a mortgage is legal or equitable will determine the priority afforded to it, that is, how the bank ensures that it can enforce the debt against the property even if it is sold or transferred. The question of priority relates to the fact that a number of different interests can exist in the same estate at the same time. If a dispute arises over who owns the property or who is entitled to share of the property or the proceeds of sale thereof, for example, the rules of priority will determine who gets what and in what order. This is particularly important in the case of mortgage lending as failure to properly register an interest in the property can result in that interest being lost.[3]

As a general rule, legal mortgages will enjoy priority over all subsequently created interests. They will also bind purchasers of the property. Equitable mortgages must be registered as a notice against the property to ensure that they are protected. Registration of such charges ensures that any potential purchaser will have notice of them and therefore ensures that the interest is protected. If they are not properly registered then they will lose priority against subsequently created legal interests, including purchase for value of the property.[4]

The most common type of mortgage is a legal mortgage. The form that the mortgage will take depends on whether the land in question is unregistered or registered.

The traditional way in which a mortgage would have been created over land would be to transfer the entire estate, whether freehold or leasehold, to the lender. This provided

---

2 Colletta Smith, 'Interest Only Mortgage Shortfall 'Big Problem' for NI' (BBC News N. Ireland, 2 May 2013) <http://www.bbc.co.uk/news/uk-northern-ireland-22378079> accessed 18 June 2013
3 See most recently *Northern Bank Ltd v Rush and Davidson* [2009] NICh 6
4 See chapter 3 for discussion of the rules of priority

security for the loan, but left the borrower vulnerable. Because title had been transferred, once the loan was repaid the lender had to go through the process of re-transferring the title. There was no guarantee that the lender would re-transfer the estate and if the lender failed to take the appropriate steps to return the property the borrower would have to take action to recover it. In addition to this practical difficulty, there were severe consequences for failing to keep up with repayments. When the loan was made, the lender would stipulate a date for repayment. This date was known as the legal date of redemption. If the loan was not repaid then the lender would be entitled not only to keep the property, but also to demand repayment of the loan.

The injustice caused by this practice led equity to intervene to recognise an equitable right to redeem. This equitable right arises once the legal date of redemption has passed and is based on the equitable maxim 'once a mortgage always a mortgage'[5]. The basic principle is that a mortgage is created as security for a loan, not as a means of transferring ownership of the property. Therefore the borrower will be entitled to the return of the property on repayment of the loan, even if the legal date of redemption has passed.

In Northern Ireland the law still allows the creation of mortgages by conveyance or assignment of estate where the land is unregistered. It is not permissible where the land is registered.[6] However it has been argued that the mortgage by conveyance, and the differing rules for registered and unregistered land, "distort the boundary between security and ownership".[7] Therefore the Law Commission has recommended that this method of creation be abolished and replaced by the charge system that applies to registered land.[8] Mortgages would therefore no longer be created by conveyance of the entire estate. While a mortgage would still create a legal interest for the lender, it would always be a limited right, a lesser interest than that owned by the mortgagor. The mortgagor therefore retains an estate in the property notwithstanding the existence of the mortgage.

A. Formalities

Any transfer of a legal interest, including mortgages, charges and leases must be executed by deed. It must therefore comply with the common law formalities for the creation of deeds. This requires that the transaction be evidenced in writing, and that

---

5   *Vernon v Bethell* (1762) 2 Eden 110, 113; 28 ER 838, 839
6   Land Registration Act (NI) 1970 section 41
7   Northern Ireland Law Commission, *Land Law* (NI Law Com No 8, 2010) para 8.7
8   Draft Land Law Reform Bill (Northern Ireland) 201[], section 58. See NILC (n 7) 179

it be signed, sealed and delivered.[9] Under the common law not only had the person creating the mortgage to sign the deed, but it also had to be sealed and delivered. Sealed under the common law may have included actions such as attaching a wax seal or a ribbon, or including a printed circle with the letters LS in it.[10] These rules continue to govern the validity of the deeds by which a large number of mortgages in Northern Ireland have been created. While these rules are long established principles of common law, the meaning of 'sealed' in the context of a deed was recently challenged in the Northern Ireland courts. In the case of *Santander UK Plc v Parker (No 2)*[11] the defendant alleged that the absence of a seal rendered the mortgage deed void. In this case the words "Signed, Sealed and Delivered in the presence of…" (the borrower) had been included, and the signature of the borrower was followed by the word "SEAL". Deeny J, hearing the appeal, held that the presence of these words was sufficient evidence of an intention to execute the document as a deed. The defendant had signed the deed, and the fact that the deed was in the possession of the lender was taken as evidence that it had been delivered. Therefore the deed was held to have been duly executed.

These common law rules on the requirement that a deed be sealed were replaced by the Law Reform (Miscellaneous Provisions) (Northern Ireland) Order 2005 which relaxed the requirements in this regard.[12] The new legislation provided that a deed would be valid notwithstanding the fact that it was not sealed if it was clearly expressed to be a deed, it was signed and delivered.[13]

The relaxation of the rules reflects the underlying purpose of the seal to indicate intention and consent. An overly formalistic approach is therefore not necessary to ensure the deed is valid.[14]

B. Legal Mortgages of Unregistered Land

In Northern Ireland, if the land is unregistered and the borrower holds the freehold,

---

9   See Law Reform Advisory Committee for Northern Ireland, Discussion Paper No 7 Deeds and Escrows (2000) on the formalities of deeds.

10   This was originally taken to indicate the space where the wax seal should have been attached, but has long been recognised as sufficient in itself to constitute a seal. See *Santander UK Plc v Parker (No 2)* [2012] NICh 20 [6]-[7]

11   Ibid [6]-[7]

12   This was given effect by the Law Reform (Miscellaneous Provisions) (2005 Order) (Commencement and Transitional Saving) Order (Northern Ireland) 2005 and came into effect from 15 November 2005.

13   Ibid Art 3

14   The effect of this provision was confirmed in *Rush and Davidson* [2009] (n 3) [11]

the most common way of creating a mortgage is by sub-demise. This means that the borrower will lease the property to the lender for a fixed period, for example, 3000 years. The demise of this term of years will usually include provision for cesser on redemption of the mortgage. This means that the mortgagee's interest in the property will cease to exist once the loan has been repaid. This method has the advantage that it allows the mortgagor to retain the freehold estate while also creating a legal estate for the mortgagee. If the land is unregistered and the borrower holds a leasehold estate, the borrower will sub-lease the land to the lender for the remainder of the term of the lease, less the last few days.

Any legal mortgage of unregistered land must be executed by deed, following the necessary requirements. The deed must then be registered in the Registry of Deeds.[15]

With both types of mortgage over unregistered land, the lender becomes the legal owner of the property. However, so long as the loan repayments are made, the borrower is entitled to remain in possession. The mortgage deed will contain a 'proviso for redemption', which states that once the loan is repaid, the title to the property will be re-assigned to the borrower.

The legal position in England and Wales is governed by the Law of Property Act 1925, under which mortgages of unregistered land can be created either by sub-demise or by way of a charge.[16] If created by charge the mortgagee obtains 'the same protection, powers and remedies' as if the mortgage had been created by a long lease.[17] The charge must be made by deed and it must be declared as a 'legal mortgage made by charge'.

C. Legal Mortgages of Registered Land

In Northern Ireland if the land in question is registered a mortgage is not technically possible. Lending against registered land is secured by way of a charge on the land. The key feature of a charge is that it does not involve any transfer of the estate from the borrower to the lender.[18] The land is charged with the repayment of the loan and the charge is registered against the folio held by the Land Registry. Section 41 of the Land Registration Act (Northern Ireland) 1970 states that, "A registered owner of land may, subject to the provisions of this Act, charge the land with payment of money either with or without interest, and either by way of annuity or otherwise."

---

15 Registration of Deeds Act (NI) 1970 section 2
16 section 85(1)
17 Ibid section 87
18 Heather Conway 'Nearly, But Not Quite – Partition Actions in the Wake of Article 48 of the Property (NI) Order 1997' (1999) 50(1) NILQ 116, 116

The charge is a legal interest and follows the normal rules of registration.[19] The creation of a charge is a much simpler and more straightforward way of creating a mortgage than a long lease.

This mirrors the position in England and Wales whereby a legal mortgage of registered land can only be created by way of a charge.[20]

D. Equitable Mortgages

With an equitable mortgage, the parties still intend to secure a loan against property, however no deed is executed. Equitable mortgages can arise in various ways. If the parties intend to create a legal mortgage but the formalities are not met and the mortgage is not properly executed, then the mortgage may take effect in equity. This is possible because of the two stage process for the creation of a mortgage. If the parties enter into a valid contract to create a mortgage then the mortgage will take effect in equity even if the mortgage is not actually created.[21] In this regard a deed is not essential to the creation of an equitable mortgage. Similarly if the mortgagor him/herself holds only an equitable interest in the land,[22] any mortgage he/she creates on the security of that land can only be equitable too. Under the Statute of Frauds (Ireland) 1695, an assignment of an equitable interest held under a trust must simply be in writing signed by the assignor or made by will.

In Northern Ireland, the most common example of an equitable mortgage is what is known as the mortgage by deposit of deeds. This is where the borrower deposits the title deeds or land certificate for the property with the lender. This is possible because the creation of equitable mortgages is not subject to the same formalities as the creation of legal mortgages. The intention of the parties to create a mortgage is evidenced by the deposit of the title deeds with the lender. This is regarded as evidence of the existence of a contract and part performance thereof. In practical terms, the deposit of deeds provides effective security for a loan because the mortgagor will not be able to produce the deeds to sell the property. While the existence of this type of mortgage remains common in Northern Ireland, it is likely to become less significant in the future. There are a number of reasons for this. Lending institutions increasingly prefer not to store documents. Further the increase in electronic transactions mean that holding paper copies of documents such as land certificates is becoming less important. Finally,

---

19 See chapter 4
20 Land Registration Act 2002 section 23(1); Under the LRA 2002 the mortgage must be registered in order to take effect in law. If it is not registered it will take effect in equity only.
21 *Russel v Russel* (1783) 1 Bro CC 269
22 Akin to that held by a beneficiary under a trust.

with the introduction of compulsory first registration more and more land will be transferred from unregistered to registered land, bringing it within the scope of the Land Registration Act which does not permit informally created mortgages. For these reasons the Law Commission felt that there was no need to specifically abolish the creation of equitable mortgages by deposit of deeds, but to simply allow the practice to die out naturally.[23]

The law in England and Wales already prohibits the creation of a mortgage by deposit of deeds. This is because under the Law of Property (Miscellaneous Provisions) Act 1989 contracts for the sale or disposition of interests in land must be made in writing and signed by the parties.

An equitable mortgage can be registered as a notice against the burdened land. Equitable interests are generally more vulnerable to sale than legal interests, therefore to protect the lender's interest it should be registered against the title of the property.

13.6 Rights of the Mortgagor

As outlined, a mortgagor enjoys certain equitable protections in respect of the relationship with the mortgagee. The primary protection is that provided by the equitable right to redeem whereby the mortgagor is entitled to repay the debt and thereby discharge the mortgage. This right arises only after the legal date of redemption has passed. The legal right of redemption is set at a short period of time, usually six months, after the creation of the mortgage. This is the date on which the debt becomes due and is the date after which the mortgagee will be entitled to a remedy for default. However, in practice the loan is not usually repaid on this date. Instead there is agreement between mortgagor and mortgagee that the loan will be repaid in instalments over a specified period of years. During this time the mortgagor enjoys both the equitable right to redeem and the equity of redemption.

The equity of redemption indicates the extent of the borrower's rights in the property. It is often thought of as the difference between the value of the property and the value of the mortgage, and referred to as 'equity' in the property. This 'equity' is a valuable commodity in and of itself, and can be used to secure further borrowing on the property. However, if the value of the property falls below the value of the loan then the owner is said to be in 'negative equity'. This means that if the owner wishes to sell the property they will have to repay the outstanding mortgage debt from other funds.

---

23 Draft Land Law Reform Bill (Northern Ireland) 201[] (n 8) section 58 (5)

In order to protect the position of the mortgagor, the courts may use their equitable jurisdiction to prevent lenders from taking unfair advantage of borrowers. While some of these protections are now included in consumer protection legislation,[24] or more appropriately dealt with by regulation of mortgage lending,[25] they have evolved through the courts, and the courts retain their discretionary jurisdiction to deal with these matters.[26] Some examples of these are given.

A. Rule Against Irredeemability

It is not possible for a mortgagor to forfeit their property because of non-payment of a loan. This confirms the basic principle of 'once a mortgage always a mortgage' and that a mortgage is security for a loan rather than transfer of property. Similarly a lender may not impose unreasonable charge for early redemption. Charges may be applied only so long as they are not harsh and unconscionable.

B. Clogs and Fetters

It is a long established equitable principle that additional conditions cannot be attached to the terms of a mortgage. A lender may seek some collateral advantage to the mortgage, for example requiring that the customer maintain a current account with or purchase a life insurance policy from the lending institution.[27] However, as a general rule conditions may not be attached that gives the lender any greater interest in the property than is necessary to secure the loan. They may not, for example, include an option to purchase as a term of the mortgage.

C. Undue Influence

The issue of undue influence is one on which there has been recent development in the context of mortgage transactions. It is most often raised as a defence to an action for recovery of secured debt. Undue influence can potentially arise where the relationship between the parties to the transaction is one of trust and confidence which allows one party to put pressure on another party to enter into an agreement that is not in their

---

24 Consumer Credit Act 1974; Consumer Credit Act 2006; Unfair Terms in Consumer Contracts Regulations 1999
25 Mortgage: Conduct of Business (FSA, 2007)
26 Northern Ireland Law Commission, *Land Law* (NI Law Com CP No 2, 2009) paras 7.19-7.21
27 The Conveyancing Act 1881 (44 & 45 Vict c 41) section 19 specifies the 'Powers incident to estate or interest of mortgagee.'

best interests.[28] It is a ground for equitable intervention where unconscionable conduct can be demonstrated. This can arises in two separate scenarios. It may be the case that the mortgage lender has exerted undue influence over the borrower. More common, however, is the scenario where the borrower alleges undue influence on the part of a third party. The third party can be either an agent of the lender, or a person unconnected to the lender who is in a position to influence the borrower. The best example of this is where a husband puts pressure on his wife to provide surety for his debt. The leading authority in Northern Ireland on the question of undue influence is the decision in *Bank of Ireland (UK) plc v Crawford*.[29] In this case the court applied principles of law on undue influence established in the House of Lords case of *Royal Bank of Scotland plc v Etridge (No 2)*,[30] confirming their application in this jurisdiction.

Where it is alleged that there has been undue influence on the part of a third party the court must engage in a two-part inquiry. First they must be satisfied that there has been a relationship of trust and confidence between the parties. In *Etridge* this relationship was that between husband and wife. However this is not the only situation in which undue influence may apply. The existence of any close personal relationship may give rise to abuse,[31] as may a commercial relationship where one party relies on the professional advice or expertise of another.[32] Second, where such a relationship exists between the parties it must be demonstrated that this relationship has been abused. Therefore establishing the existence of a relationship capable of giving rise of undue influence is not enough. It must also be proved that undue influence was in fact exercised.[33] This will be a question of fact. The burden of proof will rest on the person making the allegation of wrongdoing.

In addition to the requirement that there has been abuse of a close relationship, it must also be demonstrated that the bank knew, or should have known about that abuse.

If it can be proved that a transaction was entered into as a result of undue influence the contract will be deemed to be void *ab initio* (from the outset). The consequences of this could be severe for a lender. If the contract is void they may not be able to enforce repayment of the loan. Therefore some means of striking a balance between protecting those vulnerable to undue influence and protecting the interests of the bank is necessary.

---

28 See *Bank of Ireland (UK) plc v Crawford* [2012] NIMaster 6
29 Ibid
30 [2001] UKHL 44
31 *Copeland v Knight* [2006] NICh 1
32 *Crawford* (n 28)
33 Ibid

This balance is struck by requiring the bank to make additional inquiries where certain relationships exist. This is known as putting the bank on inquiry.[34] Undue influence cannot be used as a defence if the bank was unaware of its existence. If the bank can demonstrate that they had no knowledge of the abuse of a relationship there will be no remedy for the borrower. Putting a bank on inquiry helps to protect victims of undue influence by placing an obligation on the bank to take reasonable steps to ensure that the contract is not entered into as a result of undue influence. In *Etridge* it was established as a general principle that a bank will be put on inquiry where a wife offers to stand surety for her husband's debts. Where the relationship between the parties is commercial rather than personal the threshold for putting the bank on inquiry will be higher, depending on the circumstances of the particular case.[35]

If it can be demonstrated that the bank knew of the existence of undue influence they are said to have actual notice. The result is that the contract can be held to be void. Similarly if the bank should have made inquiries and did not they will be deemed to have constructive notice of the undue influence that may also void the contract.

The underlying rationale for allowing a defence of undue influence is to provide some protection for a vulnerable borrower from the strict application of the law. Equitable intervention mitigates the effects of allowing the lender to exist on strict legal rights.

In all cases where unfair terms or undue influence arise the court has discretionary power to set the terms of the mortgage aside.

13.7 Rights of the Mortgagee

In addition to protection for the mortgagor, it has long been recognised that if finance is to be made available for the purchase of property that there must also be legal protection for the lender. There are therefore a number of legal mechanisms that exist to ensure that in the event of default the lender can recover their capital.

A mortgage is owned as a contractual debt. The lender can sue the borrower personally for it if the debt is not repaid. However, the purpose of a mortgage is to ensure that the mortgagee does not have to rely on this remedy. This is particularly important in cases of bankruptcy where a personal action against the mortgagor would be useless. The interest created by the mortgage ensures that in these circumstances the debt can be enforced not only against the mortgagor, but also against the mortgaged property. In these circumstances the legal right of redemption is important. It is only after the legal

---

34 *Etridge* (n 30)
35 *Crawford* (n 28) [17]

date of redemption has passed that the debt becomes owed and the mortgagee has any right to take action to enforce it.

It is now accepted principle that where a mortgagor defaults on mortgage payments, the remedies available to the mortgagee should only be exercisable for the purposes of protecting or enforcing its security.[36] This has led to significant policy amendments. In general terms there is an increasing trend towards distinguishing between property that is occupied as a family home and other types of property, and to affording greater protection to mortgagor's who default on payments on a mortgage secured on the family home.[37] However this protection is afforded under consumer protection legislation, and therefore the law of mortgages, and the remedies available to mortgagees, remain rules of general application.[38]

A. Enforcement of Security in Northern Irish Law

In Northern Ireland there are a number of potential remedies for mortgagees.

i. A Court Order for Possession of the Property

Where a borrower has defaulted on their repayments the mortgagee may apply to the court for an order for possession. In these circumstances the court orders the mortgagor to give up possession of the property to enable the mortgagee to proceed to sell the property. This is necessary because it will be nearly impossible to sell premises without vacant possession, particularly if they are residential properties.[39] In Northern Ireland it has been confirmed that the court has an inherent jurisdiction to make an order putting a legal or equitable mortgagee into possession. This jurisdiction can be exercised either by the Chancery Division or by a judge exercising bankruptcy jurisdiction in the Queen's Bench Division.[40]

The Northern Ireland Law Commission has recommended that where the mortgaged property is a 'dwelling house' the mortgagee should not be able to take possession without a court order, unless the mortgagor surrenders possession voluntarily.[41]

Where the mortgaged property is a 'dwelling-house', the Administration of Justice Acts 1970 and 1973 empower the court, where it seems that "the mortgagor is likely to be able within a reasonable period to pay any sums due under the mortgage or to

---

36 NILC *Land Law* (n 7) 8.12
37 See chapter 12.4
38 NILC *Land Law* (n 7) 8.14
39 *In Re O'Neill, A Bankrupt* [1967] NI 129 (QB) 130 (Lowry J)
40 Ibid 129
41 Draft Land Law Reform Bill (Northern Ireland) 201[] (n 8) section 66

remedy a default consisting of a breach of any other obligation arising under or by virtue of the mortgage", to adjourn the proceedings or suspend execution of the order. This is discussed in greater detail in section 13.8.

Difficulties may also arise where a mortgagee seeks an order for possession of property that is co-owned. Section 63(1) of the Conveyancing Act confirms that a legal mortgage will be effective only against the severable share of the co-owner that has created it.[42] This means that the mortgagee is not entitled to possession against the owner of the interests that is not subject to the mortgage.[43] In these situations, where physical division of the property is impractical,[44] the mortgagee may have to apply directly for an order for sale of the property rather than possession.[45]

ii. Sale of the Property

There are two requirements that must be met before a mortgagee can proceed to sell a property. The power of sale must have arisen, and must have become exercisable.

Under Section 19(1)(i) of the Conveyancing Act 1881, the power of sale arises when the "mortgage money has become due". Usually this will be when the legal date for redemption has passed. The legal date for redemption is the date specified in the mortgage instrument for the repayment of the loan. However, under Section 20 of the Conveyancing Act, in order for the power of sale to become exercisable, one of three conditions must be satisfied.[46] These are:

- The lender must have served a notice on the borrower requiring repayment of the loan within three months; or
- Payments under the mortgage must be in arrears for two months; or
- There must be a breach of some provision in the mortgage deed.

It is important to note this distinction between the power of sale having arisen and becoming exercisable. Where the power is exercisable the mortgagee will not be restrained from exercising the power to sell a property unless the mortgagor repays the amount due.[47]

---

42 See chapter 12.6.B
43 *Tubman v Johnston* [1981] NI 53
44 *Northern Bank v Beattie* [1982] 18 NIJB (Ch); *Ulster Bank Ltd v Shanks* [1982] NI 143; *Bank of Scotland Plc v Brogan and Another* [2012] NICh 21
45 Art 48 Property (NI) Order 1997; This is discussed in detail in chapter 12
46 The equivalent position exists in England and Wales, where section 101(1) of the Law of Property Act 1925 implies the power of sale into every mortgage contract.
47 *McCambridge v The Governor and Co of the Bank of Ireland* [2002] NICh 9 [6] (Girvan J). This is subject to the provisions of the Administration of Justice Acts.

There has been a great deal of debate over how far the mortgagee, when exercising their power of sale, can simply have regard to their own interests and to what extent they are under a duty to the mortgagor.

Section 21(6) of the Conveyancing Act 1881 states that: "The mortgagee ... shall not be answerable for any involuntary loss happening in or about the exercise or execution of the power of sale conferred by this Act ... or of any power or provision contained in the mortgage deed."

Case law has established that the mortgagee has not only a duty to act in good faith, (ie honestly and without reckless disregard for the mortgagor's interests) but also to take reasonable care.[48] This includes being under an obligation to obtain a reasonable price for the property, equivalent to the market value at the time of sale.[49] However while the mortgagee has a duty to act in good faith, they do not act as a trustee for the mortgagor. This means that if a conflict of interest arises, the mortgagee is entitled to act in his/her own interests rather than those of the mortgagor. This might arise, for example, where the timing of a sale is likely to have a bearing on the price obtainable.[50]

If the mortgagee is a building society, Section 36 of the Building Societies Act (Northern Ireland) 1967 applies. This provision states that a building society selling a property as mortgagee is under a duty to take reasonable care to ensure that the price at which the estate is sold is the best price which can reasonably be obtained. Under the Law Commission proposals this obligation will be imposed on all mortgage lenders.[51]

Other rules include that the mortgagee cannot sell the property to him/herself.[52] Likewise, he/she cannot acquire the property indirectly through an agent.[53] Although, a mortgagee does not act as a trustee in relation to the power of sale, under Section 21(3) of the Conveyancing Act 1881, he/she is a trustee of the proceeds of the sale.

The mortgagee must apply the proceeds of sale in a particular order. Any prior encumbrances must be discharged and the residue should be paid to the mortgagor, or if there is a second mortgage, to the next mortgagee.

Section 21(1) of the Conveyancing Act 1881 states that in a sale of mortgaged property, the purchaser receives "such estate and interest therein as is the subject of the mortgage,

---

48 *AIB Group (UK) Plc v The Personal Representative of James Aiken (deceased) and Others* [2012] NIQB 51 [8]-[9] (Gillen J). Citing with approval the modern English authority of *Cuckmere Brick Co Ltd v Mutual Finance Ltd* [1971] Ch 949, [1971] All ER 633.
49 Ibid [8]
50 Ibid [9]
51 Draft Land Law Reform Bill (Northern Ireland) 201[] (n 8) section 70
52 *Henderson v Astwood* [1894] AC 150, 158 (Lord MacNaghten)
53 *Hodson v Deans* [1903] 2 Ch 647, 653-654 (Joyce J)

freed from all estates, interests and rights to which the mortgage has priority, but subject to all estates, interests, and rights which have priority to the mortgage". Therefore, if the mortgage is by lease, the term of years remaining on the lease passes. In relation to a mortgage created on registered land by a charge, under schedule 7, Part 1, Paragraph 5(1) of the Land Registration Act (Northern Ireland) 1970, the estate or interest which is subject to the charge will be sold. As regards an equitable mortgage, only the equitable interest will pass unless a declaration of trust or a power of attorney has been used to allow the legal estate to pass.

In light of the move towards protecting the mortgagor, under the Law Commission proposals the power of sale will arise as soon as the mortgage is created, thus doing away with the artificial construct of the legal date of redemption, but it will only become exercisable when it is necessary to protect the mortgaged property or realise the security.[54] It remains to be seen how these criteria are interpreted.

iii. Court Order for Sale

Instead of the mortgagee bringing proceedings for possession and selling the property him/herself, he/she may bring proceedings to have the property sold by the court and the proceeds applied in discharge of the amount owed under the mortgage. The sale is carried out under the court's control. The proceeds will be used firstly to pay off the mortgagee's costs and the amount due under the mortgage; and then to pay off any second mortgagee. If there is any sum remaining, this will be paid to the mortgagor.

Where property is co-owned partition of the property may be necessary before an order for sale can be made. Article 48 of the Property (NI) Order 1997 gives lenders the power to request partition of property to allow security to be enforced against co-owned property.[55]

iv. Taking Possession

With a legal mortgage created by the conveyance or assignment of a freehold or leasehold estate in the land, the mortgagee is entitled to claim possession of the property as soon as the mortgage is created. However, if the mortgage was created by a charge on registered land, it seems that the mortgagee can only take possession by obtaining the permission of the mortgagor or by court order. In the case of an equitable mortgage, it is debatable whether the mortgagee has an automatic right to claim possession, however, he/she can apply to the court for an order for possession.

---

54 NILC *Land Law* (n 7) 8.23
55 See chapter 12 for discussion of partition

If the mortgagee takes possession of the property, he/she can use the rents and profits of the land in the payment of the interest and capital owed to him.[56] A mortgagee in possession must account strictly to the mortgagor for rent acquired whilst in possession.[57]

v. Appointment of a Receiver

Appointing a receiver achieves the same goals as taking possession, that is, more efficient management of the property to safeguard the mortgagee's interest. The power to appoint a receiver is conferred on legal mortgagees by Section 19(1) of the Conveyancing Act 1881.[58] An equitable mortgagee must apply to the court for the appointment of a receiver.

The power to appoint a receiver arises when the mortgage money becomes due. However, the power does not become exercisable until one of the three events needed for the power of sale occurs. The function of a receiver is to manage the mortgaged property and to ensure that the rents and profits are used first and foremost to pay the interest due on the mortgage. Section 24(2) of the Conveyancing Act 1881 states that: "the receiver shall be deemed to be the agent of the mortgagor; and the mortgagor shall be solely responsible for the receiver's acts or defaults, unless the mortgage deed otherwise provides."

vi. Foreclosure

Foreclosure is a proceeding by which the mortgagee seeks to have the mortgagor's right to redeem the mortgage extinguished. The mortgagee thereby becomes full owner of the property. This may mean that the mortgagee gains property that is worth more than the outstanding debt, and is therefore unfair to the mortgagor, who retains nothing.[59] However, foreclosure has not been used in Ireland for centuries and the Law Commission has recommended that it be abolished as a remedy.[60]

Thus the mortgagee has a number of potential remedies available to enforce the debt owed. However, in order to be able to enforce these remedies the mortgage must enjoy priority over other legal and equitable interests that exist in the property. In most

---

56 *Wrigley v Gill* [1905] 1 Ch 241, 255 (Warrington J)

57 *White v City of London Brewery Co* (1889) 42 Ch D 237 (CA), 243 (Lord Esher M.R.)

58 The equivalent provision in English law is the Law of Property Act 1925 S 101(1)(iii)

59 In England the Law of Property Act 1925 section 91(2) gives the court the power to order sale in lieu of foreclosure.

60 Draft Land Law Reform Bill (Northern Ireland) 201[] (n 8) section 65

cases a first legal mortgage will enjoy such priority by virtue of its legal status. However, problems can arise with mortgages created subsequent to the purchase of the property where there may be other existing legal or equitable interests. These interests may bind the mortgagee even if they do not appear on the register.[61] If a mortgage is created in respect of a property and adequate checks are not carried out to ascertain what legal and equitable interests exist in that property, the mortgagee may risk losing priority to a person who has an equitable interest by virtue of being in actual occupation of the property.[62] This is most common where property is held in the name of one person (often a husband) but is shared with another person (the wife). If the husband seeks to create a mortgage on the property and the bank does not carry out the necessary inspections to determine if there is any other person with an interest in the property the mortgage may become unenforceable, depending on the extent of that person's interest. It is common to find wives who are not named on the title deeds of the property in actual occupation of property and therefore with protected equitable interests in it. It is therefore of vital importance that the mortgagee be aware of all such interests in order to ensure that their security is protected and can be enforced using these measures. This is achieved in practice through a 'form of postponement' by which any person entitled to such an equitable interest will consent to the mortgage. This is simply a means of mitigating the risk associated with equitable interests arising from actual occupation.

While it is an accepted matter of public policy that mortgagees be able to enforce debts against property, recent years have seen significant legislative intervention to protect borrowers who fall behind with repayments.

13.8 The Administration of Justice Acts 1970 & 1973 and the Powers of the Court

In this next part of the chapter we examine the interesting jurisdictional differences in the jurisdiction of the court in relation to applications for possession of a dwelling-house and in particular in the case law involved in the interpretation of the Administration of Justice Acts of 1970 and 1973 which place statutory limitations on the contractual rights of mortgagees. This was briefly touched upon earlier. The provisions of the Administration of Justice Acts have application in Northern Ireland by virtue of

---

61 Land Registration Act (NI) 1970 section 38, providing for burdens that affect land without registration. These include the rights of those in actual occupation of the land.
62 See most recently *Swift Advances Plc v Maguire and McManus* [2011] NIQB 55 [3]-[9] (Deeny J)

Section 36(6) of the 1970 Act which empowers the High Court of Northern Ireland to hear such cases. This power may also be delegated in appropriate circumstances.[63]

Section 36 of the Administration of Justice Act 1970 gives the court discretionary powers in respect of mortgage remedies. These powers are designed to help mortgagors who have fallen behind with mortgage repayments. They include the power to adjourn proceedings or suspend action for possession if it appears that the mortgagor would be able to repay arrears within a reasonable time.

The question to be considered by the court is how to exercise its discretion. There have been different approaches taken by the courts in England and Wales to those in Northern Ireland in relation to proposals made by mortgagors to the discharge of arrears over a period of time and to sell the property to discharge the mortgage. In England the practice was to consider two years a reasonable period, in Northern Ireland it was regarded as a 'relatively limited' period with an outer limit of four to five years.[64]

However this approach was changed fundamentally with the decision in *Cheltenham & Gloucester Building Society v Norgan*[65] in England and Wales. In *Norgan* the court outlined the factors that should be taken into consideration. These included:

- How much can the borrower reasonably afford to pay, both now and in the future?

- If the borrower has a temporary difficulty in meeting his/her obligations, how long is the difficulty likely to last?

- What was the reason for the arrears which have accumulated?

- How much remained of the original term?

- What are the relevant contractual terms, and what type of mortgage is it, when is the principal due to be repaid?

- Is it a case where the Court should exercise its power to disregard accelerated payment provisions (Section 8 of the 1973 Act)?

- Is it reasonable to expect the lender, in the circumstances of the particular case to recoup the arrears of interest (1) over the whole of the original term, or (2) within a shorter period, or even, (3) within a longer period ie by extending the repayment period? Is it reasonable to expect the lender to capitalise the interest, or not?

---

63 *Abbey National Plc v McGreevy and Another Northern Ireland* (Ch, 3 December 1997) (Girvan J)
64 *National Provincial Building Society v Lynd and Another* [1996] NI 47, 56-57 (Girvan J)
65 *Cheltenham & Gloucester Building Society v Norgan* [1996] 1 All ER 449 (CA)

- Are there any reasons affecting security which should influence the length of the period for payment?

The court stated that in establishing the reasonable period the court should as its starting point take the balance of the term of the mortgage and ask could the borrowers pay the arrears over that period of time.

In Northern Ireland the opportunity to consider the decision in *Norgan* came in *National and Provincial Building Society v Lynd*[66] in the High Court.

In *Lynd* Girvan J considered the concept of reasonable time as discussed in *Norgan*. While he agreed that the remaining term of the mortgage may be a relevant factor in determining whether repayment could be made within a reasonable time, he disagreed that there should be any strong presumption that the entire remainder of the term represented a 'reasonable period' in and of itself. In essence the judge respectfully submitted that to look at the term of the mortgage was the wrong starting point. He considered that "a determination of the facts set out by Evans J [in *Norgan*] without any pre-disposition for or against the relevant period being the balance of the term of the mortgage is in my respectful view the proper approach". He also considered that *Norgan* could be distinguished from *Lynd* in that in the latter case the mortgage debt was close to or exceeded the value of the property whereas in *Norgan* it was clear that the value of the property was such that the plaintiff's security was in no way at risk.

What is a reasonable time must be determined by reference to the circumstances of the individual case. Therefore while the remaining term of the mortgage may be relevant, it should not be the determining factor. Rather than looking at the remaining term and calculating payments from that, the court should look at what the mortgagor can afford to pay and thereby arrive at the period it will take to discharge the arrears. These provisions exist to protect mortgagors who find themselves in temporary difficulties. They are not intended for those who have simply overstretched themselves financially. This is evident on the emphasis placed on the repayment of arrears within a reasonable time rather than over the remaining term of the mortgage. Determination of a 'reasonable time' in this context must now also be made in accordance with the Provisions of article 8 of the European Convention on Human Rights. This includes the need for the decision to be proportionate and will tend to favour protection of the family home where possible.

A test of proportionality will also allow the court to take the conduct of the lender

---

66 *Lynd* (n 64)

into account. So for example if the lender has lent recklessly and this has resulted in hardship for the borrower, the lender may have to wait longer to have the arrears repaid.

A. Proposals to Sell the Mortgaged Property

Another proposal frequently put before the court at a mortgage repossession hearing is that the borrower intends to sell the property. Under the Administration of Justice Act 1970 the court has the discretion to suspend an action for recovery to allow the mortgagor to sell the property. This is clearly a benefit to both parties, as sale on the open market is more likely to yield a better price than a sale that has been forced through the court.[67] What then should the attitude of the court be to such a proposal? In the Northern Ireland case of *Northern Bank Ltd v Jeffers*, Girvan J suggested:

> "The court will have to take into account all the relevant circumstances which may include the court's view as to the genuineness of the proposal to sell, the steps taken to enable the sale to be effected, the likely value of the property if sold by the mortgagors as compared to the value if sold by the mortgagee, the conduct by the mortgagor in the past, at the time of the making of the order and since the making of the order and the increase or decrease of the mortgage debt since the making of the order."[68]

The lender often is anxious to ensure that the borrowers undertake all reasonable measures to market and sell the property as soon as possible as there is a danger that the borrowers will delay the sale if they are still in possession of the property. Furthermore, if the borrowers are not in a position to make even the monthly instalments due on the mortgage account never mind any contribution to the arrears, the level of the arrears on the account will increase during the period of adjournment or stay of enforcement. Therefore if a mortgagor seeks to stay an order for possession or adjourn proceedings on the grounds that he intended to sell the property, the Court must be satisfied with material 'of sufficient weight' that the mortgagor shall be able within a reasonable period to pay sums due under the mortgage.[69]

In the English case of *National and Provincial Building Society v Lloyd*[70] Neill LJ indicated that if there was clear evidence that a completion of a sale of a property, perhaps by piecemeal disposal, could take place in six or nine months or even a year

---

67 *Northern Bank Ltd v Jeffers and Another* [1996] NI 497, 504 (Girvan J)
68 Ibid, 504
69 *National and Provincial Building Society v Williamson and Another* [1995] NI 366, 374 (Girvan J)
70 [1996] All ER 630 (CA), (1996) 28 HLR 459, 466 (Neill LJ)

then he could see no reason why a court could not come to the conclusion that the borrower was likely to be able within a reasonable period to pay any sums due under the mortgage. The question as to what is a reasonable time is a matter for the court in each individual case.

Therefore when deciding whether or not to suspend proceedings the court will also consider whether or not the sale of the property will raise sufficient funds to discharge the mortgage.

In Northern Ireland the guidance has been more specific. In the case of *Northern Bank Limited v Mallett,*[71] Girvan J considered that the evidence which a borrower should produce when seeking an adjournment or stay on an order for possession pending sale by the borrower. What is required is a letter from a reputable estate agent acting in the sale stating:

- that the property has been placed on the market for sale
- the asking price for the property
- whether the asking price is realistic in the light of comparable prices in the area
- if there are any perceived difficulties in the sale of the property
- whether any offers have been received
- the likely timescale of the sale

In *Mallett* the value of the property and the likelihood of sale were such that the question of whether the sale of the property would be sufficient to discharge the arrears was not at issue. However English case law has provided some guidance on this question.

The decision in *Cheltenham & Gloucester Building Society Plc v Krausz*[72] is authority for the proposition that the court can only adjourn or suspend an order for possession to facilitate a sale of the property by the borrower if the court is satisfied that the proceeds of sale will be sufficient to discharge the entirety of the mortgage debt. In other words the court cannot do this if there is negative equity. However the court must look at all the circumstances of the case. Certainly if the only security afforded to the lender was the property to be sold and there is a negative equity the court has no power to adjourn or suspend. However the question will be different if the lender has other security or if the borrower has the means to add to the proceeds of sale, perhaps from the sale of another property that is not mortgaged.

---

71 [2001] NIJB 225
72 [1997] 1 All ER 21 (CA), [1997] 1 WLR 1558, 1566 (Phillips J)

13.9 Human Rights and Mortgages

As with many other areas of land law, the Human Rights Act exerts an increasing influence on decision making in this area. Many actions requesting partition or sale of property involve family property.[73] When mortgage payments fall into arrears in these circumstances the lender may apply for property that is jointly owned to be partitioned to allow for enforcement of the debt against the share of the indebted party.[74] As an alternative the court may order the sale of the property in lieu or partition.[75] This will happen where partition of the property – dividing it into two physical shares – is not appropriate. This would clearly be the case where the property in question is a family home which cannot be divided to allow one part to be sold. In this type of case the court has the discretion to order sale in lieu of partition "unless it sees good reason to the contrary".[76] These cases can be read alongside cases to be decided under Section 36 of the Administration of Justice Acts in that they both require the court to exercise its discretion as to whether granting an order for sale of the mortgaged property is a fair approach. Although there has yet to be a decision on this issue in the Northern Ireland courts, article 8 of the Human Rights Act, which protects the home, is likely to be a relevant consideration when deciding both whether to re-schedule debt to allow repayments to be made on a mortgage of a family home or whether an order for sale is an appropriate response to mortgage arrears.[77]

---

73 See chapter 12
74 This is possible under article 48 of the Property (NI) Order 1997. See generally Conway (n 18)
75 Partition Act 1868 (31 & 32 Vict c 40, amended 39 & 40 Vict c 17) section 3
76 Partition Act 1868 (31 & 32 Vict c 40, amended 39 & 40 Vict c 17) section 4
77 See generally S Nield and N Hopkins, 'Human Rights and Mortgage Re-possession: Beyond Property Law Using Article 8' (2013) 33(3) *Legal Studies* 431

CHAPTER 14

The Law Relating to Wills

14.1 Introduction

A will is a formal document setting out how assets will be disposed of after death. It is said that a will is 'ambulatory' by which it is meant that it takes effect only on death. The party making the will remains free to dispose of his/her assets during his/her lifetime. Legislation provides that a 'will speaks from death.'[1] This means that the property referred to in the will is to be construed as if the will had been executed immediately before the death of the testator.

The person making the will is termed the testator (or testatrix) and those to whom it is intended the assets will be given in accordance with the will are the beneficiaries. Where there is a failure to dispose of assets by will either because no will has been made or because the will that has been made is invalid an intestacy occurs and the estate is distributed in accordance with legislation[2] rather than the express wishes of the deceased. A partial intestacy occurs when a person effectively disposes of only part of his/her estate by will.

Whilst wills can give burial instructions these are not binding on the executors, unlike the instructions in the will as to the distribution of the estate. Wills can also contain provisions setting up trusts within which assets will be held (and appointing trustees to manage the trusts) and appointing guardians to be responsible for minor children of the deceased after his/her death.

Those persons responsible for implementing the will are executors or personal representatives. The role of an executor is:

---

1   Wills and Administration Proceedings (Northern Ireland) Order 1994 article 17
2   Succession (Northern Ireland) Order 1996 article 3

- gathering the assets of the estate
- paying the debts
- distributing the remainder in accordance with the will

The main legislation in Northern Ireland relating to the law of wills is the Wills and Administration Proceedings (Northern Ireland) Order 1994, which applies – with some exceptions, *infra* – to wills made both before or after 1 January 1995.

Some provisions of the Wills Act 1837 (which also applied in England and Wales) continue to apply in Northern Ireland even to wills made after 1 January 1995. In particular Section 1 which provides a definition of the testator's 'personal estate' and Section 11 which makes specific provision as to the wills of soldiers and mariners who die 'in actual military service' and some of whose assets may be gifted without the full formalities otherwise required of a will.

The general rule is that any kind of property and interest in property may be the subject of a gift by will. Interests which cease on death, notably joint tenancies (which pass by the rules of survivorship) and life interests cannot be gifted by will. Both legal and equitable joint tenancies are treated in the same way for the purposes of a will. Legacies (bequests) contained in a will may be general or specific. A specific legacy is a gift of a particular asset of personal property (for example "my diamond ring") whereas a general legacy is a legacy which does not amount to a gift of a particular thing (for example a general legacy of money: "£500 to my niece Alice"). The residue of an estate (ie the balance of a deceased's estate after payment of all debts bequests or legacies) is another form of bequest commonly found in wills.

In *Henry v Henry* the High Court has held that a will, although otherwise confidential, is not a document to which legal professional privilege applies. It can therefore be examined by the court when the interests of justice so demands. A will may therefore be discoverable in proceedings where the validity of the will is not itself in issue (for example in an estoppel claim) before or after the death of the maker.[3]

14.2 Formalities

A will must meet certain formal requirements in order to be valid. Some of the main requirements are prescribed by article 5 of the Wills and Administration Proceedings (Northern Ireland) Order 1994. This provides that:

---

3   *Henry v Henry* [2007] NIQB 67 (Deeny J)

- a will must be in writing
- it must be signed by the testator, or by some other person in his/her presence and by his/her direction
- the testator's signature must be either made or acknowledged by the testator in the presence of two or more witnesses present at the same time
- each witness, in the presence of the testator (but not necessarily in the presence of the other witness) either confirms the testator's signature or the testator's acknowledgment of his/her signature and signs the will or acknowledges the testators signature

A codicil, a document which amends but does not replace a previous will (for example adding a further bequest) must meet the same formalities as a will.

Whilst it is essential that the will be in writing there is no specific requirement that the will be in any particular form or length. It does not matter whether it is typed or in handwriting. There is no legal requirement that the will be prepared or written by a professional person and there is no requirement that a will be dated.

A signature can be made in a variety of ways. In *Re Estate of Parsons*[4] the testator executed his will by using his thumb as a mark. This was a sufficient execution. Initials may also suffice.[5] Where a person suffering from illness was physically unable to complete his/her full signature it has been held that the unfinished signature was also sufficient.[6] The testator must either sign or acknowledge that the signature is his/hers in the presence of both witnesses at the same time.

A particular issue upon which the Wills Act 1837 continues to have effect is that a will executed before 1 January 1995 must bear the testator's signature *at the foot or the end* of the will.[7] The Order has abolished this requirement for wills made on or after 1 January 1995.

The witnesses must either witness the signature being made or witness the testator acknowledge that it is his/her signature. It will sometimes be the case that witnesses complete an 'attestation clause' (which might typically set out "signed by the testator in our presence and attested by us in the presence of him and each other") although there is no express statutory requirement for this. It also follows that the witnessing must be after the testator has signed. It may be noted that whilst it is permissible that a proposed executor of a will also be a witness to it, a beneficiary (or the spouse or civil partner of a

---

4   *Re Estate of Parsons* [2002] WTLR 237
5   *Re Savory's Goods* (1851) 15 Jur 1042; (1851) 18 LTOS 280
6   *Re Chalcraft (deceased)* [1948] 1 All ER 700
7   Wills Act 1837 (7 Will 4 & 1 Vict c 26) section 9, 21

beneficiary) should not be a witness as this will cause the gift to the beneficiary or his/her spouse or civil partner to fail.

When a court adjudicates upon whether a will meets the formal requirements there is 'a presumption that everything has been done correctly' unless there is specific evidence of irregularity, *per* Carswell J in *Grieve v Grieve*.[8] In that case the Court rejected the validity of a will *inter alia* because it was clear from the evidence that the rule requiring that the witnesses to a testamentary document must attest *after* the testator has signed or acknowledged his signature was not complied with.

The document purporting to be the will of the deceased was also unusual in *Grieve v Grieve*, as it comprised an ordinary cheque from the deceased's Northern Bank cheque book. On the cheque had been written "The will of James Grieve" and the statement "I bequeath all my earthly goods to my nephew." The document bore the genuine signature of the deceased on the part of the document where a cheque would normally be signed and the apparent signature of two witnesses. Although it was highly unusual that a cheque was used as the document upon which the will had been created the Court did not think that this was in itself necessarily objectionable, as it might have been explicable in an emergency. However the Court was not satisfied that the document was genuine. The evidence pointed to the conclusion that the opportunity had been taken by someone to write the purported will on a blank but signed cheque which was found after the death of the deceased.

14.3 Testamentary Capacity

Article 4 of the Order provides that no-one under the age of 18 may make a valid will unless he/she has been a spouse or civil partner.

A testator must be of sound mind when executing his/her will. This has been considered in *Re Thompson's Estate (Deceased)*:[9]

> …The classic test as to the validity of a will where doubt has been cast on the testator's mental capacity is set out in the judgment of Cockburn CJ in *Banks v Goodfellow* (1870) LR 5 QB at 256.
>
>> "It is essential that a testator shall understand the nature of the act and its effects; shall understand the extent of the property of which he is disposing;

---

8   *Re Grieve* [1993] 6 NIJB 34 (Fam)
9   *Re Thompson's Estate (Deceased)* [2003] NIFam 3 [23]

shall be able to comprehend and appreciate the claims to which he ought to give effect and with a view to the latter object, that no disorder of the mind shall poison his affections, pervert his sense of right or prevent the exercise of his natural faculties – that no insane delusion shall influence his will in disposing of his property and bring about a disposition of it which, if the mind had been sound would not have been made."

Thus there are three things in particular that the testator must comprehend, namely (a) the nature of the act and its effects, (b) the extent of the property of which he is disposing and (c) the claims to which he ought to give effect.[10]

Girvan J emphasised that a sound mind does not mean a perfectly balanced mind. There is only a limited overlap between unsoundness of mind for the purpose of will making and what would be classed as mental abnormality leading to a person being detained in a psychiatric institution. Nor would it be "conclusive to a sound disposing mind that the testator was capable of understanding complicated business or following his professional calling. Mere eccentricity or irrationality are not in themselves enough to deprive someone of the ability to make a valid will."[11]

Accordingly in *Donaghey v McGlone*[12] the deceased had suffered depression most of her adult life and had previously received psychiatric care. She had been suffering from a terminal illness and in hospital care when she made the will. Nicholson LJ was nonetheless satisfied having heard evidence from a hospital doctor and a nurse and the deceased's solicitor that she capable of making a will. She was able to understand what she was doing and she was able to execute the will in the full knowledge of its contents and of its effects.

In summary the three issues that will be considered in assessing whether there is sufficient mental capacity to make a will are:

- Did the testator understand that he/she was giving his/her property to the beneficiaries identified?
- Did he/she understand and recall what property it was that he/she was giving?
- Did he/she understand that he/she was including some and excluding others?

Where capacity is challenged before a Court a number of legal presumptions will apply. If the will is rational on its face there is a presumption that the testator had testamentary capacity, although this can be rebutted by evidence to the contrary. If there

---

10 Ibid [23]
11 Ibid [24]
12 *Donaghey v McGlone* [2006] NIFam 3

is evidence of prior mental illness or unsoundness of mind, there is a presumption that this state was continuing when the will was executed. This presumption is rebutted if it can be established that the will was executed in a period of continuing lucidity or after recovery from the illness.[13] In instances of senile dementia the courts in Northern Ireland have considered it important to note that persons suffering from such a condition may alternate between periods of confusion and lucidity.[14]

14.4 Knowledge and Approval

A will must reflect the testator's free and genuine wishes. Where a testator has been misled in some way, where there has been a fraud upon or undue influence over the testator, it cannot be said that the testator had knowledge and approval of the contents of the will. The gift or the will may be invalid in consequence.

Undue influence in the creation of a will – for example a claim that a beneficiary has wrongly procured a gift from the testator – does not precisely mirror the law of undue influence in other fields of law. There are for example no legal presumptions of undue influence based on the type of relationship (such as solicitor and client; religious advisor and follower) as are found in the law of contract.

The test for undue influence contained in *Wingrove v Wingrove*[15] has been cited with approval[16] in Northern Ireland:

> "To be undue influence in the eyes of the law there must be – to sum it up in a word – coercion…
>
> The coercion may of course be of different kinds, it may be in the grossest form, such as actual confinement or violence, or a person in the last days or hours of life may have become so weak and feeble, that a very little pressure will be sufficient to bring about the desired result, and it may even be that the mere talking to him at that stage of illness and pressing something upon him may so fatigue the brain, that the sick person may be induced, for quietness' sake, to do anything. This would equally be coercion, though not actual violence."[17]

---

13 *Re Thompson's Estate (Deceased)* [2003] NIFam 3 [25]
14 *McCullagh and Others v Fahy* [2002] NIFam 21 [31] (Coghlin J)
15 *Wingrove v Wingrove* (1885) 11 PD 81
16 *Re Potter (Deceased)* [2003] NIFam 2 [20]-[24] (Gillen J)
17 *Wingrove* (n 15) 82-83 (Sir James Hannen)

It is not enough to establish that a person has the power unduly to overbear the will of the testator. It is also necessary to prove that in a particular case the power was exercised and that it was by means of the exercise of the power that the impugned will has been produced.[18]

Whilst there is a presumption that the testator had knowledge and approval of his will, this will not apply if any suspicion as to the execution of the will exists. In those circumstances the party propounding the will must adduce evidence to remove the suspicion and satisfy the court that the testator knew and approved it.[19]

In the case of *Scott v Scott*[20] Morgan J considered that:

> "Suspicion could be aroused in varying degrees, depending on the circumstances, and what was needed to dispel the suspicion would vary accordingly. The standard of proof was always the normal civil standard. In this case the defendant contended that the suspicion was aroused by the fact that the deceased was profoundly deaf and that the beneficiary was in the room at the time of the execution of the will."

Having heard the evidence the Court in *Scott* was entirely satisfied that the reason for the beneficiary remaining in the room was to assist the testator's solicitor in ensuring that he accurately recorded the testator's intentions in the will.

In the case of mistake the Court has the power pursuant to article 29 of the Order to rectify a will if it is satisfied that:

> "a will is so expressed that it fails to carry out the testator's intentions, in consequence –
>
> (a) of a clerical error; or
>
> (b) of a failure to understand his instructions"

This power has been judicially considered by *Brown v Alexander*.[21] Morgan J considered that:

> "the term 'clerical error' is not limited to errors in transcribing but extends to cases where the draughtsman has not appreciated the significance or effect of the inclusion or omission of the words in issue."

Rectification of a mistake was therefore granted in the case of *Re Heak*[22] where an error occurred because the solicitor's transcription of his client's instructions adopted the wording of an inappropriate precedent.

---

18 *McCullagh* (n 14) [37] (Coghlin J)
19 *Re Thompson's Estate* (n 13) [28]
20 *Scott v Scott* [2007] NIFam 2 [8]
21 *Brown and Others v Alexander and Others* [2004] NICh 5 [11]
22 [2001] NICh 14

14.5 Revocation and Alteration of Wills

A will once made can be revoked or altered by a number of methods.

Revocation can arise by operation of law where the testator subsequently marries or enters a civil partnership.[23] For wills made on or after 1 January 1995 article 12(3) and (4) of the Order provides an exception to revocation in this way where it appears from the will itself that the will (or a specific gift within the will) was made in the expectation of marriage/civil partnership to a particular person and that the will or gift should not be revoked by the marriage/civil partnership to that person.

The Order also governs the circumstances where a testator divorces or has his/her marriage/civil partnership annulled after having made his/her will. The effect of article 13 is to treat the former spouse as having died at the date of divorce or annulment. The general effect is that gifts contained in the will in favour of the spouse fall into the general residue of the will (if there is one) or the rules of intestacy will apply. If the gift to the former spouse contained a share of residue, the residue is divided to the exclusion of the former spouse.

More generally article 14 of the Order provides that a will or a part of a will shall be revocable by:

- another will; or

- some writing, declaring an intention to revoke the will, executed in the manner in which a will is required to be executed; or

- the testator, or some person in his presence and by his direction, burning, tearing or otherwise destroying the will, with the intention of revoking it.

Another subsequent will can revoke previous wills although it will not necessarily do so. It is possible that several wills which are not wholly inconsistent may be read together to constitute the last will of the testator. However if a later will demonstrates an intention on the part of the testator to dispose of his/her property in a manner different from that in the earlier will or if it is unambiguous in dealing with all of his/her property the effect will be to revoke the prior will. The position will be the same if it includes a revocation clause. If an express revocation clause is included within a later will no particular form of words must be used, although it has been held that words simply

---

23 Wills and Administration Proceedings (Northern Ireland) Order 1994 article 12(1); Wills Act (n 7) section 18

describing the later will as "the last will" of the deceased would not necessarily revoke the former will if not inconsistent with it.[24]

A formal instrument of revocation need not take any particular format but must be executed in the same manner and with the same formalities as a will itself.

The destruction of a will must be with the requisite intention to revoke. This may be inferred from the circumstances or may be express. There must be the same capacity for understanding the revocation as accompanies the making of a will. The mistaken or accidental destruction of a will by the testator will therefore not suffice to revoke it.

14.6 Ademption and Lapse

A specific gift is said to be adeemed if it ceases to be part of the testator's estate between the date of the will and death. This can happen in a number of ways. Most obviously if the testator has disposed of the asset during his/her lifetime, or if it has been destroyed or lost. Sometimes the subject-matter of the gift may be altered giving rise to ademption. In *Slater v Slater*[25] the Court of Appeal determined that a gift of an investment in the Lambeth Waterworks Company was adeemed because that company had been acquired by the Metropolitan Water Board prior to the death of the testator. It is open to a testator to make provision within his/her will to prevent ademption in such an eventuality.

A gift is said to lapse if the intended beneficiary predeceases the testator. Article 19 of the Order provides that in these circumstances the gift shall be included in the residuary gift (if any) contained in the will unless a contrary intention appears from the will. The main exception to this is where the gift is to a child who dies before the testator. In those circumstances the gift takes effect as though it were a gift to the "issue of the intended beneficiary [who] are living at the testator's death."[26]

14.7 Construction of Wills

The meaning and intention of the words used by the deceased or his/her draftsman may not always be self-evident. The courts have developed methods of construction to assist in "the anxious task of elucidating a testator's expressed intentions."[27]

---

24 *Simpson v Foxon* [1907] P 54, 57 (Sir Gorell Barnes)
25 *Slater v Slater* [1912] 1 Ch 29, 32
26 Wills and Administration (n 1) article 22
27 *Heron v Ulster Bank Ltd* [1974] NI 44 (CA) 45 (Lowry LCJ)

In *Heron v Ulster Bank*[28] a testator who died on 9 April 1924 by his will left a fund of money on trust to be divided into as many equal shares as he had children surviving him. The trustees were directed to pay the income to the testator's children and to distribute the fund to the children of such children. The will provided that if an interest in the trusts should fail then the share affected should "accrue by way of addition to the share or shares of my other children . . ."

In 1961 a daughter of the testator died unmarried and without children being survived by five brothers and sisters and the children of another daughter of the testator who had died in 1947. The Court of Appeal was required to decide whether the will meant that the share of the daughter who had died should be shared in *fifths* between her siblings, or in *sixths* between her siblings with a sixth to the children of the daughter who died in 1947.

The decision depended upon the meaning of "my other children" in the will. Did the testator intend that if one of his children died with issue that those grandchildren should stand in the shoes of a parent for the purposes of this distribution?

Lowry LCJ set out the procedure to be followed in construing a will:

> "I consider that, having first read the whole will, one may with advantage adopt the following procedure:
>
> 1. Read the immediately relevant portion of the will as a piece of English and decide, if possible, what it means.
> 2. Look at the other material parts of the will and see whether they tend to confirm the apparently plain meaning of the immediately relevant portion or whether they suggest the need for modification in order to make harmonious sense of the whole or, alternatively, whether an ambiguity in the immediately relevant portion can be resolved.
> 3. If ambiguity persists, have regard to the scheme of the will and consider what the testator was trying to do.
> 4. One may at this stage have resort to rules of construction, where applicable, and aids, such as the presumption of early vesting and the presumptions against intestacy and in favour of equality.
> 5. Then see whether any rule of law prevents a particular interpretation from being adopted.
> 6. Finally, and, I suggest, not until the disputed passage has been exhaustively studied, one may get help from the opinions of other courts and judges on

---

28 Ibid

similar words, rarely as binding precedents, since it has been well said that "No will has a twin brother" (per Werner J. in Matter of King 200 N.Y. 189, 192 (1910)), but more often as examples (sometimes of the highest authority) of how judicial minds nurtured in the same discipline have interpreted words in similar contexts."

This approach has been approved more recently in *Moffatt v Moffatt*.[29] Girvan LJ added[30] that:

"The only qualification which I respectfully suggest might usefully be made to that approach is that where a term or phrase has been the subject of a clear judicial determination, if that term is used subsequently by a professional draftsman, it is both likely that he would have intended the term to have the same meaning and would have advised the testator accordingly."

Reading both the immediately relevant portion of the will and the other parts of the will the Court in *Heron v Ulster Bank* discerned that the "other children" encompassed not only the children who survived the daughter who died in 1961 but all the children who survived the testator, and so included the issue of the daughter who died in 1947.

Article 25 of the Order permits the admission of extrinsic evidence as an aid to construction where a part of the will is apparently meaningless, or ambiguous on the face of it, and article 26 of the Order provides statutory definition of certain terms, for example defining 'land' to include buildings and other structures.

There are many different rules of construction and presumptions as referred to within the process of construction set out in *Heron v Ulster Bank*. They include presumptions against intestacy and that a presumption that a will is intended to be rational and not capricious. In the application of these presumptions it remains cardinal that where the words used by the testator are unambiguous in the context it is not for the Court to put a different meaning on them simply because it considers the outcome unreasonable.

---

29 *Moffatt v Moffatt* [2011] NICh 18
30 Ibid [10]

CHAPTER 15

Intestacy And The Inheritance (Provision For Family & Dependents) (Northern Ireland) Order 1979

15.1 Introduction

Where a deceased has not made a valid will or has made a will that disposes of only part of his/her property an intestacy or partial intestacy arises. The property not disposed of by will is distributed in accordance with statute. The legislation in Northern Ireland containing the rules for this distribution is the Administration of Estates Act (Northern Ireland) 1955.[1]

Rules of Court[2] define who is entitled to carry out the role of administering the intestate's assets (the administrator or personal representative). In the first instance this will be his/her surviving spouse or civil partner; if not his/her children, or the issue of any child who has died during his/her lifetime; if not his/her parents; if not his/her brothers and sisters; and so on.

The role of the administrator is to:

- gather the assets

- pay debts (including funeral testamentary and administration expenses and taxes)

- distribute the remainder (the net estate)

As where the deceased has made a will interests which cease on death such as joint tenancies do not form part of the estate for the purposes of intestate succession.

---

1   As amended by the Succession (Northern Ireland) Order 1996; the Civil Partnership Act 2004 (Amendments to Subordinate Legislation) Order (Northern Ireland) 2005; the Administration of Estates (Rights of Surviving Spouse or Civil Partner) Order (Northern Ireland) 2007
2   The Rules of the Court of Judicature (Northern Ireland) 1980, SR 1980/346 Order 97 Rule 20

15.2 Intestate Distribution

The 1955 Act prescribes formulae for the distribution of the estate as between the intestate's relatives. The distribution will differ dependent upon which relatives survive and the size of the estate. In general terms, the spouse or civil partner of the deceased is provided for first, then his/her children, and then other relatives including parents and siblings.

A. Spouses or Civil Partners

The 1955 Act firstly makes provision from the estate for the surviving spouse or civil partner[3] of the intestate although only where he/she has survived the intestate by 28 days.[4] Former spouses, meaning those who had by the time of death *completed* a divorce or a dissolution of civil partnership[5] or who had their marriage or civil partnership declared void or a nullity do not have any entitlement on an intestacy.

A surviving spouse or civil partner is firstly entitled to the 'personal chattels' of the intestate. These are defined[6] to include such matters as cars, domestic animals, horses, crockery, books, pictures, furniture, jewellery, musical instruments and wines, unless these were used for business or professional purposes.

The manner in which the remaining net estate is distributed to the spouse or civil partner then depends upon whether the intestate was also survived by issue or other relatives.

a. Section 7(2) of the 1955 Act provides that where there *are* children of the deceased the surviving spouse in addition to the personal chattels takes:

- where the net value of the remaining estate does not exceed £250,000 *the whole* of the net estate
- where the net value of the remaining estate exceeds £250,000, the first £250,000 and then:
    - in addition, where *only one child* of the intestate also survives, *one-half* of any residue left of the remaining estate[7]

    or

---

3 A civil partnership registered under the Civil Partnership Act 2004
4 Administration of Estates Act (NI) 1955 section 6A
5 By the grant of a decree absolute or final order; before then the spouse or civil partner will remain entitled.
6 Administration of Estates (n 4) section 45(1)
7 After providing for that sum and statutory interest thereon between the date of death and the distribution.

- where *more than one child* of the intestate also survives, *one-third* of any residue left of the remaining estate[8]

These rules also apply if a child of the intestate predeceases him leaving surviving issue so that those grandchildren obtain the share that the deceased's child would otherwise have been entitled to.

b. If there is a surviving spouse or civil partner but no issue, but there are parents brothers or sisters (or their issue) then the spouse or civil partner in addition to the personal chattels takes:

- where the net value of the remaining estate does not exceed £450,000 the whole of the net estate
- where the net value of the remaining estate exceeds £450,000, the first £450,000 and then:
  - in addition, one-half of any residue left of the remaining estate

c. Where there are neither issue parents brothers sisters (nor their issue) the surviving spouse or civil partner takes the whole of the intestate's estate, regardless of its value

It is important to note that co-habitants of the intestate, for example a long-term partner, do not have any rights of entitlement in an intestacy.

B. Children

Issue of the deceased includes children conceived but not yet born at the time of his/her death.[9] The law has also been amended[10] to ensure the child's statutory entitlement is not affected by whether or not his/her parents were married. Adopted children and children conceived by artificial insemination are treated on the same basis as other children of the deceased.[11]

The entitlement of issue will depend in the first instance upon whether there is a spouse or civil partner of the deceased. If there is no surviving spouse or civil partner the children take the net estate in full whereas if there is a spouse or civil partner they share in the remaining estate after the spousal provision has been made. In either scenario the distribution amongst issue is equal (or *per stirpes*).[12] The intestate's grandchildren

---

8   Ibid
9   Administration of Estates (n 4) section 13
10 Children (Northern Ireland) Order 1995 article 155
11 Human Fertilisation and Embryology Act 1990 section 27 *et sequitur*
12 Administration of Estates (n 4) section 8

take by representation their parent's share where the parent has predeceased the intestate.

For example, if the estate does not exceed £250,000 and there is a surviving spouse or civil partner the children have no entitlement under these rules. If the estate does exceed £250,000 and there is only one child, his/her entitlement is 50% of the remainder (the first 50% having been taken by the spouse/civil partner). If the estate exceeds £250,000 and there is more than one child, the remaining two-thirds is distributed amongst them (or their issue as the case may be).

C. Other Relatives

After spouses or civil partners and children the 1955 Act addresses the potential entitlement of parents, siblings and 'next of kin'.

Subject always to the rights of the surviving spouse or civil partner should the intestate die without issue his/her remaining estate is distributed between his/her parents in equal shares (or if only one of them has survived in a single share).[13]

If there are no issue or parents then siblings may have an entitlement. Again subject to the right of the spouse or civil partner where the intestate leaves neither issue nor parent his/her remaining estate is distributed between his/her brothers and sisters *per stirpes*. Therefore if a brother or sister has predeceased the intestate but left issue of their own those children take the share of their parent.

If there is a surviving spouse these entitlements will clearly only arise where the net estate exceeds £450,000, in which case 50% of the remainder is so distributed.[14]

In default of any of these scenarios the legislation looks to the 'next of kin'. Section 11 of the 1955 Act states:

> "If an intestate dies leaving neither spouse nor civil partner nor issue nor parent nor brother nor sister nor issue of any deceased brother or sister, his estate shall … be distributed in equal shares among his next-of-kin"

The next of kin is identified as being the person or persons who at the date of the death of the intestate stood nearest in blood relationship. This can lead to a complicated division of assets.

In *Re Patrick's Estate*[15] the High Court dealt with an intestacy where the intestate was the last survivor of her siblings, all of whom had died without issue. Her father was one

---

13 Ibid section 9
14 Ibid section 10
15 [2000] NI 506 (Ch) (Girvan J)

of 11 children, all of whom predeceased the intestate. Of his siblings 3 died without issue. The remaining 7 siblings left issue and their descendants were thus entitled to a distributive share in the intestate's estate. The question before the Court was that one paternal uncle married a sister of the deceased's mother. They had 5 children who were thus doubly related to the deceased.

In finding that those children would be entitled to a double share, the Girvan J observed that:

> "The way in which an estate should be distributed on intestacy is a matter of legislative policy and it is a question of determining the meaning of the relevant statutory provision. There is nothing more fair or more logical in allowing a double cousin to receive a single share or a double share. Indeed one can see the possibility of intrinsic illogicality in concluding that a double cousin should only receive a share calculated by reference to one parent."[16]

15.3 The Inheritance (Provision for Family & Dependents) (Northern Ireland) Order 1979

The Inheritance (Provision for Family & Dependents) (Northern Ireland) Order 1979 ('the 1979 Order') provides a form of safety-net entitling family members or persons dependent upon the deceased to apply to the Court to seek that greater financial provision be made for them from the deceased's estate. An application can be made under the 1979 Order whether or not there has been a will and accordingly the Court can vary either the provisions of a will or the statutory entitlements upon an intestacy. The touchstone for the exercise of the Court's power is whether 'reasonable financial provision' as defined by the legislation has been made for the party applying to Court.

The categories of those entitled to apply to the Court include:[17]

a. a spouse or civil partner of the deceased, or former spouse or civil partner who has not remarried

b. a co-habitee of the deceased who had been living for the two years immediately before the death of the deceased as husband or wife (without actually being married)

---

16 Ibid 511
17 Inheritance (Provision for Family & Dependents) (Northern Ireland) Order 1979 article 3

c. a child of the deceased or a someone (such as a step-child) who was treated by the deceased as a child in the context of a marriage or civil partnership

d. any person who was being maintained by the deceased

Article 5 of the 1979 Order sets the criteria to which the court must have regard in determining both whether reasonable financial provision has been made for the applicant and in what manner the Court should exercise its powers to vary the distribution of the estate. The factors of general application include:

- the financial resources and needs of the party presently or in the future (including therefore the applicant's earning capacity)

- the financial resources and financial needs which any other beneficiary of the estate or other applicant is likely to have

- any obligations and responsibilities which the deceased had towards the applicant or any other beneficiary of the estate

- the size and nature of the net estate of the deceased

- any physical or mental disability of the applicant or any beneficiary

- any other matter including the conduct of the applicant or any other person

If the Court is satisfied that the disposition of the deceased's estate effected by his/her will or the law relating to intestacy has failed to make reasonable financial provision for the applicant a wide range of orders[18] can be made including:

- the payment of a lump sum out of the estate

- the provision of periodical payments from the estate for any period

- the settlement of any property of the estate for the applicant's benefit

- an order that property be transferred to the applicant

- an order that property be acquired by the estate and transferred to or settled in favour of the applicant

The statute defines 'reasonable financial provision' as meaning "such financial provision as it would be reasonable in all the circumstances of the case for the applicant to receive for his maintenance." The dicta of Goff LJ in *Re Coventry*[19] elaborating upon the concept of 'maintenance' have been cited with approval in a number of Northern Irish cases:[20]

---

18 Ibid article 4
19 *Re Coventry* [1980] Ch 461 (CA) 485
20 *McKernan v McKernan* [2007] NICh 6, [2008] 4 BNIL 106 [25] (Deeny J); *Re Creeney* [1984] NI 397

"What is proper maintenance must in all cases depend upon all the facts and circumstances of the particular case being considered at the time but I think it is clear on the one hand that one must not put too limited a meaning on it; it does not mean just enough to enable a person to get by; on the other hand, it does not mean anything which may be regarded as reasonably desirable for the general benefit or welfare."

A. Spouses and Civil Partners

In addition to the general criteria to be considered by a Court under article 5 of the 1979 Order some specific matters must be considered where the applicant is the former spouse or civil partner of the deceased. The focus on 'maintenance' is wider in spousal cases so that the inquiry is into what reasonable "financial provision as it would be reasonable in all the circumstances of the case … to receive, whether or not that provision is required for his/her maintenance."[21]

These additional spousal factors are:

- the age of the applicant
- the duration of the marriage or civil partnership
- the contribution made by the applicant to the welfare of the family of the deceased, including any contribution made by looking after the home or caring for the family
- the provision which the applicant might reasonably have expected to receive had the marriage or civil partnership been terminated by a decree of divorce or dissolution rather than death

Similar criteria, with the exception of the reference to divorce or dissolution, are identified where the parties were not married or in a civil partnership but rather co-habited as husband and wife for two years or more.[22]

Where parties have finalised a divorced or judicial separation, or a dissolution to a civil partnership within 12 months of the death, but no financial provision or property adjustment has yet been concluded, the Court has power if it thinks just to do so to treat the surviving party as if the divorce, judicial separation or dissolution had not been made final.

(Ch) [41] (Carswell J); *Re Guidera's Estate* [2001] NI 71 (Ch)
21 Inheritance Order (n 17) article 2(2)
22 Ibid article 5(2A)

In *Re Moorhead's Estate*[23] a testator's estate comprised farmlands valued at £455,000, investments valued at £100,000, personal chattels valued at £12,000 and livestock and equipment valued £13,000. His will made no capital provision for his wife, the bequests to her comprising his personal chattels and certain life interests in trust.

In an application by his wife under the 1979 Order Weatherup J addressed in turn each of the article 5 criteria. The applicant was 80 years of age and it was apparent her own means might not be sufficient were she to become less active and require housekeeping or nursing assistance through age or infirmity. The other named beneficiaries of the estate were variously in employment, owned their own homes or had investments. The Court considered that the deceased had obligations toward his wife who upon their marriage 37 years prior to his death had given up her employment as a nurse and had looked after the deceased and the matrimonial home and assisted in the running of the farm, in addition to caring for the deceased's mother who lived in the matrimonial home for some 10 years. The net estate was of not inconsiderable value. Under the category of 'any other matter' in article 5 of the 1979 Order, the Court also had due regard to the deceased's own wishes that the lands should remain within the family and that they should ultimately pass to his nephew.

As *Moorhead* was a spousal application detailed consideration was given to what financial provision might have been made had the parties divorced. However the Court was clear that the correct statutory approach required that "a consideration of what might have been the financial provision on divorce is but one of the factors to which the court is to have regard, and although a very important factor it is not to treated as a starting point or a yardstick for reasonable financial provision in inheritance claims."[24]

The Court altered the will of the deceased transferring part of the farm to the wife absolutely, ordering that the remainder of it be held in trust for her during her lifetime whereafter it would be transferred to the nephew of the deceased. The deceased's farm equipment was also transferred to his wife so that she could continue the farming enterprise and from the residue of the estate provided she would receive a lump sum of £40,000.00.

B. Children of the Deceased

Specific matters are also to be taken into account where the applicant is either the child of the deceased or is someone who was treated as a child of the family by a deceased

---

23 [2002] NIJB 83 (Ch)
24 Ibid [7]

who had married or entered a civil partnership. Regard must be had to the manner in which the applicant might expect to be educated or trained, and in the latter case also to whether and to what extent the deceased had assumed any responsibility for the applicant's maintenance, whether the deceased knew that the applicant was not his own child, and the liability of any other person to maintain the applicant.[25]

It may be noted that adult as well as minor children can make a claim against the estate of a deceased under the 1979 Order. However a view has been expressed that a claim made by an adult with an established earning capacity may in fact fail in the absence of other factors such as a moral obligation owed to him by the deceased or other special circumstances.[26]

C. Dependants

The other main category of person entitled to apply for provision from the deceased's estate is 'dependants'. This is defined as a person towards whose reasonable needs the deceased otherwise than for full valuable consideration was making a substantial contribution in money or money's worth. This can include the provision of a home by the deceased for the applicant.[27] In *Gibson v Bell*[28] the deceased had for a considerable time provided financial assistance in the amount of some £400.00-£500.00 per month to the applicant with whom he had a close relationship. She was financially dependent upon him but no provision was made for her in his will. On an application under the 1979 Order the Court provided that monies from the estate be held in trust and that an income of up to £6000.00 per annum be paid to her during her lifetime.

D. Property Held on Joint Tenancies and Prior Dispositions

Typically property held on joint tenancy does not fall within the estate of a deceased. Article 11 of the 1979 Order provides a significant exception to this. In an application under the Order the Court may order that the deceased's severable share of property so held, at the value immediately before his/her death, shall be treated as part of the net estate of the deceased.

---

25 Inheritance Order (n 17) article 5(3)
26 *Re Hancock (deceased)* [1999] 1 FCR 500, 506 (Butler-Sloss LJ), cited with approval in *McKernan v McKernan* [2007] NICh 6, [2008] 4 BNIL 106 [35] (Deeny J)
27 *Re Guidera's Estate* [2001] NI 71, 76 (Girvan J)
28 *Gibson v Bell* [2000] 7 BNIL 85

Article 10(2) of the 1979 Order provides that a *donatio mortis causa* shall after allowing for any capital transfer tax payable upon it be treated as part of the net estate of a deceased.

In certain circumstances the Court can also address dispositions made by a deceased within 6 years of his/her death where it is satisfied that:

- the disposition was made with the intention of defeating an application for financial provision under the 1979 Order
- the disposition was not for full valuable consideration
- the exercise of the Court's powers would facilitate the making of financial provision for the applicant

Article 12 of the Order provides that the Court can order the recipient of the property so disposed of to provide for the purpose of the making of an order for financial provision such sum of money or property as the Court shall specify.

In *Morrow v Morrow*[29] one year before the deceased's death he had transferred his farmlands to his son for less than full valuable consideration subject to a right of residence in favour of himself and his wife. Campbell J found that his intention was at least in part to make a transfer so as to defeat an application for financial provision by his wife under the 1979 Order. As reasonable provision had not been made for the wife the Court considered the case an appropriate one for the exercise of its discretion under article 12.

---

29 *Morrow v Morrow* [1995] NIJB 46

Index